The
New West
of
Edward Abbey

The New West
of
Edward Abbey
Second Edition

Ann Ronald
Afterword by Scott Slovic

University of Nevada Press
Reno & Las Vegas

University of Nevada Press, Reno, Nevada 89557 USA
Copyright © 1982 University of New Mexico Press
Afterword copyright © 2000 by University of Nevada Press
All rights reserved
Manufactured in the United States of America

Library of Congress Cataloging-in-Publication Data
Ronald, Ann, 1939–
The New West of Edward Abbey / Ann Ronald.— 2nd ed. /
afterword by Scott Slovic.
p. cm.
Includes bibliographical references and index.
ISBN 0-87417-357-4 (alk. paper)
1. Abbey, Edward, 1927—Criticism and interpretation.
2. Western stories—History and criticism.   3. West (U.S.)—
Description and travel.   4. West (U.S.)—In literature.
I. Title.
PS3551.B2 Z87   2000
813'.54—dc21
00-011170

"A Clean Hard Edge Divides" was first published in
The Redneck Review of Literature (Spring 1989) and is
reprinted here with the permission of the author.

The paper used in this book meets the requirements of
American National Standard for Information Sciences—
Permanence of Paper for Printed Library Materials,
ANSI Z39.48-1984.
Binding materials were selected for strength and durability.

First Printing

09 08 07 06 05 04 03 02 01 00   5 4 3 2 1

To L.A.S.

Contents

Acknowledgments

I owe thanks to the University of Nevada System Board of Regents for the sabbatical leave, 1980–81, that gave me time to prepare the manuscript of *The New West of Edward Abbey*, I also thank the University of Nevada/Reno Library, the University of California/ San Diego Library, the San Diego County Public Library, and the C.O.L.G.C.

All quotations from Edward Abbey's books are used by permission as indicated in the following list.

Preface

The cover of *Abbey's Road* shows a homemade wooden sign with the words "TAKE THE OTHER" printed crudely across it. In a chapter of an earlier book, *The Journey Home*, Edward Abbey explains how he and an erstwhile fiancée came upon such a sign in 1953, while exploring Big Bend National Park in West Texas. There they found a fork with two choices equally alluring. To the left, marking a northeasterly road "up a rocky ravine into a jumble of desert hills," was a handpainted sign: "Hartung's Road—Take the Other." "A good sign," Abbey acknowledges. "One would have liked to meet Mr. Hartung but his road was not our road" that day. Staked in the middle of the other fork was an authoritative board that insisted "No Road," and that way looked even more appealing. Respecting the rights of the individual and defying the official command—that is, behaving characteristically—Abbey chose the righthand fork. He "pulled up the No Road sign, drove through, stopped, replaced the sign," and headed on "cautiously but steadily, over the rocks and through the sand, bound for Rio Grande Village—an easy fifty-mile drive somewhere beyond" [JH, 25]. The car proceeded slowly, into and out of gulches, around and over stones and sage despite mixed odors of burning clutch plate, boiling radiator, and overheated engine, along with sounds of flapping, shredded tire. "I had to see what lay beyond the next ridge," the author reports, even if the effort meant a permanent wreckage of auto and engagement.

"Disorder and Early Sorrow," a funny and whimsical narrative, recounts the adventure so typical of Abbey's "espirit de Ford," a foray repeated variously in many of his other essays. *Slickrock* tells of a one-hundred-and-eighty-mile dirt-road trek from Blanding to Green River, Utah, for example, while *Abbey's Road* itself recalls a solitary, cross-country safari through the Australian outback. Indeed, "anything small and insignificant on the map [draws Abbey] with irresistible magnetism" [S, 21]. His entire career has driven him to choices between "the other road" and "no road," two paths leading away from the establishment's confines and toward the open spaces necessary for explorations and dreams. "Somewhere out in the open desert of west central Organ Pipe I came to a fork in the road, with signboards. One sign said, 'Park Hdqtrs 21 Mi'; the other something like 'Primitive Road, Not Patrolled.' Naturally I took the latter, which looked more interesting and led in the direction I wanted to go" [CC, 26]. Abbey always chooses the path of most resistance, blazing the trail with a radical gesture and writing about it with unleashed enthusiasm. His way is his own, down Abbey's road and into the desert wilderness—Abbey's world—with hardly a sideways glance at trails that were scouted before him. The direction he takes, a course relatively unpatrolled, is the route we pursue in *The New West of Edward Abbey*.

His twists and turns have not always been easy to follow. Abbey's road leads not only through a jungle of political and philosophical arguments, but of literary genres too. "Polemics and Sermons" get lost among characters and setting, fiction gives way to nonfiction, while the cautious reader trudges past a slough of paradox. And even when bright signals have irradiated the literary path, the desert trails themselves have remained somewhat inaccessible. Let me explain.

Part of the joy in writing about Edward Abbey's books has been the exploration of the landscapes he describes. While I have always been a confirmed wilderness enthusiast—I think I took my first backpacking trip at age nine—the desert, for me, is a recent discovery. Only after I moved to Nevada twelve years ago did I begin to understand its lure, and even today its magnetism draws me less than the powerful pull of a flowered mountain meadow. Nevertheless, because I prefer horizons unmarred by manmade structures and any country free of industrial tourism, I found the transition from high country to canyons a compatible one. Even the horror of a legion of Sonoran ring-tailed rattlers patrolling Arizona's Superstition Mountains—*Cactus Country* warned me they would be there, "it was their kind of country" [CC, 44]—was allayed by the remarkable scenery and the personal autocracy of a solitary hiker. What I did not find, however, there or any place else in the Southwest, was Abbey's world.

The introduction to *Desert Solitaire* explains why. "Most of what I write about in this book," Abbey laments, "is already gone or going under fast. This is not a travel guide but an elegy. A memorial. You're holding a tombstone in your hands" [DS, xii]. He was right. The desert country of 1967 no longer exists in 1982 because just fifteen years have turned more canyons into silt ponds, clean air into smog—I could not see Phoenix that cloudless April day—and lonely stretches of desert landscape into copper mines and abandoned spoil banks. Even some of Abbey's trails have been transformed. In *Desert Solitaire*, for example, he tells of hiking to Havasu on the spur of the moment, then staying for five weeks. The same trip cannot be made today without a permit. When I called for one I was told the campground was filled to capacity—two hundred people per night—two months in advance! I hung up the phone, certain that even if a permit were available later, I would never go down that trail. Obviously it no longer leads to Abbey's "Eden," but points instead to an officially guarded campground overpopulated with campers.

Some of my other desert trips and vistas proved as frustrating, intriguingly like the world Abbey describes and yet just different enough to be alarming. An overnight jaunt to the wild palms of the Kofas, for example, was interrupted by an early-dawn marksman prowling illegally through the game preserve. While Abbey writes in *Cactus Country* that "our only moral obligation . . . is to do what killing we must in the proper spirit of humility, gratitude and grace" [CC, 115], he adamantly condemns trophy hunters who are endangering the bighorn sheep. Such predators do not belong in Abbey's milieu, yet they exist today in Palm Canyon. Also standing there is a sign, "Palms," with an arrow that points the tourist in the proper direction. It was planted, I suppose, for some bureaucratic reason. Even the isolation at Organ Pipe Cactus National

Monument has been touched by the 1980s, its vastness now marred by characteristics of a twentieth-century motor-home rendezvous. One can no longer camp overnight at Quitobaquito to listen to the birds sing at dawn, or backpack up to Bull Pasture where "the light seems a little more dramatic . . . than elsewhere in Organ Pipe—the sunrises, the sunsets, the moonrises, the stars a little more brilliant—and the air is almost always clean and good" [CC, 77]. Now the hiker must return before dark to the regimented campground where "big-tin-and-formica cakeboxes on wheels" are "lining up like elephants, snout to rump" [AR, 142].

Abbey, of course, would snort at such troublesome inconveniences. Turning his back on tourists and cities, he would head for the nearest lonesome expanse, the deepest canyon yet unexplored. But most of that country "is already gone or going fast," neither as easy to find nor as pollution-free as it was fifteen years ago. Where Abbey could escape on foot to the remoteness of Rainbow Bridge, tourists now make "what was formerly an adventure into a routine motorboat excursion" [DS, 217]. Where Abbey could spend a solitary day wandering the slopes of Colorado's Wilson Peak, the backpacker now encounters a host of other hikers—I counted twenty-three in one twenty-four-hour period. And where Abbey could renew his spirits, or his characters', in lonely lookout towers, even that option is unavailable because airplanes do the job instead. *"Keep it like it was,"* he pleads in *The Monkey Wrench Gang* [77] and again in *The Journey Home* [145]. Keep it like it was. It seems his warning comes too late.

But if it is impossible now to retrace his steps physically through Arches without its blacktop roads, or to drift with him down Glen Canyon before the dam—I have seen old color slides, but that is hardly the same—it is also difficult to flout convention in order to repeat his experiences. I tried. Driving up to the "Primitive Road, Not Patrolled" sign at Organ Pipe, the one that now adds "Next Towing Services, 76 Miles," I peered for a long time at the dusty option. Then I turned left, not right, toward the relative security of Arizona State Highway 85. Measuring my miles in six-packs, I ended up with all my empties cached neatly in a trash bag instead of thrown helter-skelter on the road. And even my chance for a personal anarchistic gesture got lost in a blush of propriety. The occasion was a two-week backpack trip along the Pacific Crest Trail in Washington. Miles from anywhere, I came to a newly surveyed section of trail where stark yellow stakes marked a new freeway-style track that would straighten out the old path's rocky horseshoe curves. I could not make myself pull one up. Even when coaxed by my companion—"How can you write a book about Abbey's attitudes when you can't follow his directions?" and, "Come on, if you don't want to carry the stakes in your pack, you could just hide them in the bushes"—l could not touch the official-looking posts. "Always pull up survey stakes," Abbey admonishes. "Anywhere you find them. Always. That's the first goddamned general order in the monkey wrench business. Always pull up survey stakes" [MWG, 80]. But I missed my chance, and my failure has haunted me for almost two years.

Abbey's road is a hard track to follow. In *Desert Solitaire* he warned people like me to get out of the way. "Serious critics, serious librarians, serious associate professors of English will if they read this work dislike it intensely; at least I hope so" [DS, x]. I have ignored his warning as blithely as I ignored the opportunity to pull up survey stakes. Instead, this serious associate professor of English has trundled slowly along the path toward Abbey's world, tiptoeing past the places I found incorrigible and rushing pell-mell into those I admired and loved. From the Maze of *Desert Solitaire* to *Black Sun*'s blood-red canyon, from the abyss on *Abbey's Road* and back to the Maze and *The Monkey Wrench Gang* again, I literally and figuratively have found some special spots. It would be tempting to call *The New West of Edward Abbey* my guidebook there. But it is not; like *Desert Solitaire*, it's "a bloody rock. Don't drop it on your foot" [DS, xii].

And like any book about somebody else's writing, this one necessarily remains twenty steps behind its subject, letting Edward Abbey set the pace and scout the path. The only real way to join him—to see his country, to find Abbey's world—is on foot through the imagination, to read his books over and over again. We must go "up there among the red cliffs and pinnacles, in those immense gulfs of space under the mountain's rim, where the air is cool and sweet with the odor of juniper and lightning, where the mockingbird and the canyon wren and the mourning dove join with the phantoms in their useless keening" [BC, 7–8], and we must keep walking, past "rock and water, huge cliffs and delicate details" [S, 60]. Each narrative tale and personal history takes a different turn— sometimes plunging ahead, sometimes even backtracking—but each

charts a course I choose to follow, the one that leads toward the author's personal domain of the imagination.

The last of the afternoon sunlight had long since vanished from the
upper walls. I walked through lavender twilight, through the sounds of
flowing water, rasping toads, swaying willows, the papery rustle of cottonwood leaves. It was time to make camp if I wanted to cook before
dark, but the charm and magic of this canyon were so great I didn't want
to stop. Each turn in the walls promised some new delight; exploring such
a place is like exploring the personality of a new friend, a new love. [S,
60–61]

The path down Abbey's road, leading far away from *Jonathan Troy*
and stretching out past *Good Neus*, follows a virgin trail. While *The
New West of Edward Abbey* may sign some way-stops, the best chance
to find the route is to hike by Abbey's side, "to get out of the goddamned contraption and walk, better yet crawl, on hands and
knees, over the sandstone and through the thornbush and cactus.
When traces of blood begin to mark your trail you'll see something.
Maybe" [DS, xii]. Not traces but a profusion of my own blood at-
tests—off in that direction lies the track toward Abbey's world, the
New West of Edward Abbey.

Part I

Footloose

The Early Fiction

Entering Edward Abbey's world, the reader steps inside a western landscape carefully reshaped and repainted by a master. "Suddenly, unexpectedly, the view open[s] wide and the whole western world" stretches to infinity: "the canyon dropping down step by step like an imperial stairway for gods, the gaunt purple foothills, the mesa rolling out for miles, the faint gleam of the river, the vast undulant spread of the city ten miles away, transformed by the evening dusk into something fantastic and grand and lovely, a rich constellation of jewels glimmering like the embers of a fire—and beyond the city and the west mesa and the five volcanoes another spectacle, a garish and far more immense display of clouds and color and dust and light against a bottomless, velvet sky" [BC, 201]. Such pictorial prose has been the foundation of Abbey's widespread appeal for almost three decades. Foremost among Southwest writers, this observant, articulate author paints a vivid scene. More than that, however, he pictures a world painstakingly designed to expose contemporary values in conflict. Whether superimposing his sense of the Old West on his vision of the New, denouncing the corporate greed that he sees desecrating the land, or assessing the fate of the individual caught in the crush of the twentieth century, Abbey raises questions crucial to anyone who has seen the frontier shrink and the American dream begin to fade.

Repeated themes, along with an ability to express them cogently, emerge in his first three novels. Although *Jonathan Troy* (1954) pours forth an ejaculation of adolescent longings, it also contains a stylized prose and certain political and philosophical interests that distinctly foreshadow the writer Abbey will become. *The Brave Cowboy* (1956) improves upon *Troy*, not only introducing more interesting characters engaged in more dramatic activities but raising serious ethical questions as well. Those questions are reassessed in *Fire on the Mountain* (1962) and, while Abbey still finds no answers, he tells a well-constructed story set in evocative surroundings. Although these tales are not as effective as his later ones, without them his writing—fiction and nonfiction alike—would have been quite different. Indeed, without the experience of writing *Jonathan Troy*, *The Brave Cowboy*, and *Fire on the Mountain*, Abbey might never have progressed to the solid achievements that have followed.

It is worthwhile, then, to look at these early efforts, at their artistry, themes, flaws, and successes. First—the prose itself: Abbey's characteristic style appears in these books, but with irregularity. A major reason for his popularity today, particularly among those who favor his essay accompaniments to such Southwest photographers as Philip Hyde and David Muench, is his ability to picture a scene in fresh and original language. Occasionally evident in *Jonathan Troy*, that talent emerges and matures in *The Brave Cowboy* and *Fire on the Mountain* until, in the latter two books, Abbey's western landscape breathes with almost more life than his characters.

Second—the thematic concerns: already the author's major interests are apparent. *Jonathan Troy* introduces Abbey's first anarchist, stars his first male chauvinist, and predicates his first environmental broadsides, although he pursues none of the issues at length. More important, the book announces his belief in the healing, regenerative powers of the western landscape. When its rebellious young protagonist stops running in circles and heads West to the land of his dreams, Abbey controls his materials for the first time, making the novel's ending the novelist's beginning. *The Brave Cowboy* follows directly. Setting the entire story in the West, Abbey plays the romantic against the real in a form more satisfying than his first attempt. A tighter plot and more appealing and believable characters make the total effort more coherent. *The Brave Cowboy* also opens its author's lifelong crusade against the constrictive powers of "the establishment," a theme which becomes the core of Abbey's point of view as well as a major source of his popularity. *Fire on the Mountain* battles even more fervently against conglomerate bureaucracy and one man's impotence against it. Although the book's passion never stirred readers as much as Abbey's later writing, *Fire on the Mountain* clearly indicts the despotism he hates.

Another theme, familiar especially to readers of western fiction, appears in these first novels. Not in *Jonathan Troy* but in the two New Mexico books that follow, Abbey considers the relationships between past and present, between the Old West and the New. Both the anachronistic brave cowboy and *Fire on the Mountain's* beleaguered cattleman are characters born out of their psychological times who run headlong into the frustrations of the twentieth century. While Abbey never champions a retreat to another age, he recognizes the absurdity of living without learning from the past. Through his fiction, he draws comparisons that illuminate both the pros and cons of a western heritage—its chivalrous code, its frontier mentality, its individualism, its greed. While these first books offer no answers, they raise puzzling questions about the mistakes of the past and the consequent problems of the future.

Third—the design: from the absence of structure in *Jonathan Troy*, Abbey moves, in *The Brave Cowboy*, to a form suitable for all his writing. Most readers discern in it, and in *Fire on the Mountain*, a pattern borrowed from the western novel, with recognizable characters —the mysterious stranger who rides in from nowhere, the sheriff, his posse, the embattled rancher, the innocent boy who is educated by his cowboy experiences—and with familiar scenes. Abbey, however, has twisted them all, confounding conventions of the past in order to reassess the present and the future. But in a discussion of Abbey's books as probing social commentaries, we ought to explore another design. *The Brave Cowboy* and Abbey's subsequent books are patterned like romances. This archaic structure allows Abbey to simplify his story lines and to exaggerate certain qualities of character while attacking those elements of modern society which disturb him. Perhaps the major achievement of this early fiction is the discovery of a form compatible with his talents and imagination.

The three books, of course, are far from perfect. *Jonathan Troy* is unmemorable, while *Fire on the Mountain* evidences more anger than artistry. Even *The Brave Cowboy*, which contains much of what

Abbey does best, is not as good as his later writing. The interplay between the Old West and the New, the ironies of mountain granite juxtaposed against yellow smog, and the excitement of an individual defying the establishment are overshadowed by a thematic inconclusiveness and a melodramatic ending. Still, *The Brave Cowboy*, along with the other two, gave Abbey confidence. From the awkward opening of *Jonathan Troy* to the sharp prose of *Fire on the Mountain*, we see a remarkable change in his writing. A developing assuredness in his characterizations, a certainty of point of view, and a mastery of style combine to improve Abbey's tales noticeably. And even though these three lack the resolution of his later books, they do raise some pertinent questions. These fledgling efforts set their author off down a path that ultimately will lead him to the forefront of western writers.

1

Bootprints

Jonathan Troy

Quicksand awaits the reader whose initial step along Abbey's road begins with *Jonathan Troy* (1954), a fictional morass of adolescent hopes and fears. But in three significant ways, this novel does mark the beginning of a successful career. First, it offers an early glimpse of Abbey's greatest strength—the power of his prose. Even though early portions of the novel are badly written, the last chapters show steady improvement and give hints of his growing professional style. Second, suggestions of future themes arise; both anarchy and ecology are mentioned, along with a number of lesser interests. Third, and most important, *Jonathan Troy* ends with a vision of the West that will pervade the author's subsequent writing. He will reassess that vision until, in its mature guise, his conception will anchor his entire system of beliefs. The most important reason for discussing Abbey's first book, then, is the metaphorical presence of the American West.

The plot itself is indefensible. Its hero is a blond, green-eyed, handsome, egotistical nineteen-year-old who uses and abandons friends and enemies alike. Despite his physical attractiveness, the young man alienates nearly everyone. A random series of unfortunate encounters defines his progress. For example, even as he enchants his English teacher, Feathersmith, by the sensitive way he reads Whitman and Shakespeare aloud, he derides him as "the little pink fairy." And after seducing his first girl friend, the unattractive but available Etheline, Jonathan discards her for a more glamorous love, even though Etheline probably is pregnant. He disdains his peers, Fatgut and the other high school students, and shows no compassion for anyone other than himself. Finally, he scorns his father, a pathetic, one-eyed, pseudoanarchistic Wobbly who moves peripherally through the novel until his unexpected demise at the end. Leafy, his second girl friend, is the only person Jonathan treats decently, but even their intimacy is emotionally unconvincing because Abbey posits the relationship in such adolescent tones. In short, Jonathan painfully inches toward manhood while intrinsically arrested in static, immature dealings with others.

The climax of the novel, however, incorporates the youth's encounters into a surprising explosion. After the high school staging of *Macbeth*, in which Jonathan enthralls the audience by his impassioned acting in the lead role, he heads toward Leafy's house in anticipation of a night of love. En route, he stops in the Blue Bell Bar where he inexplicably drinks too much beer; then, unable to leave, he sits and watches an outbreak of violence that culminates with the death of his own father. Finally wrenching himself from the bloody scene, the frightened young man runs aimlessly through the night, sick, exhausted, alone. In a piece of stylized staging, Abbey intersperses scenes of other characters in agony—Etheline, pregnant and afraid, weeps in the darkness of her room; Fatgut, sitting on a distant street corner, dreams of food and girls and shoves "the waist of his trousers down an inch to give his belly more room."[1]

Only Leafy escapes Jonathan's curse, although she does not understand it at the time. When he fails to appear at her house, she thinks he has abandoned her just as he abandoned Etheline. But he, knowing his father's death has freed him, chooses to free Leafy as well. By not seducing her that night, Jonathan performs the single commendable act in the book. He leaves, then, catching a ride with a truck driver bound for Cincinnati, anticipating further rides that will take him west and far away from the tiny Pennsylvania town of his adolescence.

The causes for *Jonathan Troy's* failure are many. There is little plot, other than Jonathan's own slow fumbling toward maturity. But since he is no Stephen Dedalus, nor even a Tim Hazzard, although some of his lovesick longings sound like Walter Van Tilburg Clark's trembling hero, the story moves ponderously. In fact, it is difficult to summarize the action because not much happens. Jonathan himself is part of the problem too, for he is not a very likable character. Too self-centered and self-serving, he stumbles from one painful encounter to another, seemingly with little purpose. Meant as a *Bildungsroman*, a novel of a youth's progression to maturity, *Jonathan Troy* succeeds only in expressing an erratic pattern of growth that never persuades the reader of real character development.

Analysis of the book's inadequacies could fill many pages, but a synopsis of them is conveniently enumerated by Feathersmith, the novel's English expert, when he speaks of his own embryonic work of fiction, *The Lyric Cry*, and what it lacks: "consistency of characterization, narrative continuity, scrupulous clarity in presentation, credible psychological motivation, integrity of purpose, authenticity of dialog and description, and the orderly development of structural elements" [192]. Ironically, Feathersmith's difficulties match his author's. Abbey could almost be that sophomoric writer; *Jonathan Troy*, his "lyric cry." Of course he could be making fun of himself too, since his sense of humor lies close to the surface of his other books and a joke on his own narrative travails would amuse him. But because *Jonathan Troy* is a remarkably humorless book, it seems more likely that *The Lyric Cry* is simply Abbey's recognition of the problems awaiting any beginning author.

Rather than dwell on those problems, however, we should move on to the significance of the book. While the bulk of the text is far from memorable, occasional passages mark its author's potential. The final section, in particular, shows Abbey in control of his material instead of the reverse. The entire passage describing Jonathan's flight after old man Troy's precipitous death is too long to quote in its entirety, but a sample portion indicates the power of the prose:

That way he ran, toward the trees and the grass, obeying something more profound than impulse, more elemental than the unthought desire for solitude, something as sure and as deep as instinct. He was gasping for air now and his heart hammered like an engine but still he ran, not slowing, past the parked Chevrolets and Plymouths, past the dark porches where old men and old women sat waiting to die, across an intersecting

street and under the light, into the black tunnel under the elm and wal-
nut trees, past the telephone poles and a mail box, past the squared-off
hedges and white fences, past a boy and girl leaning together over a low
gate, past somebody just backing out of a garage, running across another
alley and past and under the last streetlight and beyond the last of the
parked automobiles, running in the moonlight now past the unshaded
unpainted shacks and bungalows at the end of the street and off the concrete onto the stones and rutted mud at the street's end, over a sagging
barbed-wire fence and then up the slope over the burnt stubble of the
field toward the huddled young trees of the woods. When he was among
them, with them at last, safe in the warm womb-darkness of the woods,
he flung himself down on the dead leaves and the weeds and lay there
panting and gasping like an athlete fighting for his life. [348]

Here for the first time, in breathless, long-winded sentences, Abbey
brings form and content together in meaningful juxtaposition. The
diction reinforces the meaning through specifically evocative
images—"old men . . . waiting to die" reminds the reader of Nat
Troy's recent fate, "the black tunnel" suggests Jonathan's immediate
future, "the boy and girl leaning together" harks back to the youth's
lost night of love, and "the womb-darkness" remains all that is left
for him now. Choosing words and phrases to trigger genuine responses, Abbey elucidates Jonathan's experience with sympathetic
treatment.

   Unfortunately, the success of this passage comes more from the
power of the prose than from either the structural design of the
book or the psychological inevitability of the story. Beginning with
a headlong rush out of the Blue Bell Bar through the streets of the
tiny Pennsylvania town and out past stubbled fields to the sanctity
of Leafy's home where the boy waits and watches without ever
revealing his presence, until his return to Powhatan where he tries
to hop a train and fails, Abbey's style mirrors his hero's energies
and emotions. "Crazily, hopelessly, Jonathan ran after the freight
train, running over the sharp cinders on the lane between the
tracks, panting badly, not thinking, while the black smoke from
the engine drifted low, burning his eyes, depositing ashes in his
hair, shrouding the stationhouse behind him" [367]. Until the close
of the novel, those hellish, melancholy lines continue in "long banshee howls," echoing the locomotive that is pulling away from the
frustrated young man. The effect of the diction and syntax does
little, however, to camouflage the book's intrinsic weaknesses.

   The entire sequence fades abruptly into a scene in an all-night eatery followed by a puzzling encounter between Jonathan and the stolid truck driver who offers him a ride. When Abbey's characters interact with each other in this first novel, his prose turns lifeless and uninspired. Rarely in his career will his dialogues be as persuasive and evocative as his descriptions, but the problem will never plague Abbey as devastatingly as it does on the final page of *Jonathan Troy*. A vibrant paragraph describes the atmosphere inside the truck: "the engine roared and bellowed like a monster in Hell and the whole cab, bucking and swaying, vibrated in steel sympathy." Then a single, listless line culminates the story: "What? What'd you way? I didn't hear ya—" [374]. The truck driver's question has little effect, except to underscore Jonathan's inability to communicate. Neither a denouement to the boy's growth nor structurally integral to the pattern of the book, the last page dissatisfies the reader and, in fact, detracts from the quality of the preceding twenty-two in which the language resuscitates the narrative. Despite its flat ending, however, the novel's climax distinctly foreshadows such tense sequences as the brave cowboy's flight up a mountain escarpment, or Will Gatlin's descent under the canyon's black sun, or the Monkey Wrench Gang's last death-defying chase.

Other qualities of Abbey's language foreshadow his future books too. Already, in his search for specificity, his pictorial descriptions focus on naturalistic details. The caricatures, in particular, are memorable in *Jonathan Troy*. Although overstated, certain paragraphs prefigure the mature author. An example is Abbey's description of Etheline, the girl whose seduction reveals Jonathan at his most atavistic level. The first time the two teen-agers go to bed together, the author sees Etheline as

fattish; the breasts that had once seemed so full and promising when encased in their nylon hammocks turned out to be quite flabby when unsupported; when she lay on her back they spread gelatinously over her chest. Her buttocks were lumpy, full of unexpected folds and wrinkles, and near the bottom, on the sat-upon portion, of a pebbly rough pimpled texture, like pigskin. He had never expected that. Besides, she had, in Jonathan's opinion, an excessive amount of pubic hair and an annoyingly damp groin. And at irregular but frequent intervals she belched, grunted, or hiccupped. [111–12]

Because of this aggrandized treatment of her physical flaws, Etheline elicits no pity at all. Dickens long ago showed that grotesque characters can evoke compassion, and this young girl could do so too, especially when she weeps alone near the novel's close. Yet her poignancy is lost because Abbey not only withholds the depth necessary to make her more than one-dimensional but also tags her with shallow lines (and hiccups) that turn her into a cartoon sight gag. Nevertheless, she exposes a corner of her creator's imagination. Such men as *The Monkey Wrench Gang's* Bishop Love and the Chief in *Good News* grow from the same fictional source, as do some nonfiction figures, like *Desert Solitaire's* "Cowboys and Indians."

When he wrote *Jonathan Troy*, however, Abbey was just learning his craft. The same errors of excess he makes when caricaturing Etheline, he repeats with his first tentative descriptions of scenery. Filled with generalized shapes and colors, his pictorial frames evoke atmosphere more than actuality, telling rather than showing the reader what to feel.

He got up and went to the window and looked down at the glistening street, at the asphalt shining with an almost immanent wetness and lucency, at the blurred lights glowing through the undersea daylight. The air was surprisingly dark, filled with a mist of drizzling rain, gloomy and green, a marine atmosphere fathoms down where the bent light from the sun, submerged in a liquid air, floated and swayed, exiled. [38]

This passage differs from Abbey's later portrayals of the western landscape—one hardly expects a drizzling marine atmosphere there —but certain characteristic ways of viewing scenery are apparent. Qualities of light and dark combine with a sensitivity to his surroundings, so the pictorial coincides with the emotional. In this case, though, the slightness of the sentiment undercuts the paragraph.

More significant than his embryonic style is Abbey's awareness of changes in the landscape. While *Jonathan Troy* insists on no overt environmental message, concerns about protection for the earth's resources are present. The best example occurs in the description of a leisurely drive through the Pennsylvania countryside, when Jonathan and Leafy spot the Deerlick mine.

The monster was quiet now, empty, the brain abandoned for the day, but beyond the railroad and on the other side of the slow sulfurous creek the coke-ovens were alive, flaming and smoking, and a small mine-car crept across their tops over the narrow rails. Smoke came in through the windows of the car and with it the smell of burning coal and hydrogenous gasses. Jonathan rolled up the windows. They drove past the long row of the coke-ovens and past hills of burning slag—great boney piles of waste from the mines, of yellow rock and red ash, with flames creeping like blue spirits from pits and craters in the smouldering mass. [279]

Leafy thinks the name of the mine site must be a joke, but her companion explains that, "About fifty years ago, so I'm told, this was a green place with grass and real trees and a stream of clean cold water where that yellowish sewer is now. . . . The place used to be swarming with deer coming to get a good taste of that salt. They don't come any more—maybe they don't like sulfur" [279–80]. To cover his discomfort at what he sees, Jonathan laughs ironically; then the author swiftly changes the subject. In later years Abbey, not content with terse generalities, will devote entire chapters to such visual atrocities as the mine's black tipple, "towering . . . like a Martian monster, complicated, skeletal, sooty-eyed, with countless brittle legs and a long angular snout burrowing into the side of the hill" [279]. And he will berate incessantly those companies and corporations perpetrating such destruction. For now, however, because the heart of his story lies elsewhere, he merely acknowledges his displeasure at a mad machine.

Other characteristic topics arise in *Jonathan Troy* as well, but in each case the author digs no deeper than a comment or two allows. The hero's father, for example, represents failed anarchy in its most pathetic state. Despite the opportunity for dissection, however, Abbey says remarkably little about the man's inadequacies, choosing to concentrate instead on the son's perceptions. Even when the author gives Nat Troy a moment for oration, he sets the aging man in front of a Salvation Army gathering, fills his mouth with foolish phrases, and then lets the chapter drift to a benign close. Equally inaccessible are the politics of Feathersmith and his friends, a windy group of philosophers accused of being "Communist bastards" by the rednecks who frequent the Blue Bell Bar.

The bar scenes contain other elements suggestive of later Abbey portrayals. The brawl preceding Nat Troy's death, for example, foreshadows Jack Burns's fistfight with the one-armed man, George Hayduke's enthusiastic battles with everyone in sight, and numerous nonfiction adventures like *Abbey's Road*'s "In Defense of the Redneck." In this first novel, however, the beginning writer overworks his prose: "He was going through the doorway now, pushing rapidly through the smoke and noise and smells and mass of converging bodies, immersed in them but sealed off from them, his nerves waiting, listening for just one thing while his body thrust forward like a blinded animal, dumb and mute and urgent" [344].

Two generalizations should be made. First, the descriptive, emotional, and evocative sections of *Jonathan Troy* are wordy and convoluted. Second, paradoxically, the more serious thoughtful portions are cut off before they have been fully developed. A lack of revision probably accounts for some of the problems, but more likely the focus of the novel creates the chief difficulties. Abbey's later books will be designed around concrete themes—wilderness and freedom in *The Journey Home*, for example, or the individual's anarchistic duty to protect those basic needs in *The Monkey Wrench Gang*. In *Jonathan Troy*, however, an unformed young man is the center of attention and his nebulousness leads the author into trouble. Only when Abbey concentrates on a vision of the West as metaphorical habitat, as a place necessary for psychological well-being, does he bring order to his handling of characters, narrative line, and theme.

The spirit of the western landscape, not its concrete physical presence, penetrates the book. Abbey confines the story to Powhatan, Pennsylvania, a small eastern community. The West enters only through the imagination, when Jonathan's states of mind—his hopes, his fears, his dreams—need assessment. At those rare moments, Abbey both controls his novel and elicits the reader's sympathy for the protagonist by making the West a metaphorical trigger for empathy and understanding.

As early as page 3, Jonathan imagines an abstracted desert landscape. Sitting in the Blue Bell Bar and listening to the mournful sound of its jukebox, he daydreams about the singer's words. With "quivered" heart and "jellied emotion," the boy talks under his breath to the absent voice. "I know just how you feel, old dawg, old hound . . . Me too. I'm homesick too. Sick for the home I've never seen. Beyond the farthest hills, towards the evening sun, under a magic moon, away out West where the coyote howls." Adding to his reverie, "he remembered the postcards in his father's trunk, the lush-colored scenes of desert sunsets, silhouetted cactus and joshua trees, red cliffs, sandy old roads winding under cottonwoods. Good God but I'm homesick" [3]. This place is accessible only in Jonathan's imagination, a jumble of incompatible locales and picture postcard scenes conjuring wide-open spaces far from the bleak perimeters of the present. Thus Abbey introduces the young man to the reader and initiates his longings for a rebirth that can take place only in the fancied freedom of the Western landscape.

Ironically, Jonathan's inspiration comes from his father. The old man keeps a "great wooden trunk with . . . [a] treasure of trophies from past years and places far away—the stuffed horntoad, Indian beadwork, a crumpled black Stetson, the walnut-handled revolver, high-heeled boots, a jewelbox containing rattles from a rattlesnake, a piece of petrified wood, a skeletal fragment of cane cactus, a lump of ore," and a host of other memorabilia [38]. Throughout the book, Jonathan draws upon that storehouse whenever his immediate surroundings seem too dismal, envisioning a figurative landscape where he can be free. His father dozing over Edward Bellamy's *Looking Backward* and then nagging his son about the future, uneaten pork chops congealing while the two Troys bicker, Jonathan stuffing a rag in the washbasin drain before he begins to clean up—such images darken the boy's moods, until "quite suddenly, like a pang of heartache, sharp with longing" comes a vision of the West to ease the squalor of the Powhatan present.

A dim road . . . an old wagon trail curving, winding slowly, dust-colored, among giant boulders shaded purple in the shade, golden in the light; twin paths parallel by strange and solitary trees with fluted trunks and thorny unleaved limbs, dry-green, pale-green tinged with yellow from the sun, leading into distance under a tremendous sky washed with violet and turquoise-blue toward a mountain red as iron with cliffsides and level top, toward the mass of clouds shot through with fire-orange, amber, bordered with gold and banked before the sinking western sun . . . [10]

The emotive Zane Grey diction communicates Jonathan's adolescent longing for sensuous beauty and his intense yearning for freedom. For both Jonathan and his creator, only the western desertscape gives latitude to those dreams.

Because *Jonathan Troy* is not autobiography, however, distinct differences exist between the author's and the character's interpretations of the western scene. The boy has no sense of reality, so he envisions only a romantic world of make-believe and reconstructs a Hollywood imitation of the literal West. Midway through the novel, that fanciful perception takes concrete shape, when a movie called *Desert Blood* captures his imagination and draws him vicariously into its action. Again, Abbey uses italics to set the daydream off from reality.

Red as hatred. Yellow as fear, the sun stood noon-high, a burning star too bright for any camera, and far below, caught alive in the pitiless glare, treading on his own black shadow and looking backward without hope—walked Jonathan Troy. [108]

The youth fashions an inflated Gary Cooper–High Noon image of heroic grandeur—"and in the man, the dying outlaw, he saw himself. . . ." This role playing, unlike the inspiration Abbey draws from the desert sun, epitomizes the limited range of Jonathan's perceptions. While he "watched and drank and breathed it in, proud with the loveliness and romance, a powerful resolution formed and clenched and knotted in his heart" [108–9]. That resolution remains unspecified, but, if stated, it would be Jonathan's promise to himself to go west where his mirage awaits, to seek the American dream. His simplistic notion of the frontier—movie-star heroics followed by a romantic ride off into the sunset—carries him only as far as a picture postcard's boundaries. But Abbey's concept is kaleidoscopic and ever-expanding. The West, with its inherent freedom and wilderness, becomes the wellspring for his creative imagination; a new American dream becomes his goal.

It would be a mistake to equate Abbey's philosophy with Jonathan's, just as it would be inaccurate to see the man in the boy. But certain facets of the two lives coincide. Like his protagonist, Abbey grew up in a small town in Pennsylvania, and some details from the boyhoods are surely the same. More important, the author's own decision to head West matches his character's, although different reasons impelled him. When Abbey was seventeen, just before his induction into the army, he hitchhiked around the country "from Pennsylvania to Seattle by way of Chicago and Yellowstone National Park; from Seattle down the coast to San Francisco; and from there by way of Barstow and Needles via boxcar, thumb, and bus through the Southwest back home to the old farm" [JH, 1]. In the essay "Hallelujah on the Bum," published first in *The American West* in 1970 and reprinted as the opening chapter of *The Journey Home* in 1977, Abbey outlines the three-month adventures of that "wise, brown, ugly, shy, poetical . . . bold, stupid, sun-dazzled kid, out to see the country before giving his life in the war against Japan. A kind of hero, by god!" [JH, 1–2]. Although that last line may ironically link Abbey to Troy, the point is not to draw analogies between the two youths but to discover the seeds of the mature author's philosophy. Jonathan's unformed and idealistic notion of the West as a place where his dreams might find substance shows a germination of Abbey' attitudes. It does not, however, replicate them.

What Jonathan envisions is less sophisticated. His Zane Grey imagination locks him into superficial dreams, while Abbey's burgeoning creativity is unleashed by the western landscape. Because the youth never sees the real West in the novel, he never has the opportunity to experience its impact. Like many easterners, he perceives it, of necessity, figuratively rather than literally. His author, however, has firsthand knowledge. The second page of "Hallelujah on the Bum" characterizes Abbey's own experience—"a magical vision, a legend come true: the front range of the Rocky mountains. An impossible beauty, like a boy's first sight of an undressed girl, the image of those mountains struck a fundamental chord in my imagination that has sounded ever since" [JH, 2]. The desert struck an even louder chord—"all of it there, simply *there*, neither hostile nor friendly, but full of a powerful, mysterious promise" [JH, 11; italics Abbey's]. Perhaps no other lines of Abbey's so fully express the intangible source of his prose.

Certainly that "powerful, mysterious promise" propels the best-written parts of *Jonathan Troy,* and that same power will be the force behind all the books that follow on down Abbey's road. Perhaps Jonathan imagines the regenerative West somewhat superficially, but Abbey agrees in principle with his character's perception. If no other point is made by this first novel, it at least envisions the West as a metaphor for possibilities, heading both Jonathan and his creator in the right direction. Empowered by the landscape, Abbey now stands ready to focus on the western scene.

Meanwhile, one might argue that *Jonathan Troy* had best be forgotten. With its ill-designed plot, its unbelievable characters, and its foolish eccentricities, the book rarely transcends its limitations. Nevertheless, its embryonic virtues will find articulation in Abbey's subsequent writing, and for that fact alone this novel merits some attention.

2

Forward, March

The Brave Cowboy

The Brave Cowboy (1956) shows how much Edward Abbey learned from his struggles with *Jonathan Troy*. Published just two years later, it sounds as if it had been written by a different man. The author controls his characters and molds their responses in this second book, creating psychologically consistent people engaged in coherent and credible actions. The plot moves quickly, slowing only when Abbey needs to build a complexity of character or to underscore a critical motif. Unlike his first effort, this work of fiction traces a clearly conceived pattern, and its ending, although abrupt and oversimplified, is inevitable.

Most readers believe Abbey borrowed his master plan from the traditional Western novel. While *The Brave Cowboy* is set in the twentieth rather than in the nineteenth century, with an ex-college-student-sheepherder protagonist rather than a mythic cowboy hero, its pattern still reflects one pursued in most modern horse operas. A man of mysterious origins rides into the novel for the purpose of redressing certain ethical wrongs. Confronted by a host of enemies and by a hostile land as well, the man prevails through actions both chivalrous and brave. This simple pattern—successful for Zane Grey in *Riders of the Purple Sage* and for Jack Schaefer in *Shane*, imperative for all pulp writers of lesser talents and imaginations—gives Abbey a comfortable formula on which to rely. Whether a straightforward imitation or an ironic inversion of that master plan, *The Brave Cowboy* obviously borrows a time-tested structural foundation from Western writers both past and present.

The surface similarities between this book and its predecessors are self-evident. Abbey's hero is "the brave cowboy," Jack Burns, born in Missouri but raised in New Mexico by a feisty old grandfather, bred in the twentieth century but psychologically attuned to an earlier age. His story begins when he rides out of nowhere, from an unnamed wilderness camp to the civilized world of Duke City—Albuquerque—in order to rescue an old college friend from jail. There Paul Bondi awaits transferal to a federal prison where he has been sentenced for refusing to register for the draft. There, too, Burns gets himself locked up so he can better aid his pal. The quixotic mission fails, however, for on principle Bondi refuses to be saved, and Burns now must extricate himself from his own imprisonment. He escapes, but in so doing becomes a fugitive tracked by the sheriff, an official posse of dullards, an unofficial cadre of beer-drinking voyeurs, an indifferent Indian tracker, and a fanatical helicopter crew. After a thrilling chase sequence reminiscent of hundreds of Western movies, up the escarpment from the plains around Duke City to the plateau above, Burns miraculously escapes his pursuers. Then Abbey unceremoniously eliminates him in a ludicrous accident: a truck carrying bathroom fixtures strikes the brave cowboy while he crosses a freeway in the night.

Such a brief outline neither indicates the power of Abbey's prose nor includes any of the details that provide the emotional impact of the story. It shows, though, why so many readers have perceived *The Brave Cowboy* as a variation of the typical Western. Despite his sad demise, Jack Burns resembles Lassiter or Shane or a thousand other knights-errant of the ranch and desert scene, while his performance reminds the reader of their idealistic posturings and subsequent heroism. Translated to the screen, he might well be a Gary Cooper or a John Wayne. In fact, a fine movie based on Abbey's text—*Lonely Are The Brave*, starring Kirk Douglas as the cowboy and Walter Matthau as his pursuer—was produced in 1962, and a look at that film does nothing to undermine a conviction that the story springs from a traditional source.

Yet to read *The Brave Cowboy* only as a variation on a familiar theme is too easy, for Abbey's imagination ranges wider and his intellect goes deeper. A stronger formulation than Owen Wister/ Zane Grey heroics extends this book and his later ones beyond the confines of popular fiction and moves Abbey himself into the front ranks of Western writers. This pattern, taken from Shakespeare's time and earlier, from Elizabethan England and the medieval world beyond, gives him the appropriate mythos. In that distant place, like Nathaniel Hawthorne and Herman Melville a century before him, this modern author finds a mode for speaking to his own generation. Edward Abbey designed *The Brave Cowboy* not like a romantic Western but like a formal romance.

By definition and by practice, a romance opens its audience's eyes to a unique way of looking at the immediate world. Its purpose is twofold—a celebration of life, of freedom and survival, and a celebration of life's possibilities, of dreams both marvelous and visionary. To achieve those ends, the romancer must first create a self-sustaining world, isolated from tangible reality but still suggestive of it. He must populate his microcosm with figures whose stylized behavior patterns remind us of our own less predictable modes but whose actions would nevertheless be extraordinary in conventional society—"experience liberated," says Henry James. It is this "disconnected and uncontrolled experience" that frees the characters to overstep their boundaries into a twilight realm of the fantastic. By exaggerating their behavior traits, by intensifying their experiences, and by relying upon sensory impressions to heighten their tale, the author fabricates the world of the romance. Such a creation must not be mistaken for fantasy, however, because the romancer also calls into question the ethical, social, and moral assumptions of his age. The resulting exorcism of values, conceived in idealism but processed as revolt, fulfills for him his need to re-hammer the unmalleable world in which he lives.[1]

The romancer's tools are those of any writer, but the freedom with which he wields them separates him from the conventional novelist. While that novelist must maintain the texture of actual experience, the romancer can more fancifully redesign characters and reorder experiences in any way he chooses. First, however, he must postulate his world. Edward Abbey selects the West—New Mexico, in *The Brave Cowboy*—a specific environment that he carefully describes before he sets his characters in motion. Superficially, his stage resembles an Albuquerque of twenty-five years ago, and indeed, old-time residents acknowledge the resemblances. But if this is the world of a romance, there must be differences too, for such a world must suggest, but not replicate, the real.

Duke City lies "waiting, stirring faintly but in silence—vague wisps of smoke and dust, glint of reflected light from moving objects, a motion of shadows . . . an undifferentiated patch of blue and grey shadow . . . edges ill-defined . . . extremities invisible."[2] It looms into Jack Burns's vision when he rides down out of the wilderness to begin his aborted venture. Yet as he looks around the perimeters of this great city, Abbey stresses its unreal qualities. Here is a world haunted by "pale phantoms dying of nostalgia," a silent desert "troubled, vexed by . . . vagrant spirits," a mysterious realm, "this valley of ghosts and smoke and unacknowledged sorrows." Here is a melancholy miasma that seems real but is not, a place where "the Rio Bravo comes down from the mountains of Colorado and the mountains of Santa Fe and flows into the valley, passing between the dead volcanoes on the west and the wall of mountains on the east . . . flows past the cornfields and mud villages of the Indians, past thickets of red willow and cane and scrub oak, through the fringe of the white man's city" and beyond, vanishing "at last into the dim violet haze of distance, of history and Mexico and the gulf-sea" [7]. Yoking his specificity with a visionary aura, one defined by "phantoms hissing and moaning with the wind," Abbey draws his audience not into modern-day New Mexico after all, but rather, inside the restructured universe of the long-forgotten romance.

Many readers, of course, assume that any Western will be located in "virgin territory." Part of the appeal of hundreds of pulp stories has come directly from their generic settings in the untamed and largely unknown West. Escape fiction in general frees readers from their everyday experiences by taking them off to imaginary realms, and Westerns, set in the "wide-open spaces," do so most energetically. Offering a spectrum of frontier possibilities, they graphically portray heroics in a harsh land. But the scenery of *The Brave Cowboy* imitates neither Zane Grey's rainbow trail of sun, sand, and sage nor the lesser worlds of six-gun paperbacks. Instead, Abbey restructures reality in such a way that he turns the ostensibly romantic into the nether world of the romance.

A word of caution is necessary here, for the "romance" and "romantic" are not synonymous. A pulp Western writer drops an overlay of perfectability on an apparently severe environment. He pictures life romantically. The writer of romance, however, pursues a different goal with different means. He hopes to expose certain problems of his age by projecting imagined but correspondent trials on an imagined but correspondent world. It is imperative to differentiate from the outset between the two modes, the one frivolous and the other consequential. Abbey and other serious romancers direct their energies toward an analysis of the contemporary scene, while pulp writers offer only escape. To put it another way, Abbey picks an apple, finds the worm inside, looks for its source, predicates the damage it will cause. His opposite number simply turns the apple to the other side and gives the reader an unexamined, although tasty, bite. While both are dealing with apples—or with the western landscape, in this case—the serving differs extraordinarily.

Thus, in *The Brave Cowboy*, Abbey offers Duke City, an unpleasant conglomerate of smog and overcrowding, a facsimile of its model's real-world decadence. Filled with "fat automobiles gleaming like toys . . . , horns blaring challenges, white faces staring from behind their glass" [25; an image repeated at the novel's close], and strangled by its own "liquescent oozy mud with the consistency of warm gruel, an unplumbed deposit of fine silt that had once been a part of the tilth and topsoil of Colorado and would eventually become the property of the Gulf of Mexico" [22], Duke City defines the urban West after overbuilding and overpopulation have encroached upon its open spaces. A quarter of a century later, we know the truth of Abbey's vision, for in fact suburbs now creep up the mountain outside Albuquerque where once the brave cowboy imaginatively fled.

The county jail, backdrop for the middle section of the novel, is pictured in terms equally foul. Burns spends his first night in the Hole, locked behind steel grating in a "steel cubical: bare gray walls, no window, no light, no furnishings but a bare steel bunk and a washbasin and a toilet bowl without a seat" [76]. Bondi's larger space appears no more desirable, "the cage of bars and the steel walls and the dreary light filtering through the dust and cobwebs and dried spit encrusted on each window" [79]. Abbey emphasizes the dirt, the stagnation, the hopelessness of the jail setting as analogous to the plight of the men incarcerated behind its walls. The author draws parallels, too, between the atmosphere of the jail and the atmosphere of Duke City, both places shadowed by twentieth-century dust and grime. This repetition in *The Brave Cowboy* marks Abbey's growth as a novelist, for he now filters key images from scene to scene, letting their meanings reverberate and echo.

And just as dirt darkens both Duke City and its county jail, so do the walls that imprison men there recur later to diminish the relative freedom of the mountains. Burns escapes from his cell only to find a similar barrier outside. The first chapter of his flight begins:

> . . . The great cliffs leaned up against the flowing sky, falling through space as the earth revolved, turning amber as whisky in the long-reaching lakes of light from the evening sun. But the light had no power to soften the jagged edges and rough-spalled planes of the granite; in that clear air each angle and crack cast a shadow as harsh, clean, sharp, real, as the rock itself—so that though they had endured as they were for ten million years, the cliffs held the illusion of a terrible violence suddenly arrested, paralyzed in time, latent with power. [189]

Enormous, impenetrable, almost inhuman, the wall looms, an awesome obstruction to freedom. Even Burns's pursuer feels the strength of its "tortured face. . . . Something in those heights of naked, perpendicular crags and cliffs made him halt in his tracks. . . . [The sheriff] stared upward, unblinking, at that implacable wall" [214]. Abbey continues to mention rocks, cliffs, barriers, walls, noting their presence in every descriptive paragraph of Morlin Johnson's trek to Burns's camp. Dust filters over the scene too, so the entire novel seems a succession of impurities and imprisoning walls.

One could argue, of course, that the mountains of New Mexico *are* steeply forbidding and that dirt abounds because it is carried constantly by desert winds. Abbey may simply describe what exists, with no thought of utilizing extended imagery and no intention of creating a world of romance. Such a literal accusation is perhaps irrefutable, because the reader sees very much as Abbey sees, but the ways in which the author approaches the three prominent settings in the book suggest that he intended more than exact reproduction. Each place—the city, the jail, the mountain—stands one step removed from reality.

In the Prologue, a vista spreads before the reader, "a valley in the West where phantoms come to brood and mourn, pale phantoms dying of nostalgia and bitterness" [7]. Abbey continues, "The river is haunted, the city is haunted, the valley and the mountains and the silent desert are haunted—troubled, vexed by ghosts, phantoms, and vagrant spirits" [7]. Surely this is not what one sees, looking toward Albuquerque, but only what one feels when Abbey leads his audience toward his own Duke City. Part I begins more tangibly, with the cowboy fixing his breakfast amid a "burnt-out wasteland" of bunch grass and Yucca. He boils his coffee, fries his mutton, rolls his first cigarette of the day. But Abbey neither reveals his name nor penetrates the "something shadowy and smoke-like about him, something faded, blurred, remembered" [17]. Just as the valley appears indistinct and haunted, so too the cowboy seems like a man from a dream. Dusty, dark children shout along his way, "Dónde va, meestair cow-*boy?* . . . Dónde va, don charro? Eh? Dónde va?" Mildly he answers, "Quien sabe? . . . Who knows? Who cares?" [23–24; italics Abbey's]. Nothing is specified, nothing concrete is said yet—only a reflection, a shadowed border zone, shimmers before the reader's eyes. Duke City mirrors the reality of Albuquerque, as is appropriate in a once-removed world of romance.

One might expect each part of *The Brave Cowboy* to appear more real than its predecessor, the jail more immediate than the city, the mountain wilderness more tactile and alive than the urban scenes. Yet the opposite is true for, as it progresses, the story moves further away from reality. The second part begins, for example, by asking the reader, in effect, to shut his eyes. Abbey delimits the jail's confines by appealing to the auditory sense rather than to the visual.

Timothy, you got the makins?
I got a half sack Bull Durham and not a single goddamn paper.
I got paper.
It's a deal, son. Save that light, Hoskins, we got two hot babies comin up. Steady boy and watch her roll, save the tobacco while I get the coal.
Thanks, Timothy.
How long you in for, boy?
Thirty days flat.
Vaggin, pimpin, or hustlin?
Went through a red light with my eyes shut. Judge called it reckless driving.
Mighty reckless drivin. Now tell me the truth, boy.
I lifted a knife at Monkey Ward's.

Ah hah. You tried to. Good knife?
Seven ninety-five plus tax.
Good, good, son. You shrewd like a chicken.
Butt, Timothy?
Butt me no butts. Already spoken for. Hoskins gets it. Rev'rend Hoskins on his Flyin Machine, waitin for Peter to open the door, got hog drunk and hit the floor.
Lay off it, Greene.
Never!
I'm tellin you.
Never! [51–52]

The lengthy quotation, although just a portion of the chorus, is necessary because the point is its seductiveness. Inverting the traditional pattern of female voices luring the traveler onto the rocks and into the depths, Abbey sings a siren song in masculine chords. Another sound then interrupts the atonal background music, "as if from far away, muffled by barriers of steel and brick and cement, the thin dim sound of . . . wild drunken singing with the quality of an Indian's wail and the wind's intoxication, the music a wolf might make if it could sing like a man." Paul Bondi sits up in his cell and cries, "I'm dreaming, I'm dreaming, I'm dreaming" [58–59].

But he is not. The voice he hears is his friend's, as he learns the next day when he sees the cowboy standing beside him. So the pattern of the second part repeats that of the first. Introducing each of his settings indirectly by stressing their dreamlike qualities, Abbey then turns the stage over to his characters and brings his shadow worlds to life. The mysterious aura remains, however, so that the effect is one of disengagement from reality, a nonspecificity of time and place appropriate for the romance. Then Abbey concludes Burns's role in Part II by sending him back into the shadows. Paul's wife watches the cowboy ride into the nether world, or out of it.

The qualities of light and space deceived her, baffled her—she felt that the figure of man and horse, now one, might recede from her, shrink in magnitude forever and yet not completely and finally disappear—if only she had the power to prevent it. And in that momentary hallucination she felt that it was suddenly terribly important that she stop them—as if the limits of her vision were an abstract, impossible barrier dividing reality from nothingness.

The hallucination passed. She peered into the gloom of the dawn and saw nothing but shadows. The cowboy was gone. [155]

Key words in these two paragraphs show the intensity of Abbey's point. "Baffled," "deceived," "shrink," and "disappear" combine with a repetition of "hallucination," a "shadow," and "an abstract, impossible barrier dividing reality from nothingness" to blur the distinctions between what is imagined and what is real. It is unnecessary, however, to define the boundaries because only the recognition of a subliminal world's existence is important.

The third part progresses still further into that limitless space. Again, precise details define the path, from the moment the cowboy starts up "the arroyo, sandy and dust-dry except for a thread of water trickling from a tiny seep-like spring near the foot of a rock ledge" [189–90] until he crests the rim of the escarpment and wildly lopes into the sanctuary of "white slim quaking aspens . . . bending in the wind, their yellow leaves chattering frantically, crazily, with all the laughing hysteria of old mad women" [264]. But the wilderness setting of the chase resembles an infernal world, not a verdant one. To the sheriff, "the mountain appeared as a great ugly eruption of granite, not only meaningless but malignant, and worse than malignant—a piece of sheer insolence" [236]; to Burns, the cliffs are hostile too, "as if he were alien . . . to the rocks and trees and spirits of the wilderness" [249]. Both men, despite their consonance with the wilderness, intuitively recognize the presence of something more malevolent than "the sliding broken treacherous rock" [250], more awesome than the brute indifference of the Sandias. Certainly Abbey has re-created not just an ordinary view of mountains to the east of Albuquerque but the range of a romance, the "dark" range, above which, "remote in time and space, the glittering stars wheeled to the beat of a cosmic drum" [268]. The labyrinth of that dark mountain path in Part III leads deep into a world leagues apart from the conventional Western scene.

Two men guide the way—Jack Burns, the mystical knight-errant, and Morlin Johnson, the flesh-and-blood sheriff of Bernal County whose name implies an Arthurian magic. A more unlikely pathfinder than either man would be difficult to find, since Abbey emphasizes their respective nonheroic statures. For example, after the introduction leads into the intangible valley of shadows, the solitary cowboy appears.

He was a young man, not more than thirty. His neck was long, scrawny, with a sharp adamsapple and corded muscles; his nose, protruding
from under the decayed brim of the hat, was thin, red, aquiline and
asymmetrical, like the broken beak of a falcon. He had a small mouth
with thin dry lips, and a chin pointed like a spade, and his skin, bristling
with a week's growth of black whiskers, had the texture of cholla and the
hue of an old gunstock. [13]

This mortal, pictured through roughcast figures of speech, with
lanky legs, unshaven profile, and skinny frame "tough as a wild
billygoat" [28], seems almost a caricature. But on the contrary, Jack
Burns is no Etheline. Intending to show a real human being emerging from the shadows of the desert, Abbey includes naturalistic
details to emphasize the earthy qualities of his man. Intending also
to portray a figure from the world of romance, the author uses those
same details to point out Burns's otherworldliness. This juxtaposition of the real with the fanciful works as well with characters as it
did with settings. Abbey, manipulating his readers in Part II, for
example, by alternating the ethereal with the base, the chorus of
voices with the filth, the siren call with the bars, manipulates his
readers now. He makes Jack Burns convincing as a knightly protagonist because he is so ordinary.

A good example of his mixed character occurs just after Abbey
reveals the cowboy's name. Burns arrives at the Bondi home in the
middle of Part I, where he affectionately greets Paul's wife and son.
At once the reader learns the nature of this Lancelot-cowboy's quest
and the relationships that have precipitated it, the impetus of love
both actualized and unacknowledged. In a narrative line reminiscent of Arthurian romance, Burns's affection for the husband barely
controls his feelings for the wife, a revelation tacitly communicated
at a mid-afternoon wine and ice-cream feast preceding the cowboy's
departure to see his friend. The episode grounds Burns in his own
humanity, while simultaneously elevating him to a nobler plane
and also reminding the reader of Sir Lancelot. To emphasize the
point, Abbey writes explicitly of "this strange wandering friend,
riding in like a knight-errant, [who] might have . . . power through
magic or valor or wit" [34]. Both novelists and critics have recognized a resemblance between cowboys and knights-errant, but only
Abbey has looked behind the label to isolate the man behind the
mask. "Who are *you*, anyway?" [41; italics Abbey's], Jerry Bondi
asks her husband's friend. Not the Lone Ranger, implies the au-

thor, not the consort from Camelot, and not the "smoky-eyed cen-
taur" [35] from another time and place, but Jack Burns, an ordinary
man bent upon performing an ordinary deed *in a romance.*

Even his ideology stems from an ordinary event in his past when
his grandfather taught him the meaning of manhood. Burns explains the formative incident to Paul while the two men sit in jail.
One day the boy had watched a "young, strong, smart, good lookin'"
cowboy cruelly and needlessly embarrass old Snye, "bald as a buzzard, pot-bellied, cranky and ugly and generally miserable"; as a
result, Burns's grandfather had physically kicked the antagonist off
his ranch. "Not that he made me like old Snye or hate Brock [the
cowboy]; it's just that then and ever since whenever it's a case of a
Snye agin a Brock I feel I gotta help out the Snye," says Burns. "Not
for his sake, but for my own, I think. Or for the sake of somethin
more important than any Snye or Brock or me" [118]. What Burns
articulates by example, Paul considers more esoterically. He calls
it "justice," even "natural justice," and wonders if he himself might
be a Snye whom the brave cowboy has come to avenge. Perhaps
Paul's interpolation from story to self holds true, but more significant is the unveiling of Burns's motivation. The force that drives
him is one of chivalric intent, of righting apparent wrongs, of
avenging friends in need.

But Jack Burns is tilting at windmills, with a brand of chivalry
no more effective than Don Quixote's. The unshaven stringbean
fails to rescue the distressed victim, not only because his friend
refuses aid but because his plan is ill-conceived from the start. He
fails to get the girl too, for in fact Mrs. Bondi is already committed
to someone else. Moreover, he completely loses—his quest and his
life—in the end. And even that fate is anticlimactic, as he rides off
not into the sunset but toward an accidental death in the darkness
of night. Just as his profile belies a standard handsome hero's, so
his actions miscarry where we expected triumph.

This troubles some readers. Anticipating a tragic hero, they chas-
tise Abbey for a failure in conception when his cowboy acts unhe-
roically. "Jack is no hero. He overcomes nothing and rights no
wrongs," writes C. L. Sonnichsen disarmingly. "He does have guts
and a horse, but they are not enough to save him from futility. It is
not fate which opposes him. He has no real tragic flaw. He is just
born at the wrong time."[3] A harsher position is taken by another
contemporary critic who states that "because of Abbey's inability

to get the most out of his themes and characters, Burns may be taken for a fool rather than a hero."[4] Both opinions are wrong. Because Sonnichsen, Milton, and others insist upon viewing the brave cowboy at least as a stock figure in a conventional Western novel, or at best as an ironic inversion of the type, they are disgruntled when he behaves uncharacteristically—that is, in ways that differ from their preconceptions. But the faults generally attributed to Abbey's portrayal of Burns—the naiveté, the single-mindedness, the one-dimensionality, the disappointing guise of hero as victim—all grow out of an insistence upon analyzing the man in traditional ways. If, instead, we consider him as a figure in a romance, though not necessarily a romantic one, his characterization makes sense.

In medieval times, characters of romances were individuals whose exaggerated traits fulfilled certain expectations. Protagonists were good and antagonists evil, often symbolically so. Gareth's mission to rescue the Lady Lyonors, wherein he decapitates the Knight of Night, called Death, who guards the Castle Perilous, is a good example. By the time American writers had translated the form to suit their nineteenth-century needs, characters had become less blatantly allegorical. *The Scarlet Letter*'s Chillingworth and *Moby-Dick*'s Ahab, although evil, differ radically from giants and dragons. Nevertheless, they remain stylized, exaggerated, intensified. They behave almost as we do, but not quite. When Hawthorne and Melville release them into their worlds of romance, they become, in effect, psychological archetypes. Abbey follows this model in designing the details of Jack Burns's persona.

The most obvious trait is the anachronistic behavior. Not only does the author subtitle his book "An Old Tale in a New Time," but he frequently alludes to Burns as a psychological throwback. The Bondis shake their heads. "Poor Jack," thinks Paul, "poor old Jack—born too late, out of place, out of time. Look at him, the scheming atavist, all wound up in reality looking for a tunnel back to his boy's dream world of space and horses and sunlight" [124]. Jerry speaks her mind forthrightly: "You can't go on like this— you're in the Twentieth Century now" [151]. To project nineteenth-century mores upon an age that has forgotten them, to show the clash between western generations, to bring a shadowy ideal into the dusty reality of today, Abbey has stylized the figure who carries the meaning of the past. His creation must be one-dimensional because, as a character in a romance, Burns must bear an archetypal weight—the libidinous overtones of chivalry, of manhood, of independence.

Burns's need for freedom surfaces almost at the beginning of his story, when he cuts the steely barbed wire that fences him out, or in. Later, he fights against the grasps of arresting officers and finds he cannot tolerate "the suffocating oppression of confinement closing in on him" [77]. He says to Paul "This ain't no place for humans" [100]. He has to break free, because jail makes him feel "kinda sick and mournful . . . uncomfortable, itchy, restless" [108], and again he cuts through steel constraints. The same force impels him up the escarpment, despite the odds against successful evasion of the opponents squeezing in from all sides. His ability to escape that pursuit seems unreal, a fact Abbey emphasizes repeatedly. "You'd think we were chasing a ghost," growls the sheriff. "An invisible cowboy with an invisible horse" [228]. Because he is not quite human and because he does not quite belong in the real world, the cowboy can scale seemingly perpendicular walls. Riding out of the shadows as the book begins, he is "smoke-like . . . faded, blurred, remembered" [17]. Burns laughs about it. When his appearance at the jailhouse surprises Paul, he jests, "What'd you expect?—a goddamned ghost?" [93]. And when Jerry worries about his plans, he boasts, "Nothin can hurt me; I'm like water: boil me away and I come back in the next thunderhead" [32].

The cowboy does, in fact, come back, not in the next thunderhead but in Abbey's later writing. The Zia paperback reprint of *The Brave Cowboy* deletes, upon the author's request, a definitive paragraph found in the Dodd, Mead first edition. After the trucker attempts to reassure the injured rider—"Don't worry, . . . you're gonna be *all right*. Everything's gonna be fine"—Abbey originally concluded:

The choking had stopped. "Sure," the woman said, all right for *him*. He's dead now." [277—the pagination is the same for both texts; italics Abbey's]

The omission of this ending makes Jack Burns's fate ambiguous, leaving him free to haunt another day. The cowboy does so anonymously as the Lone Ranger figure in *The Monkey Wrench Gang* and overtly as an aging self-parody who carries the lance against modern oppression in Abbey's latest fiction, *Good News*. Those readers who take Burns's first anachronistic appearance literally are mistaken, for the fact that Burns dies and then lives, not only from book to book but even within the pages of one story, indicates that Abbey did not design the man as a plausible cowboy hero.

Whether on horseback, in a sea of cars, or on foot in the labyrinth of mountain canyons, Burns cannot bear the weight of analysis if we try to read his character in the traditional ways. But if we see him as a man/ghost, as monomaniacal as Captain Ahab in his futile quest but as real as any sailor on the Pequod, we find him consistent, coherent, credible. As a guide into the nether world of romance, Jack Burns rides point, a successful characterization.

The same generalizations also apply to most of the other figures in the book. Paul Bondi and the sadistic Gutierrez, in particular, have been criticized as one-sided portrayals, a refutable aspersion if they are reconsidered as semiallegorical. This is not to say that Abbey wrote *The Brave Cowboy* as allegory, or that a set of one-to-one correspondences pervades the book. Rather, it is to offer an explanation and a justification for the simplicity of the characters' minds and deeds. Gutierrez, "the bear-man," exists at the basest level and displays instinctive physical violence. During the interrogation, he begins by digging "his fingers and thumb into Burns' neck, crushing nerves and blood vessels" and ends with a kick "in the small of the back with his knee" [72–73], while later he beats his defenseless prisoner. Even his verbal harassment of the hapless men at mealtime seems excessive. On the lowest rung of the law's evolutionary ladder, Gutierrez is more animal than human, but through him Abbey makes a point. At its most mindless and primitive level, the law can be animalistic, retaliatory, and sadistic. Gutierrez both exudes the law's evil and represents it, like a fire-breathing dragon. His characterization is broad, but not as overdrawn as Etheline's or that of the beer-guzzling comic-book addicts who form another branch of the posse. The bear-man functions appropriately, as long as he dwells within the confines of a romance.

Paul Bondi belongs there too, but Abbey treats him differently. Whereas Gutierrez is a physical being, with his little red close-set eyes and sweat-stained shirt, Paul is spiritual. Abbey, in fact, never really visualizes Paul's physical self. The first glimpse comes in shadows: "Bondi sat quiet on his bunk, saying nothing aloud, busy at disemboweling his own soul, examining with an attempt at a sterilized logic the soft glistening blue-veined innards of his spirit.

While darkness gathered within and around him and the bad air of the cell settled heavily under its own weight of smoke, sweat, human vapors. The sun was gone—its light was gone" [58]. And subsequent views are equally vague, for even though Abbey tells about him and lets him talk, he never shows the man in action. Paul recognizes his own passivity. "Don't think for a moment that I imagine myself as some sort of anarchist hero. I don't intend to fight against Authority" [104]. Later in his conversation with Burns he calls himself "an ironical anarchist," a man who sees "clearly enough the utter hopelessness of the anarchist ideal . . . a lost cause—one never found," and acknowledges that his own brand of protest "is just a sentimentality" [110]. No wonder readers have viewed him as an "irresolute" martyr, "something of a prig."[5] The man talks endlessly but accomplishes nothing. Yet he is designed to fit in this romance as neatly as Gutierrez does, an embodiment of inaction just as Guitierrez is of animalism.

It is interesting that Abbey chooses a passive "ironical anarchist" for his most insubstantial character. The portrayal, reminiscent of Nat Troy in a lesser context, implies that early in his career Abbey recognized the impotence of the anarchistic gesture. Although he will pursue Paul's ideals in most of his subsequent books, he will continue to expose their ineffectiveness as actual weapons against government, big business, and social institutions. Yet he cannot give up the fight. "I only know that if I don't do this, if I give in," Paul affirms, "I'll be haunted by my surrender for the rest of my life" [143–144]. So, too, would Abbey be tortured by his own conscience if he did not pursue his anarchistic impulses. Paul, of course, is a character who resembles Henry James's John Marcher; Abbey, on the other hand, is a man who seeks out his beast, through the activist prose of his own romances. Nevertheless, Paul is necessary to the structural integrity of *The Brave Cowboy*. A man whose conscience leads him blindly, whose passivity only hurts those he loves, he represents futility, perhaps the idle gesture his creator avoids by mocking his "ironical anarchism," by creating the feeble Paul Bondi.

Other characters in the book fill in the textured background of Abbey's prose. While many of them come close to caricature or stereotype—Jerry Bondi as a female victim of the futile gesture, General Desalius as an embodiment of the military establishment, Bob Barker as a sly Mephisto of the business world, Deputy Flynn as a cartoon of the inept cop—their limitations are acceptable in the context of the genre. Just as Shakespeare's romances said more about the world than did their medieval counterparts, so Abbey's creations speak more vigorously about the twentieth century than do the stick figures of popular fiction. Even a simple enumeration of their names and attributes reveals a measure of their meaning. To make such a list, however, illuminates only the obvious, and to analyze their roles is to belabor a point. Of the other New Mexico characters, it is the sheriff who merits attention.

Like Burns, Morlin Johnson appears in an almost naturalistic guise, a gum-chewing fan of girlie calendars who spends an excessive amount of time ruminating in the men's room. Abbey again approaches overstatement, for he almost overloads the man with comical and superfluous characteristics. Some readers have seen Johnson as either a caricature or an inversion of the conventional Western sheriff, a jeepstering Matt Dillon perhaps. But this view ignores the sheriff's complexities, which, although stylized, help tie *The Brave Cowboy* to the real twentieth century. Without Johnson, the world of the romance might be too remote, its characters too exaggerated; through his presence, the reader bridges the juncture between form and content.

The extent of the sheriff's role unfolds in the third part, which opens in his jailhouse office and then moves to the mountains where the chase ensues. Several subtleties about his character appear before he leaves the city—that he is brighter than any of the lawmen who work for him (he uncovers the Bondi/Burns connection and he deduces Burns's destination from the fugitive's outmoded method of travel), that he is educated, and even has a sense of humor (he smiles, as his deputies do not, at the names of Thoreau, Shelley, and Emiliano Zapata on the list of anarchist signatures), that he is honest (he does not take Barker's real estate bait, although he pauses before making the decision). In short, he is a man of mixed thoughts and diverse motives. Before the hunt begins, he looks to the mountains beyond the smoky city and considers the cowboy's plight sympathetically. "So that's where you are, Jack Burns? Out there. A shade of melancholy passed over his mind, a sweet and fragile sadness. Alone, you poor simple bastard —We'll find you . . ." [187–188]. That night, Johnson even goes to the mountain on a sympathetic pilgrimage, but the next day, his attitude modulates. "The *cowboy!* Johnson spat; his instinctive sympathy for the hunted man was darkened by a scornful pity closer to disgust than compassion" [237; italics Abbey's]. By including lines like these, Abbey reminds us constantly that the sheriff comes from the other side.

Once the chase is under way, the author continues to describe the sheriff in charitable tones, even though the lawman performs his duty methodically. Johnson plans the pursuit wisely, placing his men effectively and utilizing modern weaponry and means of communication. The failure to rimrock the cowboy is not the sheriff's fault. The lawman's humanity surfaces when he regrets sending the "vigilantes into the hills . . . more nervous, itchy trigger fingers at large" [233–234], and when he responds with anger to a query, "Shoot on sight?" [223]. His dislike for General Desalius provides more evidence. When Johnson hears Desalius bellow over the loss of his helicopter, he feels "a peculiar shame, not for himself but for his kind" [241].

Away from the others, away from his childlike employees and their technological toys, the sheriff shows a more intimate and appealing side. While climbing toward Burns's camp, "he felt as conspicuous and self-conscious as a tourist tramping into a silent cathedral, . . . the sense of being an intruder" [217] in the stillness. A few steps farther he breaks the silence and calls to the cowboy, asking him to surrender. Only a mockingbird answers. Slowly the sheriff moves up the mountain again, then pauses "on his knees before [a] spring and the blue-veined altar of rock behind it" while "a dim sweet exquisite sorrow passed like a cloud over his mind" [228]. The kinship between the lawman and the land, which recalls Burns's own accord with the wilderness, should encourage trust in this character. But, because Johnson is a means, not an end, the author maintains some distance from this "man of limited prophetic powers" [237].

Abbey has created a functional conduit, a character, like Charon, who ferries the reader between two worlds. Equally at home in his grimy sheriff's office and in the pristine mountain canyons, Johnson remains in neither place but oscillates between the two, leading us into revelations of values of each. This is not to say that the sheriff operates as an authorial surrogate. Rather, he is a device through which the author can transcend the cowboy's world and his own. Several clues suggest Johnson's purpose, but the most important is his stasis. Despite the complexities of his personality, the sheriff never changes. "Let's go home," he concludes at the end of the chase. The events have not affected him at all. In novels, characters grow and develop, but in a romance, such is not the case. *The Brave Cowboy's* world is populated by embodiments, not by dynamic human beings, so people like Jack Burns and the sheriff must forever be objects, not subjects. Johnson ruminates after he learns the cowboy has eluded the hunters:

As he watched the pink radiance deepened into lavender, retreating upward before the advance of the blue, violet and purple shadows. The night, he thought—the night is coming . . . Above the rim the eastern sky was changing from blue to a pale cold green—the suggestion of winter.
He turned to the west; the sun had gone down without glory behind a haze of smoke and dust, leaving only a dull yellow stain stretched across the sky, but to the southwest somewhere over Thieves' Mountain a fat star glimmered, flickered, rising. Venus, said Johnson to himself, Venus —evening star, planet of love . . .   .
Johnson broke off, abashed by his train of thought. [265–66]

These lines signify nothing, however. They merely reiterate the disjunction between the two skylines, between two worlds, and they repeat the sheriff's dual loyalties. They signal no permanent alteration in this complicated but consistent man.

Morlin Johnson, then, acts as a bridge, the span that unites the restructured universe of the cowboy with the real dust and grime of the twentieth century. Hence Johnson's affinity with the land and his role as a determined posseman. Caught between two worlds, cognizant of values in each, he is unwilling or unable to sacrifice one for the other; he only connects. And just as the cowboy guides us into the nether world of the romance, so the lawman ferries us back and forth between that imagined milieu and the more hostile, constricted world of the city, the jail, and the law.

Here, of course, in the nether world, is where the heart of the romance lies, where Abbey rehammers his vision of society into a palpable work of art. His focus is twofold in this book, on the land and on the law. Despising the Albuquerque he sees in the mid-1950s, he crafts a Duke City in its image. Each smoke-tainted view emphasizes and condemns the sulphurous air of urban sprawl, the "boiling shroud of yellow dust." That air faintly troubles Sheriff Johnson by "old, obscure, unacknowledged premonitions of suffocation and disaster" [237], but it bothers the author even more. Throughout his career, Abbey will drum a death tattoo over pollution's strangled corpse, and his descriptions of Duke City simply intone the first lines of the dirge. Accompanying that mournful tune, Abbey also laments a segment of contemporary society that embodies the present-day befoulment. In his later writing, that polluted segment will vary—impersonal big government in *Fire on the Mountain*, voracious big business in *The Monkey Wrench Gang*, for example—but in *The Brave Cowboy* he chooses the law. Its corruption mirrors the land's.

Like the tainted ground fog that swirls around the city, the law, at its basest level, is represented by Gutierrez, who enjoys the reactionary and sadistic pleasures of the animalistic cop. Vindictive and reprehensible, he has no redeeming qualities. Only slightly less repugnant are the dumb deputies, the radio operator, and the helicopter pilot who sounds as excited as "a beagle flushing a rabbit" [231]. Their inane comments and their intrinsic stupidity point out, perhaps too bluntly, the foolish insufficiencies of local law enforcement. Yet the law itself, which Abbey views as abstract and unrelated to everyday life, is just as imperfect, perhaps more so because it is no joke. "The District Judge, a long gaunt man with a gray mustache and the gentle unhappy eyes of an ulcerous aristocrat," isolated in his "old-fashioned 1895" office "lined with books—ponderous unreadable volumes of legal history, statute and precedent, bound in olive drab linen and lettered in gilt" [88], corresponds to the law's removal from the world of men. In direct contrast to the prisoners, who are vital even in their captivity, Judge van Heest, cadaverous remnant of another age, seems as made of dust and air as his philosophy. "The old man, bound by a thousand hoops of habit and tradition and profession, held that the law must be obeyed whatever its social or political or moral significance" [89]. Rigid, outdated, idealistic in their own ways too, both the judge and the law he represents—The Law—are the musty holdovers that supposedly give purpose to the enforcers on the sheriff's team. Abbey is suspicious of them all and uses *The Brave Cowboy* to voice his disdain.

But the options he offers are equally unsatisfactory. Paul Bondi's alternative to legal repression, "sustained by the vague but apparently limitless strength of conviction" [89], is as blind as the judge's stoic faith, his code of ethics as ethereal:

I shall never sacrifice a friend to an ideal. I shall never desert a friend to save an institution. I shall never betray a friend for the sake of law. Great nations may fall in ruin before I shall sell a friend to preserve them. I pray to the God within me to give me the power to live by this design. [106]

Paul's concern for friends does not include his wife, however. He readily sacrifices Jerry's peace of mind when he opts for jail in lieu of draft resignation. "If I had to choose between my country and my friend I'd choose my friend" [106], the ironical anarchist affirms. His idealism, though, loses force inside its grid of bars, and his incarceration becomes an empty gesture, with no more direct impact (except on his immediate family) than a puff of smoke.

The brave sheepherder suggests a third position, but one equally out of touch with the real world. Slightly more appealing than either the judge's or Paul's because Abbey anchors it in the cowboy's Western heritage, Burns's ethic is threefold. Chivalry, or respect for others, is one segment, respect for the land a second, respect for self the third. Each part manifests itself specifically and repeatedly. Respect for others appears, as already noted, through Burns's honorable treatment of Jerry and through his deferential treatment of Paul after Paul refuses to escape. The cowboy's reverence for freedom is most apparent during Part III, when he seeks his own freedom in the wilderness. His sad, funny note—"I HOPE YOU BOYS HAVE SENSE ENUF TO USE THIS . . . YOU RUSHED ME" [218]—impaled on the carcass of the deer he shot, epitomizes his esteem for the creatures of the land. He kills only what he can use, a stark contrast to the noxious consumption of light and air in nearby Duke City. Finally, Burns's respect for self is evident too, in the way he responds to Gutierrez's beatings. The cowboy's self-knowledge and self-assuredness, nineteenth-century holdovers like the judge's faded aristocratic mien, seem more meritorious than the other ethics Abbey posits and dismisses.

But we misread Abbey if we assume he advocates this shopworn cowboy code. Despite the appeal of frontier thought and its inherent individualism, the cowboy's creed is anachronistic in modern society. To expose its uselessness as a practical philosophy, Abbey focuses his critique on a vestige of archaic behavior—the inseparability of man and horse. The bonds that unite the two are well known from countless songs and stories of the heroic West, but Burns's shaggy chestnut mare, as visually unlike the prancing Sil-

ver as the cowboy is unlike the Lone Ranger, marks her master as a
man out of step with the world around him. Early in *The Brave
Cowboy*, Burns must cut barbed wire, swim a muddy river—be it
Acheron or Cocytus—cross a four-lane highway, and do it all on
horseback. People gawk at this foolish apparition, for the spirited
animal only emphasizes Burns's unfitness for the modern world.

After he escapes from jail, this same anachronistic mode of travel,
in effect, traps him rather than sets him free. Because he insists on
riding Whisky, he can head only toward the mountains, as Sheriff
Johnson logically deduces. Furthermore, even as the pursuers close
in on him, Burns refuses to abandon the mare. "You bitch," he
mutters at her. "You ain't been nuthin but trouble to me ever since
I got you." But he chooses not to leave her behind in order to escape. "He cursed again, and thought of his saddle, bedroll, venison, ammunition, all the rest of his gear—and of the horse. 'What
the hell.' He . . . went back to the mare, picked up her reins and
led her off" [258]. Man and his horse, long a romantic duo, ride
together in the world of *The Brave Cowboy*, but the combination is
simply impractical in the modern world. By roping the cowboy to
this symbol of the past, Abbey ties him to an outdated creed. Neither horse nor ethic can carry a man through the twentieth century; the one cannot compete with modern modes of transportation
while the other, idealistic and saddle-sore, cannot deal with the
complex issues of the urban scene.

Similar indications of the insufficiencies of frontier values in
modern society appear all through Part II. Burns's fistfight, his misguided attempt to free his buddy, his unsophisticated jail break,
for example, are plans conceived by a mind conditioned to a simpler world. The cowboy maintains his naive belief that a nineteenth-
century chivalric code, supported by individualistic deeds, will
prove effective inside the confines of Duke City, New Mexico. Such
is not the case, however, and Burns and his horse find themselves
demolished by powers of the modern age.

The author sympathizes more with the brave cowboy than with
either Paul or the District Judge, but that accord is one of temper-
ament rather than of philosophical conviction. For even though
Abbey's heart often beats to a nineteenth-century rhythm, he actually lives in the present, breathing its sulphurous yellow smog.
A man of mixed affinities, he sees no simple solutions. He despises
contemporary grime, he rejects its legal filth as well; but in *The
Brave Cowboy* he negates any alternatives too. After taking the reader

down Abbey's road to a new world of his own making, he deposits his audience and characters in an environment where neither thinkers nor doers succeed. Despite the advantages available to a romancer—the opportunity to create a microcosmic universe in which to address the serious questions of his age, and the consequent opportunity to pose his own solutions—Abbey avoids the commitment. Rather than stabilize his book with the underpinnings of his own ethic, Abbey only sketches in his dissatisfactions with the world around him. Given the romancer's resources and forms, he sidesteps, at this point in his career, the romancer's responsibility to offer a visionary alternative.

Abbey, looking at New Mexico and the desecration of the Southwest, is appalled. But he looks with only slightly less disfavor at the less-complicated past. After he exposes the horrors of the present and the need to clean up both the law and the land, he discredits the values of any attempt to do so. An iconoclast, he undermines the cadaverous judge, the ironical Paul Bondi, the anachronistic cowboy, and even the countervailing sheriff with almost equal fervor. Yet he offers no other option.

The mountain, which dominates Part III of the book, physically embodies Abbey's refusal to commit himself, for just as he negates each philosophical choice, so he undercuts each symbolic adumbration too. One might expect the mountain to be Abbey's symbol of freedom, a sanctuary in the midst of modern chaos where the cowboy both literally and figuratively feels at home. After all, in that direction lies safety, or so the sheepherder believes. Of course, the antagonistic posse does not belong in "this godawful stinking place" [227], nor does the helicopter crew—"Hey! . . . How do we get out of this jungle?" [237]. But Burns is hard pressed to survive there too, limping along "on the heavy dull sliding skin of the mountain" [254]. What makes the place so hellish is its dissimilarity to a real, natural haven. Instead of embodying safety, it presents barriers, trapping and terrorizing both pursuers and pursued "with its irrational bulk and complexity, its absurd, exasperating lack of purpose or utility" [235]. Instead of towering above the dirt and decadence of the city, it shudders beneath the sky and its jet-age contamination.

A flash of silvery metal moving so fast that light and distance betrayed the eye: the thing seemed to move in a series of thrusts, pulses, like a falling star. A jet plane: Burns watched it score westward in its immaculate geometrically-accurate flight; it was nearly gone before he heard the sound of its passage overhead—a thin metallic scream, demoniacal and tortured, like the wail of some Hellbound ghost. [254]

That wail could be the cowboy's banshee voice, since he too rides a tortured, Hell-bound trail. Indeed, he may already have arrived at his moribund destination—an impenetrable contemporary world where the invader on horseback effects no changes, accomplishes no goals, and fades without an imprint on our minds. It is "as if he had never existed,"[5] remarks one astute critic.

One of Abbey's strengths is his ability to describe thrilling action. Just as the best prose in *Jonathan Troy* is the portrayal of the youth's panic after his father's death, so the finest writing in this book describes the cowboy's flight up the mountainside (or, paradoxically, deeper down, into Hell). As Abbey perceives the harried man, his

throat was burning and dry, his eyes tormented by his own dripping sweat, his lungs and heart cracking, expanding, collapsing, as if a vise of iron were closing in around his ribs, stifling his breath, seeming to threaten to break him—but he kept on climbing, kept coaxing and dragging the mare and stumbling out of the way when she leaped after him, trampling on his broken heels. He didn't think about what he was doing or why; he kept climbing. He couldn't think: his brain seemed powerless, overwhelmed by the frenzy and passion of his whole body—fiery nerves, quivering muscle, the racing blood. [252]

Intense, even sensuous in its imagery, this kind of writing forces the reader to accompany Burns emotionally on his flight, but does not engage the reader intellectually. The passage oscillates between symbolic options. A sheltering haven and then a bullet-filled inferno, the mountain finally represents both, or neither. "A meadow of grama grass, with a few soft old gray boulders, mellowed by moss and lichens, sunk deeply and comfortably into the earth, each one surrounded by constellations of miniature alpine flowers" [259–260] is "followed and passed by fragments of exploded rock and the scream of ragged lead butterflies burning through the air" and "the barking stutter of the submachine gun in automatic fire, recoil, refire" [262–63]. Just as Abbey iconoclastically devalues each ethical possibility—both the practical and the ideal—so he denies each physical and spiritual sanctuary too. Neither Burns nor the reader finds a haven, only spiraling insufficiencies.

The vortex extends to Part IV. After setting the brave cowboy free, Abbey traps him again, like a spider enmeshing a fly (and with about as much prescience), proffering, at best, an ignoble and undignified death. Art Hinton is the executioner. The dyspeptic truck driver appears sporadically throughout the book—once in Part I, three times in Part II, once more in Part III—on his migration from waitress to waitress, from Joplin, Mo., to Amarillo, Tex., enroute to Scissors Canyon, N. Mex. [abbreviations Abbey's]. The fourth section of *The Brave Cowboy*, subtitled "The Stranger" and headlined by the epigraph "On the Fourth day cometh Vengeance . . .," belongs to this pseudodemon riding in from the East. He drives a truck labeled "ANOTHER LOAD OF *ACME* BATHROOM FIXTURES! AMERICA BUILDS FOR TOMORROW!" [45]. His character, too, is overstated. "His palate scalded and corroded by tankcars of boiling lunchroom brew, bitter and brackish, and by vats of cheap whisky, and rotted by tons of soft sweet mediocre food, he had forgotten the delight of hunger, the pleasures of thirst" [46]. Limited by his own mediocrity and lack of vision, Hinton feels most at home surrounded by "forty tons of steel, iron, rubber, glass, oil" [131] or else inside a plastic "chrome-plated neonized redbrick restaurant" [45]. When he steps outdoors, he either is sick to his stomach or he fails to see "the cicada in the field and frogs in the swampy ditch [who] sing hosannas to the sky" [48]. Art Hinton, representative embalmment of the twentieth century, walks "blindly" through the night. (Ironically, his role in the movie, *Lonely Are The Brave*, was played by Carroll O'Connor of subsequent Archie Bunker fame.)

To show the human side of this stylized apparition, Abbey lets the man dream. Like Morlin Johnson, the truck driver remembers his youth wistfully, and like the sheriff too, he finds modern life too mechanistic, even while he participates fully. Abbey clubs the reader with Hinton's swirling thoughts, "the scream of the city soaring over him, . . . the yellow dusty night falling on his steel shell, the weight of his eyelids growing under it" [132]. The truck driver is continually in need of "some rest, sleep, a change of rhythm," but his only repose is assaulted by nightmares.

Sleep came at last, vague fumbling sleep, and his mind rolled in it, punched and drawn and split in dreams, smoky shards of dream, reconstructions, recollections:

. . . On a redstone road, past shagbark hickories and a rail fence—

alone, or mostly alone—sometimes accompanied by a familiar but unnameable figure—silent as all dreams, soundless but troubled—and then
the splintering of barriers and a scramble, an insane charge of pigs, hogs,
monsters with red eyes, horns, gaseous withering breath, fury without
purpose, blind maniacal destruction . . . [132]

All "fury without purpose," the words spit images that frighten
Hinton by their viciousness and disturb the reader by their convo-
lution. The "insane charge," like other ambiguities found in the
book—the philosophical options, the mountain's meaning, the final
role of the cowboy himself—is imprecise in meaning. Railing at
the modern landscape of the West, Abbey offers no mature perspective on the horrors he sees. All his writing is some form of protest,
but his later nonfiction will suggest specific cures for specific ills,
and the fiction will offer genuine, although somewhat impractical,
solutions. The Brave Cowboy, however, relies on angry but finally irrelevant lines—"the city, new and terrible, rode the night, groaned
and triumphed over the night and the rolling earth" [132]—to present its assumptions.

The truck driver's role, as with other parts of this book, is di-
chotomous. Abbey views his pawn both as a demoniac manifestation of the present—nonhuman, fatalistic, horrible—and as a man
tormented by that essence too. But, after positing both facets with
equal conviction, the author commits himself to neither. Instead,
he backs away from the possibilities and designs a role for his creation that bears no philosophical weight at all. Art Hinton is merely
a deus ex machina, a puppet with his strings showing. The truck
driver dances and dangles while Abbey manipulates the controls.

The reader dances too. For the final pas de deux down Scissors
Canyon, a shift in point of view puts the reader in the driver's seat
to see the "contours of the mountain" closing in, "vast dark shapes
looming above . . . on either side—that other world, darkness,
cold, the wild empty wind howling over rock and cactus and through
the colonnades of the forest" [272]. In a kaleidoscope of images,
the wilderness becomes an alien world and the truck cab a haven
of warmth. Then, one phantasmic horseman confounds another.
Headlights strike, "and then he thought he was dreaming: he saw
a horse on the road directly in front of him, turning round and
round, a man or a devil on the creature's back, whipping it with
his hat. . . . He heard a scream, violent and inhuman." A moment

later "he could see nothing but the glare of the lights blossoming in the dark" [273].

The cowboy suddenly materializes and then disintegrates, but the instantaneous view of him is as confused as Hinton's double-edged and ambiguous portrayal. By calling the cowboy both "man" and "devil" and by implying that the horse's scream is otherworldly, "violent and inhuman," Abbey locates Burns in the universe of a darkened romance but disallows a perception of him as an allegorical or idealized embodiment of "anarchic freedom" that one might admire. Some readers, mistaking the cowboy's role, have little difficulty interpreting the meaning of the stark, violent ending. For them "the symbolism is clear. What an oppressive law has not quite done, a complex, blind technology has finished. The anarchic freedom of the nineteenth-century cowboy cannot live in modern civilization."[7] If the import of Burns's destruction is so obvious though, why is Abbey's description so mixed? Considering the blend of positive and negative images chosen to denote the cowboy's final ride, it is impossible to read his characterization as "an exaltation of frontier anarchy."[8] Unfit to bear such symbolic weight, Burns operates more superficially on these final pages. The brave sheepherder is as much a machine of the gods as Hinton, two men maneuvered by their author's tangled strings.

To end the cowboy's quest by an accident befits Abbey's avoidance of resolutions at this stage in his career. Just as *Jonathan Troy* ended abruptly, with the help of another truck driver immured in steel who swooped out of the darkness, so *The Brave Cowboy* stops short. Abbey does not struggle with loose ends—the Bondis, for example, disappear into the shadows without a trace. The book simply closes with the sounds of a horse screaming from the black arroyo and of autos passing the scene: "the traffic roared and whistled and thundered by, steel, rubber, and flesh, dim faces behind glass, beating hearts, cold hands—the fury of men and women immured in engines" [277]. These lines, although provocative, signify nothing of the fury of the book but only drop an icy, inhuman chill over the cowboy's fate. Indeed, "The Stranger" counters the powers of the preceding three sections.

Because Abbey finds no easy solutions to the problems he has raised, he forces a head-on collision between his two multirepresentational horsemen, and leaves them to a nihilistic fate. In so doing, he severs the threads that tie the Old West to the New, the nineteenth century to the modern age. Substituting an emotional climax for an intellectual one, he unravels the narrative line but leaves its issues unresolved. Furthermore, he relies on turgid prose and a sensational accident to finish his book, tactics that only camouflage the seriousness of the problems that concern him. Abbey has, however, included enough philosophical innuendos to satisfy a variety of readers. The nineteenth century is physically dead, the twentieth is spiritually dead, both are ethically dead—endless conclusions can be drawn. But one must be cautious of forcing interpretations, of drawing correspondences, of expecting this romance to resolve itself in conventional, or visionary, terms.

The Brave Cowboy does not resolve itself. In fact, Abbey strays furthest from the traditional form in Part IV. Because its ending fails to complete a vision does not mean, however, that the book fails as a romance. Throughout three-fourths of it, Abbey has utilized a compatible design to focus on those problems that will concern him in all his writing. The romance form offers him the opportunity to juxtapose one world upon another, to try different combinations of beliefs both past and present. He finds no solution in this first attempt, but many novelists struggle with unresolved conundrums throughout their careers. The kinds of characters appropriate to romance—stylized, exaggerated, at times symbolic—suit Abbey well. The static, naturalistic portrayals of *The Brave Cowboy* will ripen into Dickensian grotesques and dimensional beings who speak their author's fantasies, if not his mind. The questions he raises about individual freedom, and about man and his responsibilities to the land and to himself are issues befitting the form, too, although we must wait for later books like *Desert Solitaire* to learn his solutions.

The Brave Cowboy was a major advance, both for Edward Abbey and for the Western novel. Even those who would read it as a stock cowboy story, or as an ironic inversion of the formula, admire the powers of its perceptions. Others who consider it a new type of romance see in its technique a marriage of form and content that will empower all of Abbey's future writing.

3

Marking Time

Fire on the Mountain

Six years after the brave cowboy's apparent defeat, Edward Abbey sent another anachronistic man to confront the impersonalized power of the twentieth century. That quest, as quixotic and as unsuccessful as Jack Burns's, occurs in a book that resembles its predecessor in a number of ways. Like *The Brave Cowboy, Fire on the Mountain* (1962) is a romance, another attempt to hammer at the rigid modern world. Set over two hundred miles south of Duke City but in the same nonchivalrous, contemporary New Mexico, it too appraises the vestigial Western code of behavior. Moreover, Abbey's third narrative continues to explore the individual's role in the larger scheme of a voracious society—*Fire on the Mountain* takes on the entire United States government. Once again the protagonist loses, not only because of the establishment's superior strength, but also because Abbey nihilistically imposes a precipitous demise. This tale ends like the cowboy's, with a narrative line that fails, at the end, to sustain either the protagonist's vision or the author's. The book succeeds, however, in one crucial way. Its powerful description translates the strength of the New Mexico landscape into an artistic conception of the earth that will reappear, in another six years, in the more philosophically successful *Desert Solitaire. Fire on the Mountain*, then, is the final preparation for Abbey's mature writing.

Its plot is simple. Civilization encroaches on John Vogelin when the government wants his isolated ranch as a guided-missile test site. Vogelin refuses to sell and vows never to vacate the premises. While his neighbors gradually succumb to pressure and leave the area, he grows more recalcitrant and uncompromising. If necessary, he will fight single-handedly to protect his property. After the Air Force rounds up his cattle, sells them, and drives away his hired man and family, it aims for John Vogelin too, but the seventy-year-old rancher holds the troops off at gunpoint. When his best friend, Lee Mackie, betrays him, however, the anarchist is beaten. Forced to leave his land, he retreats to Alamogordo, where his story ends quickly. After a few unhappy nights, Vogelin sneaks back to the mountains above his ranch and dies, the victim of apparent heart failure. His grandson and Lee elect not to take his body back to town but to give him a Viking burial, a symbolic "fire on the mountain," while the U.S. marshal apoplectically looks on. Thus the stark tale ends, with another anticlimactic death of another Abbey character born out of his time.

Unlike Jack Burns's yarn, however, John Vogelin's is based on fact. A New Mexico cattleman, John Prather, indeed stood up to the United States government when it tried to take his property for the White Sands Missile Range in 1955, but Prather's resistance, better supported by local populace and press, found more success than Vogelin's. After two years of legal and extralegal maneuvering, the eighty-two-year-old Prather obtained a U.S. District Court writ exempting his ranch house and fifteen acres from confiscation. "It was a victory for the code of the Texas cowman," C. L. Sonnichsen pronounces. "John Prather's psychology was the psychology of the [eighteen-] eighties. He reacted as his forebears had reacted against any invasion of their independence and property rights. He was still fighting the battle of the little cattleman against the big ones. . . . He was the last of his kind."[1] John Vogelin, Prather's fictive counterpart, is the last of his kind too. His story differs, though, not only in its dissimilar resolution (Prather successfully resisted the military authorities for years) but in its intrinsic design. Where the real-life anarchist's last stand comes to us through impartial newspaper accounts and journalistic revaluations, Vogelin's rebellion is reported with the subjectivity of an artist. That is, the narrative line is restructured and transformed to suit the needs of a romancer.

Gerald Haslam, in his introduction to the University of New Mexico Press Zia paperback reprint of *Fire on the Mountain,* rightly points out that one of the major ways Abbey manages his artistry is through his choice of point of view. Instead of telling the tale himself, or employing an omniscient narrative voice as he did in his first two fictions, Abbey chooses young Billy Vogelin Starr, the old man's grandson, to recount the events. This selection of an innocent voice from the East suggests that *Fire on the Mountain,* like *The Brave Cowboy,* uses conventions from the popular Western novel to shape it into a contemporary romance. Through Billy's eyes, Abbey describes the land and the men who would possess it. Borrowing from a long narrative tradition that includes such Westerns as *The Virginian* and *Shane,* Abbey unfolds his story through the unformed consciousness of a narrator who must learn as the events happen, who must, in effect, be initiated and who will include the reader in that educational experience. Billy's attitudes toward his grandfather, and toward the government that opposes him, color our own, as we see the incidents and people from the black and white perspective of youth.

It is tempting to discuss *Fire on the Mountain* as a novel of initiation, a Western *Bildungsroman* in which a youth learns what it means to be a man, for there is ample evidence of Abbey's purposeful use of certain conventions. When Billy rides with his grandfather and Lee, for example, on a preliminary journey toward experience, he learns to curb his thirst and hunger because the older men jest that only Campfire Girls and Boy Scouts carry canteens. He imagines himself as "Sgt. William Starr, United States Cavalry, advancing toward the stronghold of the Mescalero Apaches, accompanied only by a single scout,"[2] then watches Lee match wits with fools from the present-day army and discovers how unpremeditated heroics can sometimes backfire. Fetching water from a nearby spring, he meets another test—the legendary mountain lion, "a pair of yellow eyes gleaming in a sleek head, . . . a dark powerful shape of unforeseeable hugeness crouched as if to leap" [67], Abbey's symbol in this book of the wilderness and freedom. On other days we find Billy racing his horse through the fields to run off his frustrations, and one time he drinks too much rum, trying to be one of the men. Abbey couches each of these episodes in terms suggestive of what it means to be an adult male. One could even view the boy's escape from the train taking him back east and his return alone to the ranch as an adventure patterned after the part of an initiation ritual which sends a youth to seek his own destiny in the wilderness. Near the story's close, Abbey underscores that masculine tenor. When Lee and Billy leave to trace John Vogelin back to the ranch, Lee announces to the boy's aunt, "This is a job for men. Get your hat, Billy." Then the youth adds, loftily, "And we left her there to wash the dishes" [195]. Although this chauvinistic exchange is overstated, it does reiterate the thrust of the narrative design.

But Abbey has chosen a boy as his narrator neither because he wants to write a novel of initiation nor to follow in a Western tradition. Rather, he has deliberately picked a naive point of view because through it he can manipulate his audience. Billy reports what he sees and reproduces what he hears, but Abbey makes the selections. The author alone determines the information to which Billy and the reader have access, so he alone chooses the directions in which the narrative unfolds. By persuading us, though, to believe in an objectivity that is shaded only by a boy's love for his grandfather, Abbey persuades us to trust his views. Thus, the author can mask his opinions under a guise of innocence. Although we may believe we see the action directly, Billy's vision is as idiosyncratic as Abbey's. Paragraphs like the following show how the presence of a youthful observer allows the author to pump more propaganda into his story.

The armed man at the wheel of the jeep kept his small pink eyes focused on us, a twitchy irritable grin on his mouth. A second Air Policeman sat in the back seat. He too watched us with shiny eyes and a face shiny with sweat.

The pair of them sitting there in the jeep, sweating, silent, motionless, holstered automatics on their wide hips, gave me a sensation of nausea. [109]

It is unlikely that a boy would note such details as "pink eyes" or "a twitchy irritable grin," but the writer who characterized men like Gutierrez and the other members of Sheriff Johnson's posse would well imagine those "shiny eyes," the "sweat," and the "sensation of nausea." For Abbey, Billy Vogelin Starr is a sophisticated tool to help project the writer's own condemnation of the modern military.

Choosing Billy, however, leads Abbey into trouble because *Fire on the Mountain*, like its narrator, lacks complexity. The short, straightforward tale has been fleshed out with several extended encounters between the rancher and those who oppose him, and with several prolonged incidents which supposedly add to the reader's knowledge of the boy. For the most part, though, the book lacks enough people and events to fill its pages, and further lacks sufficient intellectual complications. Even more than *The Brave Cowboy*, Abbey's third fiction takes a single concern—the government's right to override the individual—and works it until the author is certain the reader is thoroughly indoctrinated. This relentlessness leaves no room for nuances, which means *Fire on the Mountain* nags the reader as much as the society it attacks.

The book is a romance of a single thread. Its twin quests are direct: John Vogelin must save his ranch and Billy should grow into manhood. Its methodology is clear-cut: the cattleman will use any means available, the boy will watch and learn. Set in a particularized locale, empowered by Abbey's descriptions, *Fire on the Mountain* attacks the forces of modernity with vigor. Its author, in a newfound tactic, now wields the genre of romance more as a weapon than as a tool. The use of an innocent narrator softens his blows and camouflages his belligerence, but Billy's ingenuousness also reinforces the story's thematic transparencies.

To counteract this effect, Abbey employs a second narrative guide, Lee Mackie. Like Morlin Johnson in *The Brave Cowboy*, Vogelin's best friend is the reader's companion as well. Billy, of course, describes the action, but it is Lee who interpolates the deeds by turning his head as conveniently as the sheriff did before him. The first words Lee speaks, meant to calm the irate rancher, sound Abbeyesque in their pseudo-jingoism: "You know it won't do any good at all to get fired up about this and declare war on the Benighted States of America" [26]. Subsequent lines, however, reveal his measured understanding of the serious complexities of the issue. Lee, sitting on the romancer's fence, is able to see both sides at once. Recognizing both the symbolic worth and the sorry futility of Vogelin's gesture, he can acknowledge both the rationale and the strength of the other side. Or, he can castigate the government's tactics— "the lousiest dirtiest trick I ever heard of. Cowardly and sneaky"

[115]—in one breath and attack his friend in another. "Senile, that's the word, they think you're just a crazy old man in his second childhood. And they'll think worse than that too, if you know what I mean. Obstructing national defense. You against one hundred and eighty million Americans" [27]. Billy and the reader listen quietly to the man's balanced judgments. In fact, Lee leads everyone in different directions at once, calming John Vogelin's combative instincts, teaching Billy to be a man, and showing the reader how to assess the powers of the establishment.

Throughout the book, Lee arbitrates between Vogelin's instinctive civil disobedience and the government's authority. That is, he counters between the romance world of the rancher's quest and the harsher reality that surrounds them. "Vogelin—you're a jackass, . . . You're heading straight for trouble—and heartbreak," Lee prophesies. "You're being downright irresponsible" [88]. Lending moral and emotional, but not tactical, support to the aging anarchist, this key figure fills in the logical gaps left by Billy's often inadequate perceptions. He also performs important physical tasks; for example, he intervenes with the armed man and prevents Vogelin from further self-destruction. "You traitor!" Vogelin bellows. "Oh, Lee, you dirty traitor!" [185]. But the betrayal is an essential function of this conduit between the romance world and the real. Just as Sheriff Johnson admired Jack Burns while he systematically pursued him to the death, so Lee Mackie respects his friend but tries, without success, to bring him into the twentieth century. Lee is like the lawman in another way too: his character remains static, an object not a subject, a man who functions rather than develops.

Lee differs from his counterpart, though, in one significant way. The sheriff humanizes the villainy in *The Brave Cowboy*, whereas Lee does little to alleviate it in *Fire on the Mountain*. The United States government, in no uncertain terms, is the evil giant of this modern romance. A stream of impossible military men parades past the boy and his older companions. And no contemplative scene, such as the one between Paul Bondi and the district judge, eases the tension, because only rigid confrontations between an angry rancher and representatives of an indifferent bureaucracy take place. One such exchange occurs midway through the book, after an Army Corps of Engineers colonel cites the government's license—a "Declaration of Taking, with an order of immediate entry"—and pointedly refers to "Volume Forty, United States Code,

Annotated, Section two hundred and fifty" [89]. John Vogelin responds tersely to the jargon. "My ranch is not for sale" [90]. Nevertheless, the conversation continues with the colonel's outline of patriotic duty.

"Mr. Vogelin," DeSalius continued, "you alone and you only are holding up this project. And this project is an essential component of our national defense program. Now I understand how your emotions are involved in this place but you must understand that national security takes precedence over all other considerations. Every citizen owes his first allegiance to the nation, and all property rights"—the colonel smacked his lips with pleasure as he rolled out the rhetorical artillery—"all property rights are derived from and depend upon the sovereignty of the state. I refer you to the law of nations. . . ." [92–93]

Answering succinctly, "I've heard all that before," the cattleman widens the distance between the two views.

The colonel's position is reinforced by all the powers of government, just as his opponent's is backed up by the age-old belief that a man's property is his own. "Legal thievery," Vogelin characterizes it a few pages later, "legal thievery" [109]. But he is helpless to stop the onslaught, as the colonel points out when he comes back to the ranch to deliver an ultimatum. "Mr. Vogelin, the time has come when the Government must act. This Government can no longer wait upon your pride and obstinacy" [155]. Nor does it, for the next day the United States marshal arrives to evict the embattled old man from his home.

By now the reader's sympathies lie wholly with John Vogelin, since Abbey inserts judgmental phrases between Billy's direct reports and Billy paints DeSalius, Marshal Burr, and various other governmental representatives unfavorably. In the paragraph cited above, for example, the colonel smacks his lips while a barrage of "rhetorical artillery" rolls out. When the military man returns to the ranch to make his final plea, Billy thinks he sounds like a "pitchman for a used-car lot" [154]. And after failing to accomplish his mission, the colonel turns "sullenly away" to step out into "the naked blaze of the sun, where his skin and straw hat withered perceptibly." Like an evil fairy-tale creature, the wicked ogre shrivels when touched by the purity of the New Mexico air. "I nearly pitied him—his beautiful new suit rumpled and stained with sweat, his hat wilting, his sharp shoes coated with dust" [158]. Billy's interpretive asides, a voice of innocence crafted by a master of experience, hyperbolically reveal how monstrous this encroachment looms.

Two more observations about Abbey's technique, while not directly related to Billy's point of view, are nonetheless illustrative of how the writer manipulates audience receptivity. One involves his choice of names for his characters, the other, his choice of words to put in their mouths. By both its sound and its familiarity, the proper name can influence our reading of a book. The pompous colonel in *Fire on the Mountain* bears the same surname as the arrogant general in *The Brave Cowboy*, although the spelling differs, so surely the selection of Desalius/DeSalius for two supercilious military men was no accident. (Neal Lambert, introducing the Zia paperback reprint of *The Brave Cowboy*, suggests the name is a wordplay on Daedalus; a second possibility would be a joke on desalinization.) Moreover, there is the owner of the general store near Vogelin's ranch, Hayduke, a man seen only in passing but whose unusual name will return attached to George, the most fanatic member of the Monkey Wrench Gang. And the anarchistic rancher himself bears the same surname as Jack Burns's grandfather Henry Vogelin, who also owned land condemned by the government.

In fact, examples of similar or identical names recur often in Abbey's writing. "Through naming comes knowing," he writes in *Desert Solitaire*. "We grasp an object, mentally, by giving it a name" [DS, 288]. A paragraph from *Abbey's Road* returns to the subject.

"What is it?" we ask, meaning what is its name? This odd quirk of the human mind: Unless we can name things, they remain for us only half-real. Or less than half-real: non-existent. A man without a name is nobody. A man's name can become more important than his person. A plant, an animal, a thing without a name is no thing—nothing. No wonder we humans like to think that in the beginning was—the Word. What word? Any word. Any word at all, anything rather than the silence and terror of the nameless. [AR, 90]

To name is to make human; to make human is to ground the romance in the realistic world. Thus it is necessary for persons, places, things in Abbey's world to have names that repeat themselves, for the representation brings familiarity in otherwise strange lands. Desalius/DeSalius and Vogelin, then, become more than just names remembered from another book, but concepts that guide the reader along familiar paths. The colonel's inanities recall the general's and together they show us the author's assessment of military might. Then, if we recall Henry Vogelin, we apprehend just what that strength can accomplish. Paul Bondi envisioned "the old man . . . sitting there on the verandah of his ranchhouse waiting for the Law to come and rob him of his home" [BC, 118–19], and later he discussed with Jack Burns the desecration of the site. "The saddest, lonesomest place in all New Mexico. A good place to set off atom bombs," the cowboy replied, "everything smashed flat. Even some of the fence posts broke off. Adobe bricks scattered all to hell. Looked like a herd of wild elephants run over the place" [BC, 119]. If we recall this description from *The Brave Cowboy* and project it beyond *Fire on the Mountain,* we understand better the dangers Abbey fears. Abbey underscores that message by repeating himself from book to book, and by repeating names.

Another technical mannerism that directs our responses has been criticized by Garth McCann in his Boise State University Western Writers Series pamphlet on Edward Abbey. He writes, "If his [Abbey's] prose shows any weakness at this stage of his development, it is in his dialogue. Without prior knowledge, we would have difficulty telling his characters apart on the basis of their language, for they all sound like Abbey—without much individual differentiation, color, syntactic variation, distinct diction, or characteristic patterns of speech."[3] Certainly the conversations overheard in *Jonathan Troy* prove the truth of McCann's statement, and stilted passages like Colonel DeSalius's arguments show little improvement in the author's technique. But McCann's comments should be modified slightly. What bothers the reader is not that Abbey's characters all sound alike but that their author gives them stuffy, flat speeches to recite whenever they are engaged in serious conversation. It is not difficult, for example, to distinguish between the bombastic governmental representative and the more taciturn western rancher, but it is nearly impossible to believe in the exchange. DeSalius's words, in particular, completely lack conviction. The officer may cite a textbook case for his viewpoint—"According to the report of our Inspection and Possession Committee, the entire missile range project may suffer a serious delay if we're held up much longer by these real estate problems" [92]—but his forced phrases ring hollow. While Abbey probably means to mock the colonel's position, the stolid prose only dulls the verbal interaction.

Other conversations, even straightforward ones, are equally ponderous; Burns and Bondi in jail, or Vogelin and Mackie in the ranch house late at night, all use more stilted language as soon as they switch from banter to solemnities. Abbey lacks the grace necessary to reveal complexities of thought in such dialogues, and too often he communicates a bombastic message, even though he means to communicate his most profound beliefs. Unfortunately, this problem will plague Abbey throughout his writing career. At his best when describing, daydreaming, or echoing a short, brisk exchange of words, his prose slows and stumbles when he tries to interject philosophy into conversation.

In spite of some defects, however, *Fire on the Mountain* still measures Abbey's early strengths—his topical concerns and his pictorial powers. Its theme, a variation on the brave cowboy's search for personal freedom amid a morass of institutionalized laws, repeats key considerations about the way we live in the West today and the way we lived there yesterday. Its pages trace a rapacious, double-edged heritage from the past. "Above the desk was an oil portrait of Jacob Vogelin, Grandfather's father, the somber bearded Dutchman who had founded the ranch back in the 1870's by first defrauding and then fighting off the Mescalero Apaches, the Southern Pacific Railroad, the Goodnight Cattle Company, the First National Bank of El Paso, and the United States Government with its never-ending wars, depressions, and income taxes" [23]. Although Billy ignores the implications, the author seizes on the paradox.

"Why do they call it Thieves' Mountain?" I asked, staring up at the transmutation of bare gray rock into gold.
"It belongs to the government," Grandfather said.
"Yes, the Government stole it from the cattlemen," Lee said. "And the cattlemen stole it from the Indians. And the Indians stole it from the—from the eagles? From the lion? And before that—?" [39]

Forcing the obvious irony on an unresponsive John Vogelin, Lee continues. "Whose mountain? whose land? Who owns the land? Answer me that, old horse. The man with title to it? The man who works it? The man who stole it last?" [40]. Lee also reopens the discussion in another argument with his long-time friend.

"Look, John—" He made a vague gesture with his hand. "Does the land really belong to you? Is it really yours? Does the land belong to anybody? A hundred years ago the Apaches had it, it was all theirs. Your father and other men like him stole it from the Apaches. The railroad company and the big cattle companies and the banks tried to steal it from your father and from you. Now the Government is going to steal it from you. This land has always been crawling with thieves." [166–67]

Abbey's point is clear, if tautologic—avaricious greed, the swallowing of the frontier, is not a thing confined to the government but a very real part of the western heritage. Billy may not heed the lesson, but the reader cannot miss the implication that a smear of history blackens John Vogelin's stand as much as the government's. In Abbey's world, the Old West fathers the New.

That connection, hidden in most pulp Westerns because their authors refuse to pursue its implications, is expressed openly in this book originally titled *Thieves' Mountain*. Ambiguities remain, however. On the one hand, Vogelin's motivations differ little from his foe's—self-interest, if not greed, drives both the rancher and the government. On the other hand, Vogelin cannot transcend the changing times, so he remains separate from his fellows. Like Jack Burns, he is an anachronistic throwback to an earlier age, a man who finds the twentieth century an indecipherable puzzle. Although he does not ride a horse through the downtown streets, he is as reluctant, in his own way, to enjoy modern conveniences. His isolated ranch has no phone, for example, and he "had no use or need for electricity, but he did like ice in his drinks. The refrigerator, the pickup truck, and the disposable toothpick, he confessed, were the three great achievements of modern man" [17]. Otherwise, the rancher prefers a different age and even blasphemes himself as a modern misfit, remarking that his epitaph should read "Here Lies John Vogelin: Born Forty Years Too Late, Died Forty Years Too Soon." When Billy asks why, he answers glibly, "I figure in forty years civilization will collapse and everything will be back to normal. I wish I could live to see it" [65]. So even though philosophically he should understand the drive behind the government's actions, Vogelin emotionally remains segregated from the contemporary world. With a foot in both centuries, he belongs in neither.

To cope with that conundrum, he fights back, but without success. When the superior forces of government and the military defeat him, Vogelin can only wither and die. The denouement suggests a fairy tale gone awry, with the triumph of a wicked giant. At least the cattleman's demise is not accomplished by another machine of the gods, but it comes no more propitiously than did the cowboy's (and it seems forced when the broken-hearted rancher's heart stops beating). Given a world where options no longer exist, Abbey's characters can only stop living. And if Burns's end was graceless and ironic, Vogelin's borders on the maudlin. While Abbey seems to have intended it to be tragic, the narrowness and occasional thoughtlessness of the portrayal make it difficult for the reader to feel either pity or fear. "Grandfather . . . sat in a strange, slumping, boneless way, supported by the wall, his hands resting on the ground, his glasses missing, his eyes half open and gazing blindly at the earth between his sprawled legs. . . . A fly buzzed near the old man's face and a faint, queer odor hovered in the twilight" [204]. The tone is jarring, its naturalism inappropriate for a tragic moment. The whole last scene on the mountainside, in fact, sounds awkward and hastily written. The dialogue between Lee and the lawman who tries to stop the funeral pyre is needlessly trite.

"You're talking to a United States Marshal; you're threatening an officer of the law."
"I know it. Don't irritate me." [208]

The final sentence of the book—"Far above on the mountainside, posed on his lookout point, troubled by the fire, the lion screamed" [211]—adds little to the "posed" quality of the whole climax. Abbey leaves us feeling as if he had waved a magic wand and the world had vanished.

As in *The Brave Cowboy*, Abbey avoids commitment in *Fire on the Mountain*. Once more, he raises a meaningful issue, gives it dimension through individuals caught in modernity's maelstrom, and then avoids a sagacious resolution. The story ends with Vogelin's death, but questions remain about human responsibilities, human rights, and human freedoms. The romancer, instead of opening the reader's eyes to a realm of possibilities, has closed his own.

In some ways, *Fire on the Mountain* resembles a fairy tale more than a romance. The arbitrary end of the action, the stereotypical heroes and villains, the brevity, and the uncomplicated point of view are all symptoms of the simplicity of its romantic guise. Written hastily—"except for a few deletions the first draft was also the final one"—and "meant quite calmly and frankly for Hollywood,"[4] the story lacks subtlety. Nevertheless, to dismiss it as a twentieth-century dragon deployment is to ignore its strengths. Unlike a conventional horse opera on the giant screen, it raises serious issues. The fact that Abbey then treats these issues cavalierly does not negate the perspicacity he shows by including them in the first place. So the observation that connects Vogelin's thievery with the government's, that asks why the code of the Old West must motivate the behavior of the New, is one made by a romancer. To quote my earlier definition of romance, he "calls into question the ethical, social, and moral assumptions of his age."

Except for its final lack of vision, *Fire on the Mountain* includes all the elements characteristic of a romance. Through the deeds of John Vogelin, it celebrates the freedom found in the Old West; through the eyes of his grandson, it celebrates the possibilities for sustaining that dream. In pursuit of those ends, the old man and the boy play out their stylized roles, acting logically, even predictably, but in ways that overstep the boundaries of conventional behavior. For them, "experience liberated" includes disobeying a United States marshal and holding off his deputies, thereby raising key questions about life in the modern world. "Nobody's safe when the Government can take away his home," the rancher argues poignantly, a viewpoint Lee counters immediately. "Nobody would be safe in a world run by the Soviet Union" [166] either. While Abbey never reaches a satisfactory solution, he tinkers with the ramifications of both positions as he tries to reshape the unmalleable universe in which he lives. That reshaping, the world he re-creates, is the world of a romance.

Abbey takes the reader to that twilight zone of an imagined New Mexico on a highway of heat waves, "giving the road far ahead a transparent, liquid look, an illusion which receded before us as fast as we approached" [4]. The transparent liquidity of *Fire on the Mountain*'s scenery, reminiscent of the ethereal ambience that surrounded Duke City in *The Brave Cowboy*, is an important feature of this third Abbey fiction. The land itself—Thieves' Mountain—is both the philosophical and the emotional crux of the story, but Abbey's own New Mexico desertscape deepens and codifies the impact. The author presents this land in ways characteristic of all his future writing. His eye and pen work together, surpassing both the picture-postcard phrasings of *Jonathan Troy* and the imprecise symbolism of *The Brave Cowboy*. This is not to say that *Fire on the Mountain*'s desert descriptions are any more tangible or real than the others. Indeed, Abbey emphasizes the fantastic qualities of what Billy sees when "the heat shimmered up in palpable waves. Through the layers of heat and light . . . the dislocated outlines of the mountain ranges flow together, floating on a yellow sea of haze. In that country, fantasy and mirage were always present" [13]. "Fantasy and mirage" are always present in a romance too, so Abbey carefully draws the real world into an imagined one where Vogelin's insurrection can take place.

Just as Jack Burns scrambled up a mountainside that was alternately haven or hell, the rancher finds Thieves Mountain an oddly unsettling place. While he sees himself connected forever to the Box V Ranch—"I am the land" [40], he declares—Lee Mackie, the reader's guide, knows differently. "The world is changing," he tells Billy. "Your grandfather don't like to admit it but the world is changing. And even New Mexico is part of the world now. You'll know what I mean, Billy, pretty soon" [43]. Abbey assesses the implications of Lee's words by juxtaposing the two extremes: even though "New Mexico is part of the world now," "in that country, fantasy and mirage were always present." In his nonfiction Abbey will clarify the paradox, but in *Fire on the Mountain* he is content simply to counterbalance the green world of his imagination against the red world of reality. These two terms, borrowed from Renaissance scholarship, most clearly distinguish between his two visions of the land. Northrop Frye uses them when he writes of "the red and white world of English history, . . . [and] the green world of the Faerie Queene. . . . Shakespeare too has his green world of comedy and his red and white world of history."[5] The green world, idyllic and imagined, counterbalances the red, a real and often unpleasant milieu. Likewise, Abbey's red world is a graphic one of the historical present, as protrayed in harsh and unforgiving words.

I saw new placards made of steel shining at me from the gateposts:
PROPERTY OF U.S. GOVERNMENT
KEEP OUT
They were talking about our ranch. [106]

In contrast, Abbey's green world comes to the reader imaginatively and pictorially, although sometimes euphuistically. "We sat on the verandah and watched the spectacular death of day in the sky beyond the mountain range: cloudy islands of auburn, purple and whisky-tinted snow, swan-necked birds with fiery wings as long as the mountains, golden lakes, seas of silver and green" [158–59].

Neither characters nor author can effect a union between these two worlds in *Fire on the Mountain,* for that separation is part of the unanswered issue at the book's core. Unlike Shakespeare, who utilized one world to explicate problems of the other, Abbey has not synthesized his troubled vision. Red and green either clash violently or else keep distinctly apart. When they clash, an act which provides the tension in Abbey's writing, the discord takes two forms, literal and figurative. The more physical, literal form, as denoted by the jeep-riding G.I.s and their "slim, silver-gray, beautiful and dead body of a coyote" [53]—the red-world army men murder the free spirit of a green-world animal—is bad enough. But the second kind of moral conflict, because more subtle, is even more horrible. "You know," Colonel DeSalius muses,

I can understand your affection for this desert country. I can't share it but I can understand it, even sympathize with it. This country is—almost sublime. Space and grandeur, a spacious grandeur that's overwhelming. And yet—yet it isn't quite human, is it? By that I mean it's not really meant for human beings to live in. This is a land for gods, perhaps. Not for men. [150]

Respecting the land for all the wrong reasons, honoring its power more than its presence, the military man patronizingly reveals his shallow percipience. Abbey implies that DeSalius represents all his fellow employees of bureaucracies that would desecrate the land. His red-world infringement violates the very spirit of Abbey's green-world milieu.

Despite the sobering message, *Fire on the Mountain* still manages to sound optimistic when describing the land by itself. As soon as Billy separates himself from his grandfather's troubles and melts into the "transparent, liquid look, an illusion" that characterizes the New Mexico landscape, he comes close to Abbey's heart.

Those mountains—they seemed at once both close and impossibly remote, an easy walk away and yet beyond the limits of the imagination. Between us lay the clear and empty wilderness of scattered mesquite trees and creosote shrubs and streambeds where water ran as seldom as the rain came down. Each summer for three years I had come to New Mexico; each time I gazed upon that moon-dead landscape and asked myself: what is out there? And each time I concluded: *something* is out there— maybe everything. To me the desert looked like a form of Paradise. And it always will. [4; italics Abbey's]

Even though Paradise, in this book, exists solely in Billy's imagination, it is Abbey's effort to touch that world that infuses spirit into his writing and attracts his many readers. Something *is* out there beyond the red-world limitations, maybe everything, not only in the desert but in Edward Abbey's writing as well.

He never specifies that "something," even though *Fire on the Mountain* comes closer than *The Brave Cowboy* to doing so, and his nonfiction comes closer yet. On the Box V Ranch, the mountain lion connotes the spirit. While the animal's presence paralyzes young Billy, the memory sustains him. It nourishes Abbey, too, as he explains many years later in *The Journey Home*. The chapter called "Let Us Now Praise Mountain Lions" treats the beast figuratively—we need them "because they are beautiful" [JH, 133]—while another chapter recalls a real-life confrontation with a big cat and describes his secret urge to know it better.

I haven't seen a mountain lion since that evening, but the experience remains shining in my memory. I want my children to have the opportunity for that kind of experience. I want my friends to have it. I even want our enemies to have it—they need it most. And someday, possibly, one of our children's children will discover how to get close enough to that mountain lion to shake paws with it, to embrace and caress it, maybe even teach it something, and to learn what the lion has to teach us. [JH, 238]

Billy, recognizing the beauty and values of the desert, is at least metaphorically ready to shake hands with that lion, to assimilate green-world qualities into a red-world existence. That he does not come any closer to doing so is part of his tale's inconclusiveness.

The similarity between Abbey's experience and the boy's is not limited to the mountain lion episode. While we must be wary of seeking autobiography in Abbey's writing, we nevertheless can recognize another parallel. Again, it has to do with the landscape, and this time it is closely related to the source of the power of Abbey's prose. "Brightest New Mexico," begins *Fire on the Mountain*. "In that vivid light each rock and tree and cloud and mountain existed with a kind of force and clarity that seemed not natural but supernatural," Abbey writes with his romancer's pen. Then Billy takes up the theme. "Yet it also felt as familiar as home, the country of dreams, the land I had known from the beginning" [3]. "Hallelujah on the Bum," where the mature author recounts his first youthful venture into the West, "full of a powerful, mysterious promise" [JH, 11], echoes Billy's words. Like the boy, Abbey was struck by both the intuitive familiarity and the imaginative auspiciousness of what he saw. "Across the river waited a land that filled me with strange excitement," he exclaims:

crags and pinnacles of naked rock, the dark cores of ancient volcanoes, a vast and silent emptiness smoldering with heat, color, and indecipherable significance, above which floated a small number of pure, clear, hard-edged clouds. For the first time I felt I was getting close to the West of my deepest imaginings—the place where the tangible and the mythical become the same. [JH, 5]

These lines strike to the heart of Abbey's philosophy of writing. The "West of his deepest imaginings" touched Jonathan Troy slightly, when he sketched picture-postcard possibilities for escape, but that first vision of the West only hinted at Abbey's sense of the land. By the time he wrote *The Brave Cowboy* he handled the physical details more competently but was less certain of their meanings. So he charged the cowboy up an infernal mountainside through alternating levels of heaven and hell or freedom and pain. *Fire on the Mountain's* landscape is paradoxical too—hostile, unforgiving, but "so beautiful it broke your heart knowing you couldn't see it forever" [97], a thieves' Paradise, "the country of dreams." There, however, for the first time, Abbey acknowledges the tangible and the mythical as separate entities, the red world and the green, and begins the lifelong task of putting them artistically together.

Not yet the West of his deepest imaginings, the land in *Fire on the Mountain* nevertheless underlies Abbey's first studied view of the isolated parts of his dream. Now he is ready to project the vision that will unite the disparate elements. Even though Billy's "season of mirage" [149] has not yet given way to Abbey's "place where the tangible and the mythical become the same," the author is working toward a vision of the land that ultimately will shape his prose and synergize the romances he designs.

Part II

On Desert Trails

The Nonfiction

Edward Abbey's nonfiction, rather than his fiction, first drew the reading public's attention to his work. Six years after he finished *Fire on the Mountain* he published *Desert Solitaire* (1968), a popular success still in print today. During the next decade he followed this best-seller with seven other nonfiction books about the wilderness— five extended pictorial essays describing especially scenic corners of the United States, and two collections of articles published previously in magazines and journals. Meanwhile, he continued writing numerous shorter pieces which advance the point of view first outlined in *Desert Solitaire,* the book that is the cornerstone of his creative output.

In many ways *Desert Solitaire* is more a work of fiction than of nonfiction, a re-creation of the desert environment into an imagined universe where Abbey can contemplate the wilderness, the individual, and the relationships between the two. Containing true experiences, far-fetched anecdotes, effusive descriptions, some polemics, and some imprecations, the book presents a composite vision of a modern man struggling to exist in a shrinking natural world. While the book focuses on southeastern Utah, its spirit embraces any wild corner of the country where humans remain cognizant of the intrinsic powers of the land. As in his later writing, Abbey tries to put man in a perspective that balances his insufficiencies against his strengths and that also celebrates the omnipotence of his environment.

Because Abbey focuses both on man and on the land around him, and because he does not want to be driven into the "literary corral" of nature writing [AR, xviii], he calls his nonfiction "personal history." He spotlights Ed Abbey, an ordinary man operating on an enormous natural stage whose individual role shrinks and expands according to a backdrop of natural law. To enter Abbey's world is to set foot in a Darwinian universe, a place red in tooth and claw yet tempered by his artistry. The mood, the tone, the point of view, and the substance of that universe are established in *Desert Solitaire* and reaffirmed in the two collections of essays, *The Journey Home* (1977) and *Abbey's Road* (1979). In these three books, Abbey sets forth his political and personal philosophies of surroundings and of self. Richer and more complex than his earlier fiction, they interpret his vision of the twentieth-century West—his love for the land and his fears for its desecration, his faith in the frontier spirit and his dismay at its inherent destructiveness, his belief in mankind and his horror at man's selfishness. His philosophy of life and liberty, articulated at last, stretches his writing far beyond its previous limits.

Desert Solitaire begins the exercise. After that, the most aggressive polemical of the personal histories, *The Journey Home,* argumentatively spreads Abbey's ideas, while the third, *Abbey's Road,* ranges afield to Australia, Mexico, and forgotten corners of the United States. Like *Desert Solitaire,* the latter two investigate the powers of the land, of those who would destroy it, of the individual who must balance the needs of the present against the needs of the future. Throughout, Abbey argues vociferously for the land and its received respect. By utilizing fictional techniques in a nonfiction format, and by conjoining those special tactics available to a writer of romance, Abbey effectively communicates his point of view. These works contain both nostalgic personal recollections and harsh attacks against problems of the present. But even when his words sound most brutal, they maintain an idealistic posture.

He alludes to that combination of savagery and sublimity when he explains why he must pursue the "wearisome job" of writing. *Abbey's Road*'s introduction gives five reasons, beginning with the simplest—money. The more serious include his desire "to share ideas, discoveries, emotions" and "to record the truth." "Most importantly," he writes "to defend the diversity and freedom of humankind from those forces in our modern techno-industrial culture that would reduce us all, if we let them, to the status of things, . . . to the rank of subject." Finally, he writes "for the pleasure of it. For the sheer ecstasy of the creative moment, the creative act" [AR, xxiii]. Because of Abbey's own needs, he shares an "endless monologue written on the wind," his vision of the modern world as it is, and as he thinks it ought to be.

> A weird, lovely, fantastic object out of nature like Delicate Arch has the curious ability to remind us—like rock and sunlight and wind and wilderness—that *out there* is a different world, older and greater and deeper by far than ours, a world which surrounds and sustains the little world of men as sea and sky surround and sustain a ship. The shock of the real. For a little while we are again able to see, as the child sees, a world of marvels. For a few moments we discover that nothing can be taken for granted, for if this ring of stone is marvelous then all which shaped it is marvelous, and our journey here on earth, able to see and touch and hear in the midst of tangible and mysterious things-in-themselves, is the most strange and daring of all adventures. [DS, 41–42; italics Abbey's]

Abbey's task as a writer of romance is to coordinate "the shock of the real" with the "world of marvels," to touch "our journey here on earth" with his "fantastic" magic wand. He succeeds by combining his own "sheer ecstasy of the creative moment" with the sheer energy of the land around him, itself shaped marvelously.

His five other books of nonfiction project the same vision, although they were written for the more superficial picture-book format. *Appalachian Wilderness* (1970), the only one about the East, displays the photographs of Eliot Porter. *Slickrock* (1971), a piece of Sierra Club propaganda, is as much a volume of Philip Hyde's camera work as of Abbey's writing. Even *Cactus Country* (1973) gives equal weight to prose and pictures, although the photographers are only footnoted in this Time-Life book about the Sonoran Desert. In Abbey's latest two, his name actually appears second to the photographers—John Blaustein, whose camera leads Abbey down the Colorado in *The Hidden Canyon: A River Journey* (1977), and David Muench, whose pictures dominate *Desert Images* (1979).

While the five essays in these books underscore the attitudes posed in the three personal histories, they say little that is new. They are important chiefly because they demonstrate the powers of Abbey's prose. His style moves with a fluidity and grace that, in these books, merges with the photographers' perceptions. Sometimes Abbey sees the world through the confines of a microscope and sometimes through a wide-angle lens, but he constantly weds diction and syntax in ways that juxtapose his own vision of the land with the camera's.

That vision has much in common with other writers' work, too. Even though Abbey disdains categorizing and hates being slotted with his predecessors and peers, he nonetheless reveals many similarities. From Henry David Thoreau to the present, American essayists have considered the role of the individual in relation to his environment, the obstacles to human peace brought by progress, and the best course to bring self and surroundings into harmony. Like John Wesley Powell and John Muir in the nineteenth century, Abbey carefully examines the world around him, and like Mary Austin and Joseph Wood Krutch in the twentieth, he does so in order to learn more about himself. Like few others though, he rails against much of what he sees and argues incessantly that technocracy gives us more to fear today than in the past, sounding a more radical note than has been heard before. Yet Abbey belongs in the ranks of America's nonfiction masters. His eight nonfiction books from *Desert Solitaire* to *Desert Images* draw his readers back again and again. In their pages, his romancer's eye reenvisions the western scene, transforming it finally into the land of his deepest imaginings, "the place where the tangible and the mythical become the same" [JH, 5].

4

Trailblazing

Desert Solitaire

In *Desert Solitaire*, the reader enters a non-fiction environment no less imaginative than Abbey's first three novelistic worlds. While the book appears wholly factual, with its first-person point of view, its detailed pictures of real places and people, its qualitative statements about the twentieth-century American West, *Desert Solitaire* is as much a fictional re-creation as *Fire on the Mountain*, as much a romance as *The Brave Cowboy*. In his most substantive effort to date, Abbey transposes an imaginative trek through the grime and beauty of the Southwest desert into a dynamic exploration of its solitary universe. "Standing there, gaping at this monstrous and inhuman spectacle of rock and cloud and sky and space, I feel a ridiculous greed and possessiveness come over me," announces the author/ narrator of *Desert Solitaire*. "I want to know it all, possess it all, embrace the entire scene intimately, deeply, totally."[1] In this first book-length nonfiction restructuring of the desert landscape, Abbey lovingly pursues the fulfillment of his desire. That he succeeds is due primarily to his skill as a writer of romance, for only by reshaping his own desert universe into a mythic place can he finally know, possess, embrace the real one.

Since the author crafts that intangible environment, and the narrator explores it, it is necessary to examine the two before proceeding to the world itself. Only by distinguishing between the author, who is real, and the narrator, who is imagined, can we differentiate between the landscape that is real and the universe that is imagined. In other words, any discussion of Abbey's nonfiction must first dispel the myth that the narrative voice is Edward Abbey himself.

Ostensibly it is, of course. Abbey explains in his introduction to text of *Desert Solitaire* that he worked as a seasonal park ranger at Arches National Monument during three different summers, that he recorded his changing impressions of those times, that "all of the persons and places mentioned in this book are or were real" [xi–xii], although he has invented some names and relocated some others in space and time. Following the pattern of Thoreau's *Walden*, Abbey has collapsed a set of experiences into a single "Season in the Wilderness," as noted in the subtitle, in order to achieve an artistic unity otherwise missing from the diversity of three nonsequential years. By his own pronouncement, Abbey intends *Desert Solitaire* as a work of art rather than a documentary or journalistic account. The creation of a narrative voice makes the shaping possible.

To distinguish between the author and his narrator, we need a name for each—Edward Abbey we already know, the dramatized persona we can call Ed. Like Jack Burns, Ed comes to us unattached, with no apparent past. We meet him in medias res, already on the job at the monument, already possessive of his "rather personal demesne," where he is "sole inhabitant, usufructuary, observer and custodian" [5]. For the most part, Ed speaks in the present tense, as if the scenes he describes were dawning before his eyes. He greets the sun, watches the snow begin to melt, listens to three ravens cry and caw, smells his bacon frying. "That's the way it was this morning," he summarizes at the end of the first chapter, just as it was when the brave cowboy came unfettered into Duke City's haunted world.

The second chapter, "Solitaire," gives no more specific information about our guide but reinforces the transcendent qualities of the man and his world. "I became aware for the first time today of the immense silence in which I am lost," Ed observes. "Not a silence so much as a great stillness—for there are a few sounds: the creak of some bird in a juniper tree, an eddy of wind which passes and fades like a sigh, the ticking of the watch on my wrist—slight noises which break the sensation of absolute silence but at the same time exaggerate my sense of the surrounding, overwhelming peace. A suspension of time, a continuous present" [12–13]. The choice of the words "continuous present" is intriguing, since the term conventionally is used in literary criticism to label any writing that communicates a sense of the ongoing, or the everlasting. Dickens's omniscient narrator in *Bleak House,* for example, speaks in the continuous present, as does Gertrude Stein in *Three Lives* where she adroitly overuses the present participle. In both cases, those authors manipulate the continuous present to impose a timeless, eternal mood on their tales; Abbey does the same in *Desert Solitaire.*

Ed dwells in a state of universal suspension in the continuous present that Edward Abbey creates. Ed's job is to invite (and keep) the reader there with him; Abbey's is to craft the environment wherein the two can explore the Elysian hypocrisies of the modern West. They perform their duties in tandem, moving between the general and the particular, shifting with ease from present to past to continuous present once more. Ed, watching an oncoming storm, notices, "The wind is rising. For anyone with sense enough to get out of the rain now is the time to seek shelter" [136]. Then he vaguely recalls, "I have stood in the middle of a broad sandy wash . . . and looked up to see a wall of water tumble around a bend and surge toward me" [137]. And he remembers more specifically when his friend Ralph Newcomb was caught by quicksand "that gurgled a little and made funny, gasping noises, reluctant to let him go" [141]. In just five pages the verb tense changes three times and the particularity changes with it. Abbey and Ed subtly suck the reader into the quicksand of the book—a happy fate, as it turns out—by constantly shifting scene and substance in a fluid, continuous present.

Insistence upon a separation of author and dramatized narrator may sound trivial. Although such a distinction is generally made when talking about novels, most readers and critics assume that in nonfiction the two are synonymous. Beneath the solid surface of *Desert Solitaire,* however, viscosity awaits those who innocently believe the author is also the main character. Ed is an original creation, like Billy Vogelin Starr, manipulated by Abbey in similar ways and for similar purposes. The author can thus control his audience's attitudes and responses more easily and more effectively. The technique works the way escape fiction does, but with more radical success.

The reader knows little about Ed's life or his ties to other people. He is "still young, . . . enjoying good health, not yet quite to the beginning of the middle of the journey" [94; Abbey was forty-one when *Desert Solitaire* was published]; he has a brother named Johnny; he leaves a wife and loved ones back in Albuquerque when he drifts down the Colorado with Ralph, although they do not seem to be there when he leaves Utah at the book's close. But Ed remains astonishingly free from external demands. Not only does his family float vaguely in the background, but even friends in the foreground fade into insignificance whenever their demands clash with Ed's desires. Riding to L.A. one summer, Ed decides to "see Havasu immediately, before something went wrong somewhere. My friends said they would wait. So I went down into Havasu—fourteen miles by trail—and looked things over. When I returned five weeks later I discovered that the others had gone on to Los Angeles without me" [221]. No other reference is made to these acquaintances. Like a Jack Burns, a Lassiter, or a Shane, Ed bears no apparent responsibilities other than the ones in the continuous present of *Desert Solitaire*. He frets more about wildlife and tourists than he does about wife and family.

In a romance, this stance is appropriate. The knight-errant, the idealistic park ranger, must be free to joust quixotically with the bureaucratic windmills of the United States Park Service. To encumber him with responsibilities would be to limit his freedom of movement, of spirit, of radical thought. Without visible restraints, Ed can behave like an apprentice to the Monkey Wrench Gang, leveling a billboard with a bucksaw borrowed from his employer, or pulling up wooden survey stakes and cutting bright little ribbons that mark what will be a new road into his Arches domain. The anarchistic gesture, unbecoming for a solid citizen with a wife and sons, or ironically inconsequential for a Paul Bondi, has more impact when performed by the unfettered Ed. Jocular, almost tongue in cheek, the voice of *Desert Solitaire* lets the reader join him on metaphorical raids against the establishment. We enjoy the fun vicariously, just as we delight in the antics of escape-fiction heroes when they successfully assault their foes.

Ed's complete freedom explains not only the ease with which we absorb radical thought in this and other of Abbey's books, but also the confusion we feel about the narrator's thoughtless, sometimes selfish, deeds. When Abbey's characters toss beer cans out on the desert, for example, many readers feel genuine irritation.

Indeed, they find such behavior totally paradoxical. Yet who among us has not been tempted to do the same, just once? Instead, we lean back in our chairs, breathe secondhand the fresh desert air, and turn another page as we might with any Western pulp paperback.

Abbey's world is not, however, a frivolous one. Most of the time he and his narrator lure the reader into more meaningful confrontations with the Southwest landscape. Conducting an experiment with an innocent rabbit, for example, Ed brains a cottontail with a stone, killing it in the name of science.

For a moment I am shocked by my deed; I stare at the quiet rabbit, his glazed eyes, his blood drying in the dust. Something vital is lacking. But shock is succeeded by a mild elation. Leaving my victim to the vultures and maggots, who will appreciate him more than I could—the flesh is probably infected with tularemia—I continue my walk with a new, augmented cheerfulness which is hard to understand but unmistakable. What the rabbit has lost in energy and spirit seems added, by processes too subtle to fathom, to my own soul. I try but cannot feel my sense of guilt. I examine my soul: white as snow. Check my hands: not a trace of blood. No longer do I feel so isolated from the sparse and furtive life around me, a stranger from another world. I have entered into this one. We are kindred all of us, killer and victim, predator and prey, me and the sly coyote, the soaring buzzard, the elegant gopher snake, the trembling cottontail, the foul worms that feed on our entrails, all of them, all of us. Long live diversity, long live the earth! [38–39]

The apparently senseless experiment, highly inappropriate if conducted by a man with a family in tow, allows Abbey to draw a series of behavioral generalities from the specific deed. He considers the euphoria one feels after committing an uncivilized act, he thinks about his own guilt (and rejects it), he wonders about the more esoteric kinship between killer and victim, and finally he comes to a more personal understanding of self and soul. While it is unlikely that any reader will feel compelled to repeat the test, it is probable that most will join Ed in spirit, "no longer so isolated from the sparse and furtive life." The paragraph naturalistically drags reader and narrator alike into the Darwinian world.

Ed intrinsically prefers his separation from others, although "there are lonely hours. How can I deny it? There are times when solitaire becomes solitary, an entirely different game, a prison term, and the inside of the skull as confining and unbearable as the interior of the housetrailer on a hot day" [109]. He affirms, however, "that a man can never find or need better companionship than that of himself" [111]. To prove his point, Ed often wanders in the desert alone because he finds "that in contemplating the natural world my pleasure is greater if there are not too many others contemplating it with me" [226]. Perhaps too many of us lack the courage (or foolhardiness) to explore the desert by ourselves, but to do so with a free-spirited companion, like the voice of *Desert Solitaire*, is to do so under the best of circumstances. With Ed's guidance, we touch corners and canyons of which we might otherwise only dream.

We can experience similar sensations if we turn to one of Abbey's favorite souls, a young man named Everett Ruess who disappeared into the desert wilderness more than forty years ago. After a futile year in college, Everett chose to wander through the Southwest alone with his burro, pausing only to make friends with other isolated fellows and to write and to draw. Neither a prospector nor an anthropologist, but an explorer, an observer, and a dreamer, he roamed for almost three years before he vanished amid the folds of the Waterpocket. Friends later collected Everett's letters, poems, and drawings, and published *On Desert Trails* (1940), a slim volume that pierces the heart of a spirit who wanders the slickrock country alone. More poignant, adolescent, and naive than Ed, Everett reveals the romantic heart of a true desert rat. His words—"I have gone my way regardless of everything but beauty"[2]—suggest a little more about Abbey and his narrator too.

The "solitaire" of *Desert Solitaire* differs from the solitude on desert trails in that Ed acknowledges the paradox of his unwillingness to escape permanently. Although his ties to the civilized life are minimal, he cannot stay away from "the rat race *(Rattus Urbanus)*" [298] forever. At the book's end he ironically explains that "duty calls. Yes, I hate it so much that I'm spending the best part of a paycheck on airplane tickets." He confesses, too, that "unlike Thoreau who insisted on one world at a time I am attempting to make the best of two. After six months in the desert I am volunteering for a winter of front-line combat duty—caseworker, public welfare department—in the howling streets of Megalomania, U.S.A." [298]. Still, Ed disappears into the sunset of the continuous present as magically as the Lone Ranger at the end of a six-gun adventure. "The sun goes down, I face the road . . . The car races

forward through a world dissolving into snow and night" [303].
As with any guide through the maze of a romance, the narrator
remains mysterious and unfettered to the shadowy end.

Just as we do not imagine the Lone Ranger with a wife and children at home, we must not picture Ed too specifically in a grimy
New York/New Jersey metropolitan environment—the euphemistic "Megalomania, U.S.A." will do. Several chapters earlier, Ed hyperbolically trumpeted a paragraph of italicized (and parenthetical)
fancy about that world so vaguely shadowed at the book's close.

(My *God!* I'm thinking, what incredible *shit* we put up with most of
our lives—the *domestic* routine (same old wife *every* night), the stupid and
useless and degrading *jobs*, the *insufferable* arrogance of elected officials,
the crafty *cheating* and the *slimy* advertising of the businessmen, the boring wars in which we kill our buddies instead of our *real* enemies back in
the capital, the foul, diseased and *hideous* cities and towns we live in, the
constant *petty* tyranny of automatic washers and automobiles and TV machines and telephones—! ah *Christ!*, I'm thinking, . . . what *intolerable*
garbage and what utterly *useless crap* we bury ourselves in day by day,
while patiently enduring at the same time the creeping strangulation of
the clean white *collar* and the rich but *modest* four-in-hand garrote!) [177–78;
all punctuation Abbey's]

Beer can poised to toss into the imagined sage, rock clasped, tie-tight collar unbuttoned for just a moment, the reader breathes again
the fresh air of Abbey's prose. Just as we were unwilling to repeat
Ed's other deeds, we hesitate to spout our frustrations at the "incredible *shit* we put up with most of our lives" too. We let the voice
of *Desert Solitaire* do it for us. And he complies, in crude words
chosen carefully to shock, to electrify, to jar, to prod.

Does this argumentative man sound like the same one who threw
a rock at a passing rabbit? Conversely, is he the same human who
lives placidly with a gopher snake that by day "curls up like a cat
in the warm corner behind the heater" [21]? Yes, despite his occasional contradictory or eccentric behavior, Ed remains essentially
consistent throughout the book. The snake and the rabbit interludes,
for example, are both expressions of his relationship to animals,
and thus of man's relationship to the animal world. These and other
passages, in fact, show the narrator, like any character in a romance,
static rather than dynamic, one who changes minimally from start
to finish. The man who drives into a snowstorm at the book's close

is the same one who woke from "a cold night, a cold wind, the snow falling like confetti" [3] three hundred pages earlier. Through the episodes between, Ed's attitudes, his reactions, his likes and dislikes, remain the same, with a rigidity more attractive than irritating. And because he has no permanent relationships with others in the world of *Desert Solitaire*, we neither expect growth and development in that arena nor do we find any. Ed acts just as any medieval knight would, in a stylized and unchanging manner, with ethics, politics, and convictions that remain intransigent.

Like the hero of a Zane Grey novel, the untrammeled narrator invites us to share vicariously his experiences in the untamed West, and like other characters of Abbey's fiction, Ed comes from the shadows and leaves in the night. Such a distanced point of view allows the author to include acts and statements that may be exaggerated, unsupportable, even libelous, without forcing him to shoulder the inherent responsibility. In a sense, Ed is Abbey's radical gesture, a mouthpiece for the ironical anarchist, a safety-valve for the author's anger and disgust at the changes he sees occurring in the West of the twentieth century. Finally, the narrator is a dramatized persona who leads us into the maze, not of southeast Utah, but of Abbey's world. The author maintains that *Desert Solitaire* is "a book of personal history, one man's odyssey in search of Ithaca" [JH, xiii]. The statement might be modified to read: 'a book of *dramatized* personal history, Abbey's *and* Ed's *heretical and romantic* odyssey in search of their *dreams in the American West.*'

Where they lead us, though, is no more real than Ed himself. Abbey admits as much in his introduction when he explains his methodology. "What I have tried to do . . . is something a bit different. Since you cannot get the desert into a book any more than a fisherman can haul up the sea with his nets, I have tried to create a world of words in which the desert figures more as medium than as material. Not imitation but evocation has been the goal" [x]. While such an endeavor differs from the conventional nonfiction nature or ecology book, it is similar to the evocative process undertaken by the creator of a romance who quickly spins from reality into a fully imagined ambience. It also mirrors the procedure followed by Abbey himself in a fictional tale like *The Brave Cowboy*. A return to the passage about the flash flood, alluded to earlier as an example of Ed's shifting sense of past and present, demonstrates how powerfully that process of evocation works. Following the lines, "I have stood in the middle of a broad sandy wash," Ed describes the vision he "looked up to see":

A wall of water. A poor image. For the flash flood of the desert poorly resembles water. It looks rather like a loose pudding or a thick dense soup, thick as gravy, dense with mud and sand, lathered with scuds of bloody froth, loaded on its crest with a tangle of weeds and shrubs and small trees ripped from their roots.

Surprised by delight, I stood there in the heat, the bright sun, the quiet afternoon, and watched the monster roll and roar toward me. It advanced in crescent shape with a sort of forelip about a foot high streaming in front, making hissing sucking noises like a giant amoeba, nosing to the right and nosing to the left as if on the spoor of something good to eat. Red as tomato soup or blood it came on me about as fast as a man could run. I moved aside and watched it go by. [137–38]

The passage is not a photographic reproduction, but a tactile evocation of all the senses. The taste and smell of tomato soup, the texture of pudding or gravy, the sounds of hiss and suck, the sights of tangling cresting tamarisk, brush-stroked with blood and bloody froth—the images of the picture converge into a single "sense." More real than the actual turbulence, Abbey's flash flood sweeps the reader into its rush and roar, nightmare and chaos, truth and fiction.

How many of us would stand there voluntarily, "surprised by delight," while we watched such an unleashing of nature's strength, or would recall the event with such metaphorical particularity? Most, indeed, would flee too quickly, missing the "queer vibration in the air and in the ground," ignoring the comparison with "a freight train coming down the grade, very fast." Our guide into "southeastern Utah: the canyonlands; Abbey's country" [69] can, and does. That is part of his job too.

Throughout *Desert Solitaire*, Abbey works hard to make Ed communicate Abbey's own sense of the slickrock world. He does so according to a careful design that alternates not simply verb tenses and specificities but kinds and intensities of experiences too. The word order of the last quotation evidences a recurrent pattern—from geographic locale (southeastern Utah) to generic world (the canyonlands) to generalized universe (Abbey's country, the heart of the matter). The author has designed most of the chapters in this way, and then has put those chapters together in a structured manner. We spend the first several alone with Ed, becoming acquainted with Arches—its geology, its plants, its animal population. Inventoried by a poet's eye, each "living organism stands out bold and brave and vivid against the lifeless sand and barren rock" [29]. Next, Ed voices his first polemic, a personal plea against "industrial tourism" and for "freedom and wilderness." After this overview, he proceeds to a series of individualized episodes that reveal the desert more intimately. Some tales star Ed himself; others belong to local Southwesterners. Each, however, interprets some facet of the land. In these chapters, Abbey distinguishes *Desert Solitaire* from the typical book of natural history by focusing, as he says, on evocation, not on imitation, by turning it into a romance.

One exemplary chapter, entitled "Rocks," begins in "southeastern Utah" with a detailed account of the treasures found there. "The very names are lovely—chalcedony, carnelian, jasper, chrysoprase and agate" [69]. After depleting his list, Ed continues with some introductory comments about mining and the government's role in such endeavors. Leading us deeper into "the canyonlands," he quotes John Wesley Powell's 1869 description of the rapids below the confluence of the Colorado and the Green, then recounts the misadventures of two greenhorn prospectors searching the same area for uranium almost a century later. But the best is yet to come. With the turn of a page, we careen from the swirls of Cataract Canyon into the treacherous eddies of Abbey's country where the evocative story of "Rocks" begins.

In all those years of feverish struggle, buying and selling, cheating and swindling, isolation, loneliness, hardship, danger, sudden fortune and sudden disaster, there is one question about this search for the radiant treasure—the hidden splendor—which nobody ever asked. It is necessary, therefore, to relate one more story concerning the uranium strike, a story based on events which may or may not have actually happened but which all who tell it will swear is true. [76]

Like an old-timer spinning a yarn, Ed thus introduces us to Albert T. Husk and family, and their business partner, Mr. Graham.

No synopsis could do justice to the windy, naturalistic tale. The two men, the East Texas dupe and Chuck Graham the speculator (who seduces first Albert into his questionable mining company and then Albert's wife into his bed), end up dead in the canyons while Billy-Joe Husk (the son) floats down the Colorado on a fantastic voyage precipitated by a flash flood which recalls Ed's own vision of "a red snout of liquid mud, . . . swaying from side to side in the rhythm of its pendulous momentum, like a locomotive on uneven rails" [89]. Billy-Joe dies too, leaving Mrs. Husk as the survivor and inheritor of "a 40 per cent interest in a group of uranium claims known as the Hotrock Mountain Mineral Development Company." A slick lawyer from Austin tries to negotiate.

Mrs. Husk said how much? The lawyer said that he had been authorized to offer Mrs. Husk $4500—twice what her late husband had paid for them. Mrs. Husk said that she would settle for $150,000. The lawyer smiled and said that he was quite serious. Mrs. Husk said that she was serious too and that on second thought perhaps $237,000 would be a more reasonable figure. The lawyer smiled again and revealed confidentially that he had been authorized to offer, *if absolutely necessary,* as much as $15,000. Mrs. Husk said that $192,761 seemed to her a fair price. The lawyer offered her a cigarette. She took it. He lit it for her with a trim-shaped lighter bearing on its fuselage the emblem of the USAF. They agreed shortly thereafter on the sum of one hundred thousand ($100,000) dollars. [92; italics Abbey's]

With flat understatement, the tale ends, as does the chapter.

Condensation may weaken the flavor of the prose, but the point remains clear. The final paragraph, with its revelation of the victors of the tale (few prospectors in the dusty desert earned money from uranium speculation) and the ensuing disputes and bargains (specificity makes $192,761 the funniest offer of all), indicts the United States government more surely than any diatribe could. The question "which nobody ever asked" is posed, and tacitly answered, with the flick of a tiny cigarette lighter. With hyperbolic understatement, a careful blending of exaggeration and immediate undercutting, Abbey has effectively satirized the power of the "Rocks."

No less meaningful are the chapters which focus on Ed rather than on the natives he sees around him. "Down the River," for example, launches the narrator and his friend Ralph on a personal exploration of the Colorado before "the beavers had to go and build another goddamned dam" [173]. Through Glen Canyon before it was drowned, the two men drift into the world of the romance. Ed, one arm dangling over the side of his rubber boat, enjoys a special kind of intimacy with the river while the current grabs his craft. "Something dreamlike and remembered, that sensation called *deja vu*—when was I here before? A moment of groping back through the maze, following the thread of a unique emotion" [176], and the trip begins in earnest.

Following his standard format of shifting from the land to a mystical evocation of it, and from the world of Utah canyons to a better universe imagined, the author carries us downstream on a rising wave of prose. Some of the best descriptive writing in *Desert Solitaire* occurs in this chapter, as do some of the most cogent statements of Abbey's attitudes toward the modern-day West. "Down the River" is almost a synopsis of the author at his best.

> Down the river we drift in a kind of waking dream, gliding beneath the great curving cliffs with their tapestries of water stains, the golden alcoves, the hanging gardens, the seeps, the springs where no man will ever drink, the royal arches in high relief and the amphitheatres shaped like seashells. A sculptured landscape mostly bare of vegetation—earth in the nude. [187]

No one who saw Glen Canyon before its burial can deny the cast of perfectability Abbey throws on its walls. A few pages later he compares the lower Escalante to "a surrealist corridor in a Tamayo dream" [200–201]; a few pages beyond that, the rocks to hamburgers, or "piles of melted pies." Ed, looking around at the awesome scenery, announces definitively, "I am not an atheist but an earthiest. Be true to the earth" [208]. So his author is, evoking a canyon now buried under two hundred feet of water, silt, and mud, depicting a universe now alive only in the imagination.

Speculatively, the dream turns to the wilderness and freedom, touchstones in Abbey's canon of words. Rejecting the government's definition of wilderness—"A minimum of not less than 5000 contiguous acres of roadless area" [189]—with barbed irony, author and narrator try to reach a more satisfactory truth by connotative, rather than denotative, means. For them, "the love of wilderness is more than a hunger for what is always beyond reach; it is also an expression of loyalty to the earth, the earth which bore us and sustains us, the only home we shall ever know, the only paradise we ever need—if only we had the eyes to see" [190]. Succinctly, these words summarize their attitude toward the desecration so apparent in the voracious construction of Lake Powell and the attendant destruction of the free-running river.

. . . Wilderness is not a luxury but a necessity of the human spirit, and as vital to our lives as water and good bread. A civilization which destroys what little remains of the wild, the spare, the original, is cutting itself off from its origins and betraying the principle of civilization itself. [192]

Although Abbey will return to this first principle in almost every piece of prose that follows *Desert Solitaire,* he will never define it with more conviction. In his eyes, to destroy the Colorado so casually was tantamount to destroying a part of the West's very soul. His fictional equivalent would be the leveling of John Vogelin's Box V Ranch, or the more figurative elimination of Jonathan Troy's dream, but the real physical action of turning Glen Canyon into a lake looms even larger. Any civilization that would willingly ruin the land in such a way is no civilization, and so deserves no quarter. The only justifiable rejoinder, then, is anarchy, in Abbey's world.

Even while he was writing *Desert Solitaire,* monkey wrench tactics were not far from Abbey's mind. In fact, a specific formula for the ultimate dam's destruction appears in "Down the River." If

some unknown hero with a rucksack full of dynamite strapped to his back will descend into the bowels of the dam; there he will hide his high explosives where they will do the most good, attach blasting caps to the lot and with angelic ingenuity link the caps to the official dam wiring system in such a way that when the time comes for the grand opening ceremony, when the President and the Secretary of the Interior and the governors of the Four-Corner states are all in full regalia assembled, the button which the President pushes will ignite the loveliest explosion ever seen by man, reducing the great dam to a heap of rubble in the path of the river. [188]

At this point, Abbey perceives the scene as only "idle, foolish, futile daydreams," but he will recall his scheme when *The Monkey Wrench Gang* begins and will replay the potential explosion in full color. Meanwhile, in the real twentieth-century American West that anchors Abbey's world, "something precious and irreplaceable [is] about to be destroyed." That something is the wilderness with its attendant freedom. Abbey's goal is to stop that destruction, although to do so may well result in some unfortunate monkey wrench destruction of his own. But according to his somewhat primitive code of retribution, the end justifies the means. "In wilderness is the preservation . . .," and we need to conserve both the land and ourselves before it is too late to salvage either. Abbey will pursue these beliefs more stridently, in *The Journey Home,* which contains a chapter called "Freedom and Wilderness, Wilderness and Freedom," and in its sequel, *Abbey's Road.* He will also suggest possible courses of action in his fictional fantasies. But it is in *Desert Solitaire* where he codifies his strategems.

A descriptive sense of the land itself supports the body of his prose. Without his visual awareness, his use of detail, and his mastery of the particular phrase, Abbey's writing would be lifeless and dull. As both the origin of his popular appeal and the trigger for his philosophical musings, the many pictorial paragraphs—those describing scenes which may be pictured, imaged and framed, in the reader's mind—account for much of his present popularity. He was virtually unknown two decades ago, but we now can find his narratives and travelogues in half a dozen different magazines. Whether rafting in Alaska [see *Mariah/Outside,* January 1980], running in Arizona [see *Running,* December 1980], or exploring in between, Abbey's lexical skills sell his writing to a large audience. It was in *Desert Solitaire* that he began to perfect the technique: "Under a wine-dark sky I walk through light reflected and re-reflected from the walls and floor of the canyon, a radiant golden light that glows on rock and stream, sand and leaf in varied hues of amber, honey, whiskey—the light that never was is here, now, in the storm-sculptured gorge of the Escalante" [200]. In his descriptions, Abbey transforms the actual world into an imagined replica, extrapolating generalized truths from the particulars of the exchange. In other words, he processes his nonfiction just as the materials of fiction or of a romance are processed.

He reproduces his version of the Southwest desert country in two forms. One shape is the metaphoric, as in Jonathan Troy's West, where the land becomes a literal figure of speech that replaces the figurative dreams. Arches National Monument, "glimpses of weird humps of pale rock on either side, like petrified elephants, dinosaurs, stone-age hobgoblins" [2], is both a concrete and an abstract place. The more complicated dimension of Abbey's domain, however, is the mythic, where the land becomes the one of his "deepest imaginings" and the intangible replaces the tangible. He began doing this tentatively in *Fire on the Mountain* by isolating the red world from the green. But when he bombarded one with the other, nothing happened. His two envisioned worlds ricocheted, effecting no permanent changes (except as the reader's attitudes may have been altered by the thrust of the prose). Just as the brave cowboy left no footprints in Duke City, so John Vogelin could not budge the government's point of view. So even though the green world and red interacted more directly in the Box V tale, no synthesis took place. Superficially the same appears true in *Desert Solitaire*— Tukuhnikivats has little to do with the United States Park Service, nor does the pristine beauty of Glen Canyon stop the completion of a cement superstructure that will dam it up. But Abbey now surpasses the simpler ways of his earlier books. The red and green do more than confront each other in *Desert Solitaire;* they begin to build toward an artistic vision. Abbey has discovered a third alternative, a distinctly different world that serves to strip bare the fallacies of the other two.

This three-step transfiguration of the land, from the literal to the metaphoric to the mythic, is best characterized by a Renaissance scholar who goes beyond Northrop Frye's dichotomies of red and green. Harry Berger, Jr., writing about More's Utopia, Sidney's golden world and Arcadia, Spenser's Faerie, Shakespeare's green world and stage world, in effect describes the sun-drenched mirage of *Desert Solitaire* as well. The essential quality of the created world, the "playground, laboratory, theater, or battlefield of the mind," is its explicit, and hypothetical, artificiality, says Berger. "It presents itself to us as a game which, like all games, is to be taken with dead seriousness while it is going on. In pointing to itself as serious play, it affirms both its limits and its power in a single gesture. Separating itself from the casual and confused region of everyday existence, it promises a clarified image of the world it represents."[3] Berger goes on to refine the kinds of worlds that may be imaged— the world inside a picture frame, for example, or the world of pastoral simplification, or even the world of the controlled conditions of scientific experiment—and explains the rudimentary utilitarianism of the technique. By creating a new world of metaphor and myth that is ostensibly a frivolous place, the author may either annihilate or affirm those tenets of the real world he images, and may do so through innuendo. Although readers may be unwilling to grant Edward Abbey the company of Shakespeare, Sidney, and Spenser, his adoption of their method is indisputable.

In a chapter like "Down the River," Abbey plays the horrors of

Glen Canyon's red world off against the ethereal unreality of his own green existence.[4] Rainbow Bridge, for example, exists in the red world as "an isolated geological oddity, an extension of that museum-like diorama to which industrial tourism tends to reduce the natural world" [217], whose approach leads through "the unmistakable signs of tourist culture—tin cans and tinfoil dumped in a fireplace, a dirty sock dangling from a bush, a worn-out tennis shoe in the bottom of a clear spring, gum wrappers, cigarette butts, and bottlecaps everywhere" [214]. The green world, on the other hand, seems idyllically preferable, with its "catfish in the mainstream and venison in the side canyons, cottonwoods for shade and shelter, juniper for fuel, mossy springs (not always accessible) for thirst, and the ever-changing splendor of sky, cliffs, mesas and river for the needs of the spirit" [183]. Ralph and Ed agree that "if necessary, . . . a man could live out his life in this place"; but could the reader? To imagine a permanent existence alone in the silent desert, or even to imagine a permanent existence under Abbey's anarchistic and free-spirited rule, would be as ludicrous as to imagine Abbey chained to a bureaucrat's desk. The green world may appear preferable to the red, but only because Abbey has appealed to our romantic instincts, not because he has modelled an environment where we might actually live.

It seems man needs a third choice, Berger's all-important alternative that subsumes parts of the other worlds into a coherent, and greater, whole. When writing *The Brave Cowboy* and *Fire on the Mountain,* Abbey stopped short of that option—painting the green and tainting the red and exposing the basic incompatibility of the two without moving on to the larger vision of *Desert Solitaire's* most original chapter.

The story of "The Moon-Eyed Horse"[5] begins in a composite red and green Utah canyon outside Moab where Ed learns of the creature's existence and vows he must have the independent cuss. A month later he returns alone to take possession. "I could hardly have picked a more hostile day," Ed begins. "Nothing moved, nothing stirred, except the shimmer of heat waves rising before the red canyon walls." Under the searing summer sun, Abbey turns the so-called green world into a pseudo-Hell, a twilight zone where the pageant of the spectral horse can be enacted. "Out of the heat and stillness came an inaudible whisper, a sort of telepathic intimation that perhaps the horse did not exist at all—only his tracks." Yet Ed must pursue the animal, and Abbey must pursue the vision.

Something breathing nearby—I was in the presence of a tree. On the slope above stood a giant old juniper with massive, twisted trunk, its boughs sprinkled with pale-blue inedible berries. Hanging from one of the limbs was what looked at first glance like a pair of trousers that reached to the ground. Blinking the sweat out of my eyes I looked harder and saw the trousers transform themselves into the legs of a large animal, focused my attention and distinguished through the obscurity of the branches and foliage the outline of a tall horse. A very tall horse.

With the mendacity characteristic of a tall tale, narrator and author visualize the beast. "He was a giant about seventeen hands high, with a buckskin hide as faded as an old rug and a big ugly coffin-shaped head. . . . His nineteen ribs jutted out like the rack of a skeleton and his neck, like a camel's, seemed far too gaunt and long to carry that oversize head off the ground." But in this land of the romance, such figurative specificity as the "coffin-shaped head" and the neck "like a camel's" is undercut in order to transform the brute into a specter—"apocalyptic, a creature out of a bad dream," a "goddamned nightmare of a horse." When Ed approaches the fleshy phantom, the tangible becomes increasingly intangible.

We stared at each other, unmoving. If that animal was breathing I couldn't hear it—the silence seemed absolute. Not a fly, not a single fly crawled over his arid skin or whined around his rheumy eyeballs. If it hadn't been for the light of something like consciousness in his good eye I might have imagined I was talking to a scarecrow, a dried stuffed completely mummified horse. He didn't even smell like a horse, didn't seem to have any smell about him at all. Perhaps if I reached out and touched him he would crumble to a cloud of dust, vanish like a shadow.

Ed groans that his "head ached from the heat and glare and for a moment I wondered if this horselike shape in front of me was anything more than hallucination." Does the creature exist? Or is he simply a construct of Abbey's mind?

Like Jack Burns before him, for example, the moon-eyed horse is both real and imagined, a spectral figure from another world that touches this one in meaningful ways. Both, in fact, represent the idyllic green world life, with its attendant freedom from responsibilities and its impractical and quixotic moods. The horse, after all, bucked off a middle-aged tourist and fled to the sanctity of the canyons just as Jack, too, freed himself from the trappings of the civilized world. The brave cowboy, the horse, even Ed the narrator, at times munch the figurative grass of a simpler, more pastoral life quite removed from the red, furious rush of the present. But where the conflict between Duke City and Jack Burns—the red and the green personified—was solved only by a contrived accident, the relationship between Ed, the moon-eyed horse, and the world beyond is knit into a textured, thematic whole.

Abbey stage-manages it by throwing a barrage of images at the reader—"the red cliffs rippled behind the veil of heat, radiant as hot iron"—that refracts the dry desert landscape in an "explosive blaze of light and heat." Then, beneath the white-hot glare of sun and dust, there comes "a glimpse of a lunatic horse expanding suddenly, growing bigger than all the world and soaring over me on wings that flapped like a bat's." The green world, despite its appeal and enchantment, can be too seductive. Its permanent freedom from restraint can overwhelm the man who seeks refuge there, for the unrelenting animalism combined with the continual introspection finally make the green undesirable. Abbey, recognizing the menace, turns the syllogism around and threatens the spectral creature with the very things that threaten the man. "The Turkey buzzards will get you," Ed predicts. "And after a couple of months there'll be nothing left but your mangled hide and your separated bones and—get this, Moon-Eye get the picture—way out in eternity somewhere, on the far side of the sun, they'll hang up a brass plaque with the image of your moon-eyed soul stamped on it. That's about all." The same fate awaits Abbey too, and all who would follow him into the box canyons of the slickrock country, for by choosing a narrow isolationism from the world, they doom themselves as surely as the horse is doomed.

Jack Burns, for example, slogged blindly up the interminable mountainside only to find death. His "old tale" ended blindly, without a vision of how his demise fit in the "new times" around him. In contrast, Ed sees complexities, opening his eyes to the limited universe of the moon-eyed monster and turning away from the kismet that could trap him there. "Enough. I turned my back on the horse," he announces. "Refusing to look again at the spectre, . . . I started homeward. . . . Once, twice, I thought I heard footsteps following me but when I looked back I saw nothing." Unlike Orpheus, Ed can manipulate his vision, tantalizing the fates and enchanting his readers with the music of his words but without destroying what he loves best. Nevertheless, he cannot remain in the wilderness forever; no flesh-and-blood man of the twentieth century can. Instead, he must depart, leaving the moon-eyed horse behind. Abbey and Ed rightly regard the whole experience in the box canyon as emblematic, looking past the artistic skeleton to see a meatier whole.

The horse stood motionless as a rock. He looked like part of that burnt-out landscape. He looked like the steed of Don Quixote carved out of wood by Giacometti. I could see the blue of the sky between his ribs, through the eye-sockets of his skull. Dry, odorless, still and silent, he looked like the idea—without the substance—of a horse.

The twice-removed comparison, from the Rocinante of a naive and idealistic Spanish knight to a representation of that horse, points out the crucial insubstantiality of Abbey's green world, the land of the moon-eyed horse where idea replaces substance and dream replaces reality. Moreover, it suggests that Abbey has looked through and beyond himself, past the quixotic gesture of the ironical anarchist and around the singular vision of the radical rebel, to see a composite alternative.

He even has words for the vision, although he does not use them in this particular chapter. "Paradox and bedrock," he calls it in *Desert Solitaire*'s first pages; "Bedrock and Paradox," he names the final chapter of the book. Even as he rejects a technique that calls for the personification of nature, he invents a mythic horse to carry the weight of dreams above its skinny, insubstantial ribs. Adopting the "dream of a hard and brutal mysticism in which the naked self merges with a non-human world and yet somehow survives still intact, individual, separate" [6], he attempts in *Desert Solitaire* to construct a third alternative to the red and green that will successfully subsume the best parts of the other two. Without fully articulating its characteristics, since to do so would be to employ a substantiality alien to dreams, Abbey leaves the reader free to imaginatively design a vision that draws from the best of both green and red, or, more specifically, to predicate an alternative world from the factors of his experiences.

Although such a process may sound abstruse, it actually is not. *Desert Solitaire* works on an emotional level in much the same way that escape fiction does, while its intellectual and philosophical levels are more complex. Designing an idyllic green hothouse that encourages man's dreams to flourish, and simultaneously negating the horrific red hell created when culture squeezes the blood from modern civilization, Abbey finally argues for neither. His is not the Zane Grey West of a mellowed sunset nor is it John Hawkes's parched wasteland but, rather, Abbey's new West is a contemporary composite that stirs readers' thoughts even as it soothes their fears, encourages readers' dreams even as it intimates they may never come true. In a romance form borrowed from an earlier age and from a different genre, Abbey has found a new way to explicate the twentieth-century West, provocatively moving beyond the strictures of red and green.

The Albert T. Husks and the moon-eyed horses of this world survive more hardily in legend than in life. But since one of Abbey's chief characteristics is his deprecating sense of humor and since one of the necessary ingredients of the green world is a rollicking sense of play, the tall-tale chapters seem more exemplary than some of the others. If we turn, though, to two of the most serious sections of *Desert Solitaire*, we will discover similar images, patterns and alternatives emerging when the paradox of dreams clashes head-on with the bedrock of reality. We will find, too, the grace with which Abbey's technique works.

"The Dead Man At Grandview Point"[6] opens sleepily. It is August. "Each day begins clean and promising in the sweet cool clear green light of dawn. And then the sun appears, its hydrogen cauldrons brimming—so to speak—with plasmic fires, and the tyranny of its day begins." As the heat intrudes on the cool of night, the red intrudes on the green. For a page or two, Abbey continues to evoke the hot summer world with more specificity than anywhere in the tale of the moon-eyed horse. Cloudbursts, elaborate sunsets, the sight of a nighthawk and sound of a coyote define the Arches environment and locate man in a natural, although slightly alien, milieu. In fact, a man's intrusion proves fatal.

The heart of the chapter sends Ed on a manhunt for a lost tourist. The sixty-year-old amateur photographer disappeared in a maze of "washes, giant potholes, basins, fissures and canyons" where the Park Service, two days later, now searches. Joining them, Ed finds himself attracted to the abyss, "the mesa's edge and a twelve-hundred-foot drop straight down to what is called the White Rim Bench." Even as he looks under junipers and overhanging ledges, and into gullies and sand-blown cracks, he cannot resist the lure of the infinite drop.

At times I step to the brink of the mesa and peer down through that awful, dizzying vacancy to the broken slabs piled along the foot of the wall, so far—so terribly far—below. It is not impossible that our man might have stumbled off the edge in the dark, or even—spellbound by that fulfillment of nothingness—eased himself over, deliberately, in broad daylight, drawn into the void by the beauty and power of his own terror . . .? "Gaze not too long into the abyss, lest the abyss gaze into thee,"

Ed quotes to himself. He might substitute with equal import, "Gaze not too long at the moon-eyed horse, lest the moon-eyed horse gaze into thee." Once more Abbey has set up a situation that reveals the dangers of the green world while projecting simultaneously its inherent allure. He does so by combining concrete details—a *sixty*-year-old tourist, a *two*-day manhunt, a *twelve-hundred*-foot drop—with the abstraction of a "fulfillment of nothingness." The specifics help tie down the floating generalities.

At once more particular and less pleasant is the actual discovery of the tourist's remains, lying "on his back, limbs extended rigidly from a body bloated like a balloon. A large stain discolors the crotch of his trousers. The smell of decay is rich and sickening," as the red world of reality makes naturalistic hash of Ed's idealized musings. Written to shock as much as to provide details, designed also to expose the paradox of the grotesque—"rich and sickening"—the lines force the reader's awareness of the hostile indifference of the universe. Then Ed's mood swings. The dead man "had good taste. He had good luck," the narrator enviously decides. "To die alone, on rock under sun at the brink of the unknown, like a wolf, like a great bird, seems to me very good fortune indeed. To die in the open, under the sky, far from the insolent interference of leech and priest, before the desert vastness opening like a window onto eternity—that surely was an overwhelming stroke of rare good luck." Balancing the minutes of panic preceding the man's death against the glory of a final moment "before the desert's vastness opening like a window onto eternity," Ed rationalizes the suffering and pain. "He may have died in his sleep, dreaming of the edge of things, of flight into space, of soaring." There is a bit of wish-fulfillment in the justification, along with a bit of Edgar Guest philosophy too, but it remains an appealing way to disguise a red world nightmare in a green world dream.

It is apparent many years later when the author/narrator of *Abbey's Road* pursues a personal expedition to the edge that Abbey has always been drawn to the abyss, no matter what its color. Why he did not step across in *Desert Solitaire*, and why he never will, is explained in the coda of his most recent personal history.

On this point I halt. One step further would take me into another world, the next world, the ultimate world. The longest journey begins with a single step. But I pause, hesitate, defer that step, as always. Not out of fear—I'm afraid of dying but not of death—but again, from respect. Respect for my obligations to others, respect for the work I still hope to do, respect for myself. The despair that haunts the background of our lives, sometimes obtruding itself into consciousness, can still be modulated, as I know from experience, into a comfortable melancholia and from there to defiance, delight, a roaring affirmation of self-existence. Even, at times, into a quiet and blessedly self-forgetful peace, a modest joy. [AR, 194–95]

The reader cannot miss the difference in tone between *Abbey's Road* and *Desert Solitaire*. Although only a little over a decade has passed between them, the more articulate Ed of 1979 reveals more and says less than the 1968 desert novitiate. "Respect for my obligations to others, respect for the work I still hope to do, respect for myself" are introspective words unlikely to be spoken by the unattached voice of *Desert Solitaire*, who may think them, but who seems immune to either desperate feelings or modest moments. The "roaring affirmation of self-existence" remains the same from book to book, however, and it is the defiant delight that sketches the alternative world so attractive to most readers, so provocative in its range of possibilities.

A lengthy sentence that is the last paragraph of "The Dead Man At Grandview Point" and one reminiscent of Stephen Dedalus's well-known notebook inscription, specifies the universality of Abbey's vision—as it originates in *Desert Solitaire* and as it will appear in his subsequent prose.

I feel myself sinking into the landscape, fixed in place like a stone, like a tree, a small motionless shape of vague outline, desert-colored, and with the wings of imagination look down at myself through the eyes of the bird, watching a human figure that becomes smaller, smaller in the receding landscape as the bird rises into the evening—a man at a table near a twinkling campfire, surrounded by a rolling wasteland of stone and dune and sandstone monuments, the wasteland surrounded by dark canyons and the course of rivers and mountain ranges on a vast plateau stretching across Colorado, Utah, New Mexico and Arizona, and beyond this plateau more deserts and greater mountains, the Rockies in dusk, the Sierra Nevadas shining in their late afternoon, and farther and farther yet, the darkened East, the gleaming Pacific, the curving margins of the great earth itself, and beyond earth that ultimate world of sun and stars whose bounds we cannot discover. [243–44]

Locating himself in the natural wasteland of the twentieth century, Ed sweeps not only the desert Southwest but the universe itself into his sights. The dead man's fate, by triggering Abbey's own intimations of mortality, causes him to stand Ed on the edge of a personal abyss where the writing can take wing or drop off, depending on the technical and imaginative skill of the author. Abbey does not disappoint us. Lines like the preceding quotation reveal that *Desert Solitaire* carries the same spirit of initiation as *A Portrait of the Artist as a Young Man* or as *Fire on the Mountain,* placing a neophyte in a larger context while developing his acumen on every page.

Actually, Abbey and Ed treat the lost-tourist experience—as they treated the stoned rabbit episode—as an experiment that leads to a greater comprehension of life's pattern. It is not always pleasant— "a ruthless, brutal process—but clean and beautiful" [242], Ed decides. Yet even his most distasteful analysis of the anonymous corpse's demise, a suggestion that the poor man's "departure makes room for the living," originates in Abbey's sense of a naturalistic pattern. This design, important in each chapter of *Desert Solitaire,* was missing before. *Jonathan Troy* was too adolescent, *The Brave Cowboy* too circumstantial, *Fire on the Mountain* too fatalistic to incorporate the vision of a natural system that overtakes Abbey's writing in this fourth book of prose. Although a green world and a red battled in each of the two Westerns, the limited results revealed little about an inevitable order. As we look back now, we can see that Abbey had not formulated, in those fictions, an intrinsically Darwinian design. That is, in the romance worlds of *The Brave Cowboy* and *Fire on the Mountain* the indifferent world of nature never was allowed to take its course. To be sure, apparently indifferent forces destroyed both Jack Burns and John Vogelin, but the instruments of their fates were red-world gadgets—an anonymous eighteen-wheeler and an empty air force dictum. And although naturalistic details appeared on many pages, the selection of details was not necessarily a natural one. In Abbey's first books survival of the fittest served as a deus ex machina rather than emerging as an innate force.

The natural order found in *Desert Solitaire*, from the rabbit and the tourist's untimely deaths to the moon-eyed horse's last stand through the universal pronouncement from Grandview Point, is quite a different, indeed, more "natural," thing. Abbey and Ed are able to assess the red world, even to design fictive versions of it, to hypothesize its green counterpoint, and then to imagine an umbrella version that lays bare, rather than shelters, the weaknesses of the other two. An alternative universe is created, one that measures the best qualities of red and green and laces the potion with Darwin. That its bedrock is one of paradox delimits its potency.

Announcing itself as a polemic, the chapter of *Desert Solitaire* that confronts the inadequacies of the Park Service plumbs Abbey's vision as deeply as any of the others, and perhaps more definitively. It opens quietly, with a subdued green overview of Ed's daily schedule and nightly activities that lulls the reader into a somnolence similar to the early mood of "The Dead Man At Grandview Point." "I was sitting out back on my 33,000-acre terrace, shoeless and shirtless, scratching my toes in the sand and sipping on a tall iced drink, watching the flow of evening over the desert," Ed's voice caresses the reader. "Prime time: the sun very low in the west, the birds coming back to life, the shadows rolling for miles over rock and sand to the very base of the brilliant mountains" [49]. Then, charging across the desert and breaking the intimacy comes the discordant, snarling whine of a jeep—U.S. Government, Bureau of Public Roads—a survey crew. The red world intrusion—the men are marking a new roadway into the Arches—leads Ed to a series of digressions about the encroaching horror of the twentieth century, "Industrial Tourism," the force destroying the national parks with "serpentine streams of baroque automobiles," electrified Comfort Stations, Coke machines, charcoal briquettes, and bumbling Winnebagos. Ed itemizes the attendant changes—in Canyonlands, in Grand Canyon (where "most of the south rim . . . is now closely followed by a conventional high-speed highway and interrupted at numerous places by large asphalt parking lots" [52]), in Navajo National Monument, and Natural Bridges, Zion, Capitol Reef, Lee's Ferry, each transformed radically during the past two decades by Industrial Tourism's demands.

Ed then shifts from the negative to the positive and suggests three Park Service policy changes that might slow the march of red world into green: 1. No more cars in national parks. 2. No more new roads in national parks. 3. Put the park rangers to work. He elaborates, arguing from the "basic assumption that wilderness is a necessary part of civilization and that it is the primary responsibility of the national park system to preserve *intact and undiminished* what little still remains" [54]. In other words, he reiterates his belief in the rock-bottom human need for wilderness and freedom. He also repeats his castigation of red world forces, changing the specific bureaucracy that embodies those forces from book to book, but never changing the thrust of his censure. This time, rather than the law or the Air Force, it is the Park Service and its two incompatible philosophies—preservation and development—that bear the brunt of his criticism. What makes the reproof distinctive, however, is Abbey's vision, which combines an idealistic view of the parks' potential with a formula for seeing those goals effected. Not content with merely maligning the onrush of Industrial Tourism, he suggests specific cures for specific ills, panaceas that might prevent the red world from devouring the wilderness. Replacing his chorus of complaints with a concrete call for action, he advocates particular changes that not only would slow the voracious red appetite but would turn the green into a more tangible reality and thus create a third, alternative environment. Even when Ed jokes about erecting a great national billboard "gorgeously filigreed in brilliant neon and outlined with blinker lights, exploding stars, flashing prayer wheels and great Byzantine phallic symbols that gush like geysers every thirty seconds" [65], behind which Smokey the Bear would recite a litany for parked cars, he communicates his sobering views about the way mechanization exploits the environment. And even while he pulls up survey stakes by the light of the moon, he seriously decries their trespass.

The paradox of our national parks—that even as the government preserves a modicum of natural beauty it simultaneously destroys while it develops—vexes Abbey immensely. Consumption of the wilderness by the very institution designed to protect it is symptomatic, he feels, of the way civilization has been cannibalized by culture. He defines the dichotomy in another chapter: "Civilization is the vital force in human history; culture is that inert mass of institutions and organizations which accumulate around and tend to drag down the advance of life" [276]. A list of specific examples follows, like "Civilization is the wild river; culture, 592,000 tons of cement," or "Civilization flows; culture thickens and coagulates, like tired, sick, stifled blood" [277]. Civilization, it seems, is analogous to the "vision," the world of possibilities, the West of Abbey's "deepest imaginings where the tangible and the mythical become the same." Culture is the encroaching, red, engulfing "other." Ironically dependent on men, although not necessarily on mankind, civilization borrows a frontier optimism from the red world and a frontier idealism from the green, then images a whole immeasurably greater than the parts. To see the modern potential of civilization, then, as it may displace "culture" in the contemporary West, is to go down Abbey's road, to seek with him his visionary world, to revel with him in his richly complex universe of the romance. And traveling down that road is to tread upon the tangible base that shores up the intangible dream—to walk, that is, upon the desert.

As the testing ground for alternatives, the desert becomes for Abbey a metaphorical background for the truly civilized world. "Behind the dust, . . . under the vulture-haunted sky, the desert waits—mesa, butte, canyon, reef, sink, escarpment, pinnacle, maze, dry lake, sand dune and barren mountain—untouched by the human mind" [272] until the writer evocatively reimages it for his new world of the romance. Why this locale above all others? "What is the peculiar quality or character of the desert that distinguishes it, in spiritual appeal, from other forms of landscape?" [270]. Ed glibly asserts that "there is something about the desert" [272], although he refuses to specify what that is. Acknowledging it "waits outside, desolate and still and strange, unfamiliar and often grotesque in its forms and colors, inhabited by rare, furtive creatures of incredible hardiness and cunning, sparingly colonized by weird mutants from the plant kingdom, most of them as spiny, thorny, stunted and twisted as they are tenacious" [271–72], he chooses diction that will emphasize the desert's alien atmosphere—hostile, indifferent, harsh. No other environment will do for Abbey's world. Neither "the restless sea" nor "the towering mountains" (both dismissed as too trite) provides the rich clarity or the strange allure, the paradox and bedrock that Abbey needs.

The desert says nothing. Completely passive, acted upon but never acting, the desert lies there like the bare skeleton of Being, spare, sparse, austere, utterly worthless, inviting not love but contemplation. In its simplicity and order it suggests the classical, except that the desert is a realm beyond the human and in the classicist view only the human is regarded as significant or even recognized as real. [270]

The dioramic key, not only in *Desert Solitaire* but in all of Abbey's best writing, is the taciturn, invincible landscape of the desert. Only there can the mythic "vital force" be felt, can the metaphoric wild river "flow." Only there, too, can Abbey search out his dreams.

"I am convinced now that the desert has no heart," Ed confesses paradoxically, "that it presents a riddle which has no answer, and that the riddle itself is an illusion created by some limitation or exaggeration of the displaced human consciousness. This at least is what I tell myself" [273]. Trying to be "rational, sensible and realistic," Abbey thinks he can hold the desert at arm's length in order to "overcome at last that gallant infirmity of soul called romance" [273]. But even as he writes those lines he knows he cannot do so. Unable to stay away for long, to resist the deep spirit of the place, he cannot displace the romance. Even when he compares the desert's unique essence to a certain "bleak, thin-textured" contemporary music—"a-tonal, cruel, clear, inhuman, neither romantic nor classical, motionless and emotionless, at one and the same time —another paradox—both agonized and deeply still" [286]—he does so in a provocative human way. The desert is the background of Abbey's world, the land of his deepest imaginings where "life nowhere appears so brave, so bright, so full of oracle and miracle" [286].

On his final *Desert Solitaire* adventure into the desert's mystery, Ed and a friend search out "The Maze," an intricate "vermiculate area of pink and white rock" that remains almost inaccessible to man. Recognizing its isolation, a border-zone of wilderness and freedom, the two men nevertheless anticipate the journey. "As with anything enormously attractive, we are obsessed only with getting *in;* we can worry later about getting out" [284], Ed decrees. So, too, the reader in Abbey's world, another border-zone of freedom and of wilderness, of metaphor and of myth. "Nobody gets in and out . . . *completely* untouched. Even the most hexproof infidels cannot escape the power of such a magic . . . , the glamor of that sinister reputation, the occult touch of all those bored and restless haunts, the spirits of the place" [CC, 51].

5

Wanderlust

The Journey Home
and
Abbey's Road

"There is *something* about the desert . . ." [DS, 272], and although Abbey elusively avoids saying what that something may be, he has continued writing nonfiction that pursues the wilderness spirit. Seven more books, as well as numerous articles and shorter observations, followed *Desert Solitaire* in the 1970s. Each examines in detail what is best and worst about the contemporary environment. Two of these examinations, *The Journey Home* (1977) and *Abbey's Road* (1979) are personal histories like *Desert Solitaire*. Abbey thinks every one of his nonfiction books belongs in that category, but even though all eight keep Ed's voice as narrator and the author's judgmental point of view as the philosophical constant, their designs and purposes differ. Where the five pictorial essays are essentially descriptive, *Desert Solitaire*, *The Journey Home*, and *Abbey's Road* are nonfiction romances that lead into crafted worlds where illusions are examined and issues defined. There Abbey clarifies his own sacred vision of the land and damns the machines that would profane it. In *Desert Solitaire* we entered Abbey's world physically and emotionally; now he leads us there spiritually and politically too.

An introduction, staking out the writer's territory, precedes each text. So many reviewers have misread Abbey throughout his career that he apparently has felt compelled to help them understand his recent efforts. As early as *Desert Solitaire* he dismissed the critical assessments of wrong-headed readers, but his tone remained jocular. Nine years later he sounds more defensive. "I am not a naturalist," begins the introduction to *The Journey Home*. "I never was and never will be a naturalist. I'm not even sure what a naturalist is except that I'm not one. I'm not even an amateur naturalist."[1] After a full paragraph of repetitive disclaimers, he explains the impetus behind his words. "The aim of this preamble is not to indulge in a foolish vanity, as might appear, but to assist those reviewers and critics who persist in attempting to read my work as studies in natural history, . . . for unless revised, [their] expectations will . . . be disappointed" [JH, xii]. Quite true. Any reader needs to chew on Abbey's own definition of his nonfiction—"redneck slumgullion," a nutritious coherent stew, "fragments of autobiography, journalistic battle debris, nightmares and daydreams, bits and butts of outdoors philosophizing, all stirred together in a blackened pot over a smoking fire of juniper, passionflower and thorny mesquite" [JH, xiv]—in order to appreciate the flavor of his work. To take up *The Journey Home* or *Abbey's Road* is to bite off chunks of words written "in Defense of the American West" by one of its most ardent defenders; to find the slumgullion tasty is to whet one's appetite for Abbey's world.

The stew analogy is an appropriate one, since both *Journey* and *Road* are hodgepodges "in the form of adversary essays and assays, polemics, visions and hallucinations, and published piece by piece in various odd places" [JH, xiv]. Abbey wrote a few new morsels for each, in order to unify the whole, but for the most part the two books contain words first printed elsewhere. Thus the style, the content, the effort, and the achievement differ from chapter to chapter and from bite to bite. The voice of the narrator and the stance of the author, however, remain constant. For example, a full paragraph from the introduction of *Abbey's Road*, "Confessions of a Literary Hobo," documents Abbey's own awareness that Ed is a created point of view who functions substantially the same way in all his nonfiction.

The writer puts the best of himself, not the whole, into the work; the author as seen in the pages of his own book is largely a fictional creation. Often the author's best creation. The "Edward Abbey" of my own books, for example, bears only the dimmest resemblance to the shy, timid, reclusive, rather dapper little gentleman who, always correctly attired for his labors in coat and tie and starched detachable cuffs, sits down each night for precisely four hours to type out the further adventures of that arrogant blustering macho fraud who counterfeits his name. You can bet on it: No writer is ever willing—even if able—to portray himself as seen by others or as he really is. Writers are shameless liars. In fact, we pride ourselves on the subtlety and grandeur of our lies. Salome had only seven veils; the author has a thousand.[2]

If writers are indeed shameless liars, Edward Abbey is even more shameless than most. Cutting through his verbiage and jokes, his counterfeiting of the already counterfeit, we see how strongly Abbey prides himself on the grandeur of his lies. That he is neither dapper recluse nor blustering macho is self-evident, yet he loves such egregious poses. That he is no photographic spokesman for the natural world, no nature writer, no companion on Annie Dillard's travels, should be obvious too, for his thousand veils swirl around an imaginative outlook more appropriate to fiction than nonfiction. Readers who see in Abbey's books only the word-pictures of an environmental writer or who hear only the polemics of a wild-country advocate have closed their eyes and ears to half his intent and accomplishment. They have forgotten his romancer's vision.

Both *The Journey Home* and *Abbey's Road* create worlds less sharply restricted than *Desert Solitaire*'s. Ranging far beyond the confines of the slickrock community, *Journey* defends most corners of the western United States (in spirit, if not in fact), and *Road* stretches as far away as Australia. Yet the blueprints of the three are similar, a steadfast pursuit of "the need to make sense of private experience by exploring the connections and contradictions among wildness and wilderness, community and anarchy; between civilization and freedom" [JH, xiv]. In other words, to go down Abbey's road, to make his journey home through the American West, is to follow a "personal odyssey" that seeks to discover how man can live respectfully within the bounds of his environment. Whether that environment is a lonely fire lookout or an arid, solitary island off the coast of Mexico, a bustling, smog-choked Arizona city or a stretch of isolated outback, Abbey is looking for the human dignity that comes when man acknowledges his physical and spiritual dependence on the natural milieu. He says he wants to expose "the rape of the West," indeed "The Second Rape of the West" [see Chapter

16 of *Journey*], but what he hopes to explore too is the potential of human experience. Thus the personal histories focus constantly on both man and his landscape because, in his mind, the two are inseparable.

As noted earlier, *Journey* opens with Abbey's first sight of the West of his "deepest imaginings," his 1944 train ride through a desert "full of a powerful, mysterious promise." Subsequent chapters of personal history take Ed back to the land itself. From the depths of Death Valley to the heights of Montana's Numa Ridge, he pursues his courtship of the planet earth, renewing his love affair with its particulars and extending his reverence for its unprofaned state. Superstition Mountain, for example, stands "gaunt and grim above the desert floor, resembling a titanic altar, ancient, corroded, rotten with the blood of gods," and contrasts sharply with the suburbs of Phoenix that float around its base in "a haze of smoke and dust" [JH, 66]. Las Vegas, with a loud "HOWDY PARTNER and the clash, roll, jangle, rumble, and rock of 10,000 concentrating mothers of America jerking in unison on the heavy members of 10,000 glittering slot machines" [JH, 68], contrasts unfavorably with a quieter place called Echo Canyon where Ed descends a "narrow gorge between flood-polished walls of bluish andesite—the stem of the wineglass. I walk down the center of an amphitheater of somber cliffs riddled with grottoes, huge eyesockets in a stony skull, where bats hang upside down in the shadows waiting for night" [JH, 77]. In random order, thesis alternates with antithesis, purity with pollution, violence with peace, solitude with noise with solitude, red world with green. Horrid spider webs become things of beauty, "each with a tiny golden spider waiting at the center," while one lovely, battle-scarred, six-point buck reminds the narrator of "the struggle for existence" in nature and, in turn, of the more appalling brutality of humans, "the horror of this planetary spawning and scheming and striving and dying" [JH, 56–57]. Without pressing his frustrations or his animosity, Abbey is content here merely to point out what seems good and bad.

If a synthesis exists in *Journey's* first several chapters, if thesis and antithesis lead to a consummate vision, it appears in the slickrock country landscape, where Abbey returns, as he always does, to the place "that has to be seen to be believed, and even then, confronted directly by the senses, . . . strains credulity" [JH, 86]. There, in the desert, he works hard to verbalize the "approximate picture," knowing that "despite the best efforts of a small army of writers, painters, photographers, scientists, explorers, Indians, cowboys, and wilderness guides, the landscape of the Colorado Plateau lies still beyond the reach of reasonable words" [JH, 86]. But Abbey's goal is metaphysical rather than pictorial. "When all we know about it," he says of the redrock canyons, "is said and measured and tabulated, there remains something in the soul of the place, the spirit of the whole, that cannot be fully assimilated by the human imagination" [JH, 86]. In order to capture that spirit, even though he acknowledges the futility of the task, he uses his romancer's vision as the mode of assimilation. He wants the reader to apprehend the land, not destroy or fear or ignore it. He argues persuasively for a personal plan that uses the desert's physical essence in more spiritual ways, as a sanctuary for the human soul where self-exploration and self-revelation can take place. Even if he cannot recapture "the soul of the place," he can help the imagination try.

His method, then, in both *The Journey Home* and *Abbey's Road*, lets Ed share with the reader a nonsequential series of personal episodes, encounters, and opinions, as the land and man affect each other. His design consists essentially of thesis/antithesis/synthesis, although he often prolongs the third step until Ed has fully exploited the first two. *Journey*, for example, moves from the intimate chapters of personal history to a section of strident and angry words, then from more chapters of loving affection for the wilderness to another section of fears for its destruction. The book then ends with a synthesis of past, present, and future in an imaginative chapter called "Dust," where the shifting scenes remind us of man's transience on earth.

Road's pattern differs from *Journey*'s in its particulars but follows the same general thesis/antithesis/synthesis structure. In a long opening section called "Travel," *Road* starts in Australia, moves to Mexico, and then wends its way north via Big Bend to Abbey's country—Canyonlands, the Escalante. Through the first nine chapters of exploration, Abbey compares the apparent abundance of still unexplored territory with the now constricted frontiers of the American West. To no one's surprise, he concludes that what has happened here can happen there too, for neither the outback nor the *barrancas* is immune to predatory inclinations. In the second, antithetical part of *Abbey's Road*, "Polemics and Sermons," the author fights for human rights while discounting the intrusions of science and technology on individual freedom. The third section continues the discussion. Its five chapters include a playful soliloquy in a redneck Arizona bar, an unhappy LSD trip in Death Valley, and a benign daydream from a North Rim lookout tower. Here Abbey combines the personal and the polemical in a semisynthesis that leads naturally to a conclusion high above the grand river. There he looks over the edge of the abyss and speculates, dreaming of man and his landscape, of freedom and wilderness. "Let others save the world for the time being," he decides, exercising his prerogative to be free. "Tonight and tomorrow and for the next few days I am going to walk the rim of Cape Solitude, along the palisades of the desert, and save myself. Without half trying" [AR, 198]. Save himself he does, whenever he seeks the heart of his beloved Southwest.

Throughout the pages of both these books of personal history, he follows his natural mode of thinking, the thesis/antithesis/synthesis pattern that informs not only the ordering of the chapters but their internal organizations as well. Turning an idea from side to side, he balances one alternative against another. He poses an idea, then abandons it, suggests its opposite, then rejects them both. Finally, he synthesizes his divergent views into a composite vision, the full perspective that was missing in the first fiction he wrote. Like past romance writers—Cervantes, for example, when he concluded *Don Quixote*—Abbey now directs his readers beyond the boundaries of his writing toward the imaginative vision that substantiates his thoughts. This crucial synthesis, present in one form or another in all his prose since *Desert Solitaire*, comes, in essence, from the land of his "deepest imaginings."

Any discussion of Abbey's vision must begin with the lines "there is *something* about the desert . . .," for that "something" is the basis of this author's whole philosophy. He comes closest to articulating what it might be when he invites the reader to "Come On In," in the midst of *The Journey Home*. "For us" (those who love the great plateau and its canyon), he writes, "the wilderness and human emptiness of this land is not a source of fear but the greatest of its attractions." Calling his favorite redrock country "a place for the free," he explains how it must be guarded, defended, and saved because there, in its spaces, human beings can "rediscover the nearly lost pleasures of adventure, adventure not only in the physical sense, but also mental, spiritual, moral, aesthetic and intellectual adventure" [JH, 88]. In other words, "something" about the desert offers the most profound pleasures a soul may experience.

Here you may yet find the elemental freedom to breathe deep of unpoisoned air, to experiment with solitude and stillness, to gaze through a hundred miles of untrammeled atmosphere, across redrock canyons, beyond blue mesas, toward the snow-covered peaks of the most distant mountains—to make the discovery of the self in its proud sufficiency which is not isolation but an irreplaceable part of the mystery of the whole. [JH, 88]

One man's *"discovery of the self in its proud sufficiency which is not isolation"* italicizes the intent of Abbey's personal histories, the reason for their existence. The one spot he loves best, "a place for the free" amid the "solitude and stillness" of "a hundred miles of untrammeled atmosphere," provides the backdrop for that odyssey. "All my life a prospector" [JH, 65], Ed characterizes himself, a pocket hunter for the mother lode of personal fulfillment; and like a true pocket hunter he sticks to the earth. "In my case it was love at first sight. This desert, all deserts, any desert," he affirms. "No matter where my head and feet may go, my heart and my entrails stay behind, here on the clean, true, comfortable rock, under the black sun of God's forsaken country" [JH, 12]. There he pokes and sifts and digs, looking for self-knowledge, self-revelation, at times for self-justification. There he finds the spiritual sustenance needed for survival.

"Why go into the desert" at all? Abbey asks in the foreword to a 1977 Sierra Club publication, *Deserts of the Southwest.*[3] On one single page he documents the answer, the pros and cons, thesis and antithesis that twist and turn the reader's own responses. Why? "That sun, roaring at you all day long," Abbey begins. "Those pink rattlesnakes down The Canyon, those diamondback monsters thick as a catskinner's wrist that lurk in shady places along the trail." Why? His narrative voice continues. "The rain that comes down like lead shot and wrecks the trail before you, those sudden rockfalls of obscure origin that crash like thunder ten feet behind you in the heart of a dead-still afternoon." And why again? "The ubiquitous vultures, so patient—but only *so* patient. The ragweed, the tumbleweed, the Jimsonweed, the snakeweed. The scorpion in your shoe at dawn. The dreary wind that seldom stops, the manic-depressive mesquite trees waving their arms at you on moonlight nights." Why?

In the typical Ed/Abbey mode, he counters by telling a story. Once, on a hike in Coconino County, Arizona, he wandered down a stream and into a canyon along a route that eventually became a "deep, narrow and dark" gorge "full of water and the inevitable quagmires of quicksand." Looking for a more comfortable way out, he found a flue he could scramble up. "No one, I felt certain," he definitively announces, "had ever left Nesja Canyon by *that* route before. But someone had." He discovers "near the summit an arrow sign," pointing north. At what? He peers into the distance, seeing first the rim of another canyon, a straight drop-off, and then scrubby clumps of blackbrush and prickly pear, a few square miles of nothingness, no indication of life. "I studied the scene with care," he informs us, "looking for an ancient Indian ruin, a significant cairn, perhaps an abandoned mine, a hidden treasure, the mother of all mother lodes. . . ." His words trail off as he gazes more intently.

But there was nothing out there. Nothing at all. Nothing but the desert. Nothing but the world.

That's why.

For Abbey, as for all other desert rats, no other world exists, not really.

To analyze nothing, to put words in the author's mouth, would be a critical faux pas, because part of this particular author's magic is his suggestive stirring of the reader's imaginative juices. He never tells us in so many words, for example, what the desert means; he only hints at its essence. "It means what it is. It is there, it will be there when we are gone. But for a while we living things—men, women, birds, coyotes howling far off on yonder stony ridge—we were a part of it all. That should be enough" [DI, 224]. It should be enough, too, that he only intimates why he goes there, for "there is nothing out there. . . . Nothing but the world." Perhaps we all should have the grace to obey Abbey's command for silence and sufficiency—"perhaps a few places are best left unexplored, seen from a distance but never entered, never walked upon," as he enjoins in a provocative tone. "Let them be, for now" [AR, 119].

It seems important, however, not only to step "Down There in the Rocks" with him but to turn over the largest boulders, those which cover the sacred, not the profane, man. Because Abbey studied philosophy in both his undergraduate and graduate days, because his reputation for disdaining easy labels is well known, and because he rejects notions of God rather flippantly in his writing, it would be presumptuous to tag him a believer in a single school of thought. Atheistic, agnostic, deistic, transcendental—none of these will do for his complex thoughts. Even "sacrality" may be slightly inaccurate, but this designation best touches on his way of looking "down there in the rocks."

Max Westbrook calls sacrality simply a "belief in God as energy,"[4] or, more abstrusely, a "belief that concrete acts, here and now, can recreate the primordial energy and meaning of the relevant cosmic or original act."[5] Not God as energy but, more accurately, energy as God, or, in Abbey's sense, land as energy as God. Man affirms his sacred self by tapping his own primal energy: that is, by literally touching the land around him, by finding (as Westbrook says) the thing in itself. "The sacred man can find his rough realistic God of energy in the beauty of a lake, the harsh heat of a desert, the blank and haunting eyes of a fresh-killed deer." Seeking not a mere symbol but the actual physical object that itself *is* the energy, he looks, in Abbey's case, not for God in the desert but for the desert that itself *is* the sacred force.

In *Desert Solitaire* and the other personal histories, Abbey looks directly at physical objects and sometimes comments only on the surface of what he sees. "Campfire of juniper and scrub oak. The smell of coffee, the incense of burning wood. Vast, lurid sunsets flare across the sky, east as well as west, portending storm and winter, but we don't care. Showers of meteors streak across the field of the stars, trailing languid flames. An old, worn moon goes down as the rising sun comes out" [AR, 119]. But at other times, perhaps just one page later, those physical objects direct him toward a primal power.

The hot radiance of the sun, pouring on our prone bodies, suffusing our flesh, melting our bones, lulls us toward sleep. Over the desert and the canyons, down there in the rocks, a huge vibration of light and stillness and solitude shapes itself into the form of hovering wings spread out across the sky from the world's rim to the world's end. Not God—the term seems insufficient—but something unnameable, and more beautiful, and far greater, and more terrible. [AR, 120]

"There is *something* about the desert," he has told us before. "Not God," he elaborates now, "the term seems insufficient," but an unnameable cosmic energy, a special sacred force which impels both the natural world and the man who lives there. Such a thesis may best be called "sacrality."

William T. Pilkington, who first suggested that sacrality might describe Abbey's beliefs, even though he dismissed the label, explains that "the sacred force can be felt but never tangibly grasped, much less defined. It is simply the unnameable energy that is the source of man's intuitive and instinctual knowledge."[6] So when Abbey eyes "vast, lurid sunsets," smells the juniper incense from his tiny campfire, juxtaposes the languid flames of burnt-out meteors against the light of a tired moon, or looks "down there in the rocks," he draws on the landscape's inherent energy to fortify his words. In the best of Abbey's writing, the power of the land becomes the power of the author. And while he never commits himself to a concrete characterization of the transcendent energy borne by the desert scene, he does commit the dynamics of the landscape to the printed page.

Thus he engages the reader in the task of interpolation. Some argue that because he alludes to a sacred fount without articulating its source, he takes the easy road. But an examination of some revised portions of "Down There in the Rocks" refutes that criticism because it demonstrates how Abbey reworked his presentation of the energy of the unnameable "hovering wings" in order to emphasize its sacrality. Most of *Journey*'s and *Road*'s chapters are verbatim reprints of earlier articles; Chapter 9 of *Abbey's Road*, for example, was published originally in the March 1977 issue of *Harper's* as a two-page piece called "Last Oasis." Although Abbey rarely changes his texts from article to book, he did so this time, altering an appositive clause in the lines just discussed, deleting a sentence from the preceding page, and adding another sentence at the end of the chapter. The first transformation concerns his notation on God. What now reads, "Not God—the term seems insufficient," originally said, "Not God—there never was a God." Apparently Abbey later felt uncomfortable with the atheism/agnosticism of the original, since he has derived, over the years, an immeasurable energy from the desert. Despite his steadfast refusal to name precisely the form of the energy, in this or in any other piece of prose, he has come to acknowledge the desert's essence more openly than he once did. He is more positive and less abrasive, more sensitive and less cynical, in a disclaimer such as "the term seems insufficient" than in the gruff assertion "there never was a God."

The second alteration connotes a similar change of heart. Where *Abbey's Road* entreats that "perhaps a few places are best left unexplored . . . let them be, for now" [AR, 119], "Last Oasis" included a pensive note with the request. "A few places saved for that last walk, that final journey from which you have neither the plan nor the desire to return. Let them be, for now."[7] Elimination of the sentence alluding to mortality strengthens the positive import of the rest of the essay. In fact, those few revisions Abbey makes between article and chapter accomplish more than just greater verbal precision; they tend to change his metaphysical stance from overt skepticism to a more optimistic, or at least neutral, outlook on life. His attitudes have not swung radically in two short intervening years, but rather his books tone down certain elements of despair found in his articles, and move instead toward the energy at the positive end of a magnetic field. The third alteration, an addition, supports this movement. The 1977 article closed with the lines, "The hawk soars, the ravens quarrel. And no man watches. And no woman hears. And no one is there."[8] In *Abbey's Road*, another sentence follows. It reads, "Everything is there" [AR, 119]. A clear indication of Abbey's feelings about the omnipresence of the desert spirit, "everything" embodies the unarticulated energy that he senses "everywhere." It announces his sacrality.

We misread Abbey, however, if we look for any specified energy, or if we regard the desert as an overt symbol for any particular God or force. Rather, the desert exists *as* energy. An emblem of sacrality, it lends to Abbey the fortifying power of the landscape, of wilderness, and of freedom. He draws on that strength whenever "there comes a day when a man must hide. Must slip away from the human world and its clutchy, insane, insatiable demands" [AR, 191]; he draws on it, too, whenever he chooses to write. His retreat to Cape Solitude to "save" himself, for example, traces the process by which he pulls the desert's energy into his own soul. "Each time I come here," he muses, "I wonder why I ever go back. Every time I go anywhere out in the desert or mountains, I wonder why I should return. Someday I won't" [AR, 192]. How different from the exorcized "final journey" that chosen step toward the desert's energy sounds. Meanwhile, until he makes that choice, he returns to his typewriter where, funneling the land's essence into words, he creates passages like the following:

The sun goes down. A few stray clouds catch fire, burn gold, vermillion, and driftwood blue in the unfathomed sea of space. These surrounding mountains that look during the day like iron—like burnt, mangled, rusted iron—now turn radiant as a dream. Where is their truth? A hard clean edge divides the crescent dunes into black shadow on one side, a phosphorescent light on the other. And above the rim of the darkening west floats the evening star. [JH, 84]

In Abbey's nonfiction, the reader finds numerous examples of sacrality. Sometimes it slips in, like the evening star floating into the west; sometimes it attacks like a bolt of lightning. "Now comes another direct hit on our lookout. First the buzzing sound, the eerie *hiss* and *fizz* directly overhead. That sinister touch, God's fingertip upon our roof. Light, deadly, an almost dainty touch, you might say. Followed by the flash of light and the *crack!* of a great whip. The building vibrates" [JH, 49], an electrifying experience. Later that same day, while dreaming about life and love, Ed derives energy from the storm to counteract the foggy sadness of the afternoon. Incorporating the earth's sacrality, he strengthens his own weaknesses; looking at "the rosy hoods of *Amanita muscaria*," he calculates "the possibility of flight beyond the sorrows of this sublunar sphere" [JH, 49]. Just as Ed pulls emotional strength from the land and Abbey draws artistic energy, so the reader gains a certain power from the exchange. Perhaps we could call the author a conductor for some undefined electrical charge that transforms the particular energy of the wilderness into the energy of pure prose.

To induce those feelings by drugs rather than natural means is both less effective and more deleterious, as Abbey learns the hard way. "Death Valley Junk" [Chapter 17 of *Abbey's Road*, 170–75] tells of one notable experiment that failed, an event tangled "in a web of alkali and phosphorescent chemicals. Years ago." In passages reminiscent of Aldous Huxley's sensuous particularity in *Doors of Perception* (1954), Ed builds a crescendo of artificial effects provoked by a synthetic substance, LSD. "The mountains across the valley, glowing in the sunset light, looked glorious, vividly palpable and tangible" until they suddenly begin to breathe, a "mile-high mass of pink lungs, alive." Paralyzed by the enervating quality of the moment, Ed feels "trapped in limbo between two worlds—a place too queasy and queer to be the waking world, too bright and definite and three-dimensional to be the world of dreams. I didn't know where I was, except that I didn't much like it." He struggles to keep in touch with himself, then loses the earth in the sky.

The stars began to move.
They moved in a kind of viscous dance, as if caught in a web. As if trapped and tangled in a quivering spiderweb with moony spokes of light radiating from the hidden center. I felt sorry for the stars. God is the Great Night Spider.
Cassiopeia was a silver blue firefly snared alive in the quilted folds of the cobweb sky. The stars were points of light shining through pinholes in that rumpled mass.

Speaking to the Great Spider in the Sky, Ed assaults mind and body until the acid trip peaks and diminishes. "But there was no sense of joy or exultation in the floating opera of my nervous system." Admitting the abortiveness of his temporary flight, he acknowledges, too, his relief at having escaped "that dreadful web in which the stars are trapped, that galactic spider out yonder in the dark attic of space." Three hundred and fifty micrograms provided no magic shortcut, no easy road to "wisdom, understanding, peace," but demonstrated instead the narrator's own preference for natural, not artificial, energies. Flippant as the appellation 'Great Spider in the Sky' may sound, it embodies the profanity of Ed's venture into a synthetic world, a profanity recognized and rejected by the author.

A second Abbey chapter about Death Valley describes a contrasting trip. In an article first printed in *Sage* (Spring 1967) and then reprinted as *Journey*'s Chapter 7, Ed drops

beneath a sea, not of brine, but of heat, of shimmering simmering waves of light and a wind as hot and fierce as a dragon's breath.
The glare is stunning. Yet also exciting, even exhilarating—a world of light. The air seems not clear like glass but colored, a transparent, tinted medium, golden toward the sun, smoke-blue in the shadows. The colors come, it appears, not simply from the background, but are actually present in the air itself—a vigintillion microscopic particles of dust reflecting the sky, the sand, the iron hills. [JH, 71–72]

The textures of the two forays into the Valley differ—the one, explosive, kinetic, artificial, enervating, and utterly horrifying and the other, minus the destructive overtones, evocative in a less violent way. The *Sage* piece pulses with life as it embraces what Ed sees. "Genealogies: From these rocks struck once by lightning gushed springs that turned to blood, flesh, life. Impossible miracle. And I am struck once again by the unutterable beauty, terror, and strangeness of everything we think we know" [JH, 77–78]. Sacrality, the belief in God as energy and in energy as God, and for Abbey the belief in the landscape as energy as God (or something), appears, with instinctive rightness, on page after page.

Because the land carries so much importance, abominations committed against it trouble Abbey more than any other man-driven acts. So the political force of his prose is second only to his notion of sacrality in thematic impact. Most chapters of *The Journey Home* and *Abbey's Road* refer at least indirectly to the twentieth century's rape of the West, and many attack the problem directly. Telluride, Yosemite, Black Mesa, Colstrip, Glen Canyon—he catalogues the landscapes changed irrevocably by science, industry, and government, all in the name of progress. Most of his polemics are angry ones, designed to underscore his resentment at the desecration of "his" West. When a giant corporation hatchets Telluride, for example, his "favorite mountain town," a Colorado haven of "rundown, raunchy, redneck, backwoods backwardness," he bitterly asks why. "One more mountain forest, virgin valley, untainted town sacrificed on the greasy altar of industrial tourism and mechanized recreation" [JH, 129]. Why must it be destroyed? "I thought of the canyon and mesa lands of Utah and northern Arizona—my country—being disemboweled, their skies darkened by gigantic coal-burning power plants, in order to provide juice and heat for frivolous plywood ski hutches like this. Sad? No, not sad," he adds indignantly. "Just a bloody criminal outrage, that's all" [JH, 128].

Abbey views strip-mining as a geographically more widespread "second rape of the West" now taking place throughout Arizona, Utah, Colorado, Wyoming, and Montana. Relying partly on research and partly on firsthand observation, Abbey throws facts and feelings at his readers in a dramatic effort to move them. Strip-mining "now consumes about 4,650 acres of American farm, forest, and rangeland each week," Ed tells us. "Each week of the year. An area the size of Connecticut, some 5,000 square miles, has already been strip-mined for coal alone" [JH, 161]. He quotes more figures, then offers a firsthand view. "I saw, as usual, the iron rigs of giant draglines looming over the landscape, digging into the earth beneath a pall of dust. On the skyline were the long gray ridges of spoil banks, the overturned soil." To contrast the mayhem caused by the machines, he looks "beyond the mined area, [where] the original landscape remains, hills of ponderosa pine rising from the rolling plains of grass" [JH, 177], and plaintively asks, a few pages later, "How could such a thing happen to so beautiful a land?" [JH, 181].

Switching his tone frequently, he shifts from one mood to another while seeking the most cogent ways to communicate. His approach varies from emotional plea to right reason, from venomous attack to a stand based on numerical data. Using any tactic he feels will work, Abbey attempts to shock the public into a realization that it is their country being destroyed, their beautiful land overturned into the long, gray ridges of spoil banks. "That's what you have to look forward to, tourists, next time you come west to enjoy what is, after all, *your* property" [JH, 162]. If it takes a tall tale to drive home his message about the land's frugality, he writes one.

"God's Plan for the State of Utah: A Revelation" [Chapter 10 of *Journey*] teaches J. Orrin Garn—Big Jake—some windy truths about Utah's deteriorating environment. An imaginary Director's henchman, Nehi, wings Big Jake high above the hills for a bird's-eye view of the potash evaporation ponds "so big and square you can see them from near anywhere," the dust and smoke from the new shale rock operation near Vernal, "all that brown-yeller smog . . . stretching for about a hundred miles from Bountiful to Cedar City" with Salt Lake City "down in the middle of it somewhere," and Lake Powell, "world's biggest silt trap, . . . world's biggest evaporation tank, and someday, before it all fills up with mud, . . . the world's biggest sewage lagoon" [JH, 107–11]. Although the image of an angel dressed in shorts, tennis shoes, and sunglasses, flapping across the skyline with Big Jake clutched to one hand, belies the seriousness of Abbey's point, the essay effectively inventories atrocities common to Utah and the other western states. Thus Abbey exposes the misguided effort to encourage growth of industry and population as a collective destruction of the land.

Recognizing the limits of the earth's resources, he goes beyond his *Desert Solitaire* panaceas for the National Park Service and argues for a larger national policy that, if enforced systematically, would keep those resources inviolate. "The assumption is that we must continue down the road of never-ending economic expansion, toward an ever-grosser gross national product, driven by that mania for Growth with a capital G that entails, among other things, a doubling of the nation's energy production every ten years" [JH, 183]. Abbey's road leads somewhere else. Without hesitation he shoots down this "expand or expire" mentality. "Growth for the sake of growth *is* the idealogy of the cancer cell" [JH, 183], he intones, begging instead for a national policy of political economy that answers man's *real* needs. "Good beer, good fresh healthy food for all," he begins lightly. "Homes and apartments for all that are well made, well designed, comfortable, durable and handsome; quick easy urban transit systems; good continental passenger train service; air that's fit to breathe, water that's fit to drink, food that's fit to eat; and now and then, when we want it, some space and solitude and silence" [JH, 187], he finishes in more somber tones. Abbey neither predicts doom for the future nor wishes to retreat to the past; he asks instead for a middle road where man respects his environment, and can therefore respect himself.

"I believe it is possible to find and live a balanced way of life somewhere halfway between all-out industrialism on the one hand and a make-believe pastoral idyll on the other" [JH, 234], he insists, as he balances the red world against the green. "According to my basic thesis, if it's sound, we can avoid the disasters of war, the nightmare of the police state and totalitarianism, the drive to expand and conquer if we return to this middle way and learn to live for a while, say at least a thousand years or so, just for the hell of it, just for the fun of it, in some sort of steady-state economy, some sort of free, democratic, wide-open society" [JH, 235]. Here, in the heart of his nonfiction, the romancer's vision finally becomes a coherent possibility. The via media between red world and green, old world and new, present and past, idealism and despair becomes Abbey's road, a carefully surveyed track that winds through the landscape without destroying it, that taps the earth's energy without stripping it.

A short essay, "Grow and Die," itemizes the steps we must take in order to traverse the proper route. "One: open our eyes. Two: rise and stand. Three: speak up. Four: reach out, assert control."[9] While these generalities would support no functional roadbed, the remainder of the article suggests some specifics that might. Returning to *The Journey Home*'s thesis, Abbey repeats that "the religion of Growth must be questioned. And opposed. And resisted. And subverted. And supplanted, before disaster overtakes us all, by something sane, healthy, and rational." He pleads for useful, creative work that builds and nurtures, as opposed to dehumanizing jobs that fabricate assembly-line junk. He calls for cessation of the flow of illegal aliens, asks for penalties against heavy human breeders, insists on an economic replacement for agribusiness. Big business of any sort, like big government, has no place in Abbey's world. The giants must be "divided and sub-divided, with all power returned to the city, the region, the community, the human family—where it belongs." Individuals must resist the blitz of corporations. "We have submitted to the domination of an insane, expansionist economy and a brutal technology—*a mad machine*—which will end up by destroying not only itself but everything remaining that is clean, whole, beautiful and good in our America. Unless we find a way to stop it" [S, 77; italics Abbey's].

In Abbey's early fiction, no one finds a way to stop it, for men like John Vogelin are impotent before the rampaging cancer cells of growth. Now, however, the romancer has conceived a more cohesive vision. Now he believes the individual can indeed stop unwarranted "progress," not by making an idle anarchistic gesture but by deliberately resisting "the mad machine." While Abbey admits that the core of his formula is utopian, he does not deny its efficacy because he firmly believes that without dreams we have nothing.

Dreams. We live, as Dr. Johnson said, from hope to hope. Our hope is for a new beginning. A new beginning based not on the destruction of the old but on its reevaluation. . . . If lucky, we may succeed in making America not the master of the earth (a trivial goal), but rather an example to other nations of what is possible and beautiful. Was that not, after all, the whole point and purpose of the American adventure? [AR, 137]

In other words, Abbey would substitute new methods for old while retaining the best part of the dream itself—the search for "what is possible and beautiful." As a western writer who has rewritten nineteenth-century frontier attitudes into a twenty-first-century vision, he bypasses his contemporaries to look into a better future. Those who have failed to make the present-day West a fit place to live he despises, not only for what they are doing to the land but also for what they have done to the original dream. Sneering at their shortsightedness, he asks, "What good is a Bill of Rights that does not include the right to play, to wander, to explore, the right to stillness and solitude, to discovery and physical freedom?" [AR, 137]. Modern developers, he is convinced, have unfortunately forgotten "the whole point and purpose of the American adventure" and have worked the land in such a way that those important rights are no longer easy to attain.

When he thinks about the destruction, both of the land and of the dream, he reacts angrily. Charging "that science in our time is the whore of industry and war and that scientific technology has become the instrument of a potential planetary slavery" [AR, 125], he blasts the establishment that has elevated the mega-monster to such a level. "There is something in the juxtaposition of big business, big military, and big technology that always rouses my most paranoid nightmares, visions of the technological superstate, the Pentagon's latent fascism, IBM's laboratory torture chambers, the absolute computerized fusion-powered global tyranny of the twenty-first century" [JH, 180–81]. Abbey prefers his own vision of the future, a romancer's superstate, a realm where Reason—"intelligence informed by sympathy, knowledge in the arms of love" [AR, 127]— prevails.

If that sounds too abstract, he agrees. "It will be the job of another generation of thinkers and doers to keep that hope alive and bring it closer to reality" [AR, 137]. He wants mainly to jolt his readers, to make them recognize what can happen when finite resources are sacrificed on the altar of Growth. Yet he no longer is as timid about stopping the immolation as he once was. Whereas earlier he castigated ironical anarchists like Paul Bondi, who transform only themselves by their protests, he now recognizes the emotional and spiritual ways individuals can effect change, even when their actions bring about no physical differences in the status quo. A 1979 article explains how his appreciation for the physiological potential of civil disobedience has modified since the days of *The Brave Cowboy*. Ed, investigating the sit-ins at Colorado's Rocky Flats nuclear facility and the subsequent trial of the objectors who blocked the railroad crossing there, develops a new perception of anarchy. These efforts were not idle gestures, he decides, but tangible demonstrations of personal conviction that moved him from cynical detachment to caring admiration. "Now I felt a guilty envy of the protestors, of those who act, and a little faint glow of hope—perhaps something fundamental might yet be changed in the nature of our lives. Crusaders for virtue are an awkward embarrassment to any society; they force us to make choices: either side with them which is diffi- cult and dangerous, or condemn them, which leads to self-betrayal.[10] While Abbey could hardly be categorized as an activist—he com- mits metaphorical rather than literal rebellion—he instinctively sympathizes with the goals and methods of civil disobedience. Be- tween 1956, when *The Brave Cowboy* was published, and 1979, the power of marches, sit-ins, boycotts, and hunger strikes has mani- festly increased. The Rocky Flats protestors, by their profound com- mitment to a cause, now prove to him that individual effort can have a real impact on others.

Both *The Journey Home* and *Abbey's Road* are devoted in part to airing Abbey's reconstructed views on the subject of what human beings, either singly or collectively, can do in a personal war against machines, technocracy, and excessive growth. The close of a *Jour- ney* chapter called "Shadows from the Big Woods" draws the battle- lines.

Meanwhile, though, the Big Woods is gone—or going fast. And the mountains, the rivers, the canyons, the seashores, the swamps, and the deserts. Even our own, the farms, the towns, the cities, all seem to lie helpless before the advance of the technoindustrial juggernaut. We have created an iron monster with which we wage war, not only on small peas- ant nations over the sea, but even on ourselves—a war against all forms of life, against life itself. In the name of Power and Growth. But the war is only beginning. [JH, 226]

To fight that war, Abbey suggests a strategy.

The machine may seem omnipotent, but it is not. Human bodies and human wit, active here, there, everywhere, united in purpose, indepen- dent in action, can still face that machine and stop it and take it apart and reassemble it—if we wish—on lines entirely new. There is, after all, a bet- ter way to live. The poets and the prophets have been trying to tell us about it for three thousand years. [JH, 226]

Now, a poet and prophet is trying to tell us about it in the twenti- eth century. This, after all, is Abbey's chief function and major contribution—not to march with the protestors or to detonate the charge, but to envision, for us, "a better way to live."

Those who mistake his intent misread the personal histories. "He certainly is no thinker," wrote one reviewer about *Abbey's Road*, "which is why the reader never gets a clear idea what Abbey's revolution would consist of, although it seems to have something to do with conservation."[11] Like others who ignore the romancer's mode, this reviewer wants the author to offer a more concrete prophetic vision, a task both inappropriate to and incompatible with Abbey's stated ends. "I am an artist, sir, . . . a creator of fictions" [AR, xxii], Abbey announced bluntly in his introduction to the very book this reviewer castigates. A creator of fictions draws no factual, formulaic blueprint. His talent is to scout out new terrain, not to settle it, to spur the reader out beyond the horizon, not to delimit a new frontier. Well-known romances of the past—*As You Like It*, for example, or *Don Quixote* or *The Scarlet Letter*—articulate no revolutionary methods, no specific outlines for violent action. Written by creators of fictions, they depict worlds where values and assumptions are questioned, where idealism is processed as revolt, but where, finally, no answers are given. Their authors hammer at the unmalleable worlds around them, effect change through artistic, rather than physical, means, as Abbey himself chooses to do.

That we can isolate his precise attitudes toward the land and toward the machines that would cannibalize it, though, documents the integrity and coherence of his point of view. The three personal histories, clearly constructed in the romance mode, communicate his belief in the sacred power of the landscape—its energy—as well as his antipathy toward the profane forces of a techno-industrial society. The three books do so in fictive ways. By narrating stories of Ed's adventures, by breathing windy tall tales, by arguing eclectically against specific ills, by shouting at what is happening and weeping for what still may occur, Abbey uses every artistic and rhetorical means at his command to convey his romancer's vision and to urge his readers to heed his romancer's prophecies.

He is at his best when he is most visionary and most prophetic, as in *The Journey Home*'s final chapter, "Dust: A Movie." There he images the twilight zone where Abbey's road may end, in a desert ghost town called Pariah, a visual emblem of Abbey's American West. "The time is today, tomorrow, or a thousand years ago" [JH, 239]. Using a narrative camera to photograph verbally a dissolving diorama of time and space, the author cuts from dawn to dusk, from man to beast, from peace to natural holocaust, from silence to silence. "Dust: A Movie" selectively ignores the profane autocracy of the "mad machine" and focuses instead on the earth's sacred energy—a frenzied storm, a swollen flood, a silent desert, a cat with burning yellow eyes. "Rocks crumble from the canyon wall. The final traces of the town, overgrown with brush and cactus, melt into the desert" [JH, 242]. Collapsing the transcendent history of the American West into a single imaginative time capsule, the surrealistic chapter effectively synthesizes Abbey's vision. Its way is the way down Abbey's road, that journey home to the American West of his deepest imaginings.

While he fears the track may be blocked by men who ravage the landscape to such an extent that the natural order will be broken, burying the Glen Canyons alive and interring the broader desertscape beneath a yellow shroud of smog, he still envisions a time when both humans and the earth may yet be free. If his readers will follow his romancer's vision, the dream may be accomplished, the onslaught of the Growth God stopped, the rights of the individual protected, the resources of the earth sanctified forever. Meanwhile, Abbey does what the poets and prophets must do—he reminds us constantly that a better way can exist. *Desert Solitaire, The Journey Home,* and *Abbey's Road* are three personal histories, three modern romances, designed to hammer physically, emotionally, spiritually, and politically at the universe, and to show us the better way. "And we see in their golden depths," at the close of *The Journey Home,* "the reflection of the sunrise, the soaring birds, the cliffs, the clouds, the sky, the earth, the human mind, the world beyond this world we love and hardly know at all" [JH, 242].

6

The Promenade

Appalachian Wilderness, Slickrock,
Cactus Country, The Hidden Canyon: A River Journey,
and *Desert Images*

Edward Abbey's remaining books of nonfiction spotlight the land-scape itself rather than the characters who populate the romanc-er's realm. The five still contain a romancer's vision, and include long passages of personal history as well as hasty political incur-sions against the establishment, but forests, mountains, rivers, des-erts, and canyons occupy center stage more frequently than not. The focus on the land occurs because these books were designed quite differently from the other three nonfiction romances. Writ-ten as textual accompaniments to photographs, these five lengthy essays mean to parallel in prose what the camera captures on film.[1]

The first volume sets the pattern, even though it is the only one whose physical landscape is the East—the Appalachian Wilderness, the Great Smoky Mountains. While Eliot Porter took the pictures that appear on almost every page of *Appalachian Wilderness* (1970), and Harry M. Caudill contributed the epilogue, Abbey wrote the central essay entitled "Natural and Human History." Divided into six chapters, his text includes a personal reminiscence about a De-cember trip to the Smokies, details about the vegetation and the animal population, musings about the human settlement of the area, concerns about the landscape's fragile future, and several long quotations from other authors whose words echo Abbey's own. On every page the words underscore and elucidate the pictures or vice versa, delimiting a single geographical region by artistic impressions of it.

Slickrock (1971), Abbey's next nonfiction venture, does the same for another part of the country. This time the writer's eye turns west, toward the fragile southeastern corner of Utah where red rocks and canyons dominate the scenery. Taking an explicitly environmentalist point of view, this Sierra Club publication calls attention to an endangered area that Abbey particularly values. We know quite a bit about Slickrock's origin from the introduction by John G. Mitchell, editor of Sierra Club Books. Mitchell describes the initial expedition that took writer, photographer, designer, and editor to the canyons where they sought a "symbiosis of word and picture" [S, 8], a trenchant association of complementary visions. They finally organized the book into different sections—"Abbey's part" and "Hyde's commentary"—so the photographs and the essay remain separate. Each distinctively projects a valid artistic response to the red rock scene. Abbey's section primarily balances the smallness of man against the enormity of the landscape. Like the prose essay of Appalachian Wilderness, it includes a measure of human and natural history, but the portion of personal history is longer, recounts more than one trip, and explores different parts of the wilderness. Abbey's Slickrock essay becomes, at the end, openly propagandistic, shooting facts and feelings at the reader in a rapid-fire barrage, confronting dreams with reality and emotions with statistics.

Cactus Country (1973), a Time-Life book in the American Wilderness series takes a different rhetorical stance. Written about the Sonoran Desert of southern Arizona and northern Mexico, it explores the region's animal, mineral and vegetable kingdoms in a gentle tone. Detailed pictures and additional editorial information about biological, geological, and botanical forms appear after each of Abbey's seven chapters. Ed conversationally narrates those seven personal explorations and takes the reader deep into the arid country —camping alone, hiking in the Superstition Mountains, working as a seasonal ranger at Organ Pipe Cactus National Monument, climbing Baboquivari, exploring Palm Canyon, and making two rugged trips to the Gulf of California. Meanwhile, the author manages to survey most of his environmental concerns as well, despite the publisher's restraints that keep him from venting his anger at any specified man-made intrusions. In fact, editorial requirements make *Cactus Country* unique among Abbey's picture-book essays, for its photographs were taken by several different men whose names appear in a footnote rather than on the title page. Their photographs illustrate the prose, or else the prose explicates the pictures, but in either case the writer and the cameramen coordinate their efforts to produce an understated, semieducational format.

After a four-year hiatus from this kind of writing, Abbey published *The Hidden Canyon: A River Journey* (1977) with John Blaustein. A personal encounter with the wilderness, the book moves into the turbulence of the Colorado River, down through the Grand Canyon. Ed's part of *The Hidden Canyon* is a diary of an eighteen-day float trip by dory from Mile 0 to Mile 277, drifting with his wife Reneé, the photographer Blaustein, and a small party of other river runners. Interspersing his own narration with excerpts from John Wesley Powell's first account of the trip, Ed lets the reader make comparisons between past and present efforts to run the rapids safely. "The gorge is black and narrow below, red and gray and flaring above, with crags and angular projections on the walls. . . . Down there in these grand gloomy depths we glide, ever listening, ever watching," wrote Powell in 1869, when his small group of men swept through Granite Gorge. "Grand, we'd agree," Ed reacts to the explorer's words, "but not really gloomy. *Glowing* is the word." He finds the canyon friendlier a century later, less intimidating. "The afternoon sun is hidden by the narrow walls but indirect light, reflected and refracted by the water, by the pink granitic sills and dikes in the polished cliffs, by the blue lenses of the atmosphere, streams upon us from many angles, all radiant. However, unlike Powell and his men, we are fresh, well fed, well supplied, secure in our bulging life jackets, confident in our dories, too ignorant (except the boatmen) for fear" [HC, 37]. The two writers, one hundred years apart, illustrate verbally the scenes that Blaustein captures graphically on film.

Abbey works in tandem, too, with noted photographer David Muench, in his next nonfiction essay about the land. *Desert Images* (1979) is a big book—expensive ($100), hefty (10½" X 17"), protracted (240 pages). As the chapter titles indicate, its pictures and prose range throughout the desert Southwest—"Sand Dunes," "Scarce Waters," "Rough Rock," "Wild Flowers," "Cactus Land," "Petrified Wood," "Desert Snow," "Saltscapes," "Mud Mosaics," "Cliff Dwellings," "Images on Rock." In each, Ed recalls an appropriate personal experience, but the content remains more descriptive than narrative and the tone more somber than frivolous. Some of the stories we have heard before, such as the one about Ed's job as an entrance-station ranger at Petrified Forest National Park, which Abbey subdues this time around; others are new, such as the frightening anecdote of Ed "riding into a blizzard and [becoming] utterly disoriented, completely lost" [DI, 167], and more than a little scared. The sobering tales seem to substantiate the physical and pictorial weight of the volume, focusing the reader's attention on the author's and photographer's impressions of the desert. Aside from its bulk, though, *Desert Images* differs little from the other four coffee-table books. In fact, it shares with them a set of characteristics that measurably distinguish the five from Abbey's other nonfiction.

First, the tone of these books is rather more didactic than that of *Desert Solitaire*, or of either collection of articles. *Cactus Country*, for example, aims to instruct the reader about the Sonoran Desert, and its format promotes that educational goal. In the fully illustrated subchapters written by the editors, one learns about "The Anatomy of a Colossus," facts and figures describing the giant saguaro cactus's dimensions and growth patterns, about "The Water Misers," a lively group of beasts and birds, and about a number of other typical plants and animals. Abbey's essays are also filled with factual information about the land and its inhabitants. Likewise, *Appalachian Wilderness* and *Slickrock* provide information about the human and natural histories of their respective areas, the former to inform, the latter more to incense the reader. Even *The Hidden Canyon* and *Desert Images* include factual details about the Colorado and the southwestern environment, although their intentions seem more descriptive than analytic. And since two of the volumes include bibliographies, their subjects can be investigated beyond the bounds of the books themselves. One of the five even features a "Geographical Table" of the area's rock formations.

In keeping with the didacticism and to communicate an even wider range of erudition, Abbey often quotes related writing by authors both little known and famous. He alluded to T. S. Eliot, William Wordsworth, Robert Frost, and Robert Burns in *Desert Solitaire*, for example, but in the picture books Abbey makes a practice of integrating other words with his own. *The Hidden Canyon* leans heavily on John Wesley Powell's journals for an elaboration of man's responses to the Colorado scenery. *Cactus Country* opens each of its chapters with an appropriate quotation from someone whose thoughts echo Abbey's—Mary Austin, B. Traven, William Hornaday, Joseph Wood Krutch, and Ann Woodin. These epigraphs not only expand our understanding of the subsequent bit of personal history but also make the author seem a little less isolated. For example, after B. Traven observes, "The glittering treasure you are hunting for day and night lies buried on the other side of that hill yonder" [CC, 42], Ed follows with a trek through the Superstition Mountains east of Phoenix, in search, perhaps, of the Lost Dutchman Mine, or of "something." Actually, each of the five picture books propagates the author's search for a treasured freedom, primarily of the wilderness but sometimes of self.

Along with the romancer's quest, however, comes the search for knowledge, and Abbey appears even more inquisitive in these pages than elsewhere. Of special interest because of its in-depth scholarship is the long section in *Appalachian Wilderness* about William Bertram, "a remarkable botanist, writer and traveler, who journeyed on horseback, mostly alone, through much of the Carolinas, Florida and Georgia in the years immediately preceding the American Revolution" [AW, 54]. Abbey quotes the 1791 book that describes Bertram's experiences and discoveries, and emphasizes the accuracy with which this early Appalachian observer noted his surroundings. He also includes replicas of Bertram's drawings, so the reader finishes this section with an educated sense of the man's accomplishments and contributions to knowledge. Other pages of *Appalachian Wilderness*, too, are filled with excerpts carefully selected from writers whose sensibilities substantiate Ed's own, men as radically different as Ivan Turgenev and e. e. cummings. Not only does this research document Abbey's range of knowledge, it also establishes him as part of a continuing tradition, the very one he glibly dismisses elsewhere.

This is not to say that Ed disappears in a slough of quotations, but his presence definitely is muted in the five books. Perhaps only a third of *Appalachian Wilderness* focuses on his personal adventures; perhaps only half of *Slickrock*. And even in a book like *The Hidden Canyon*, where Ed's diary relates nothing but his personal responses to the walled environment, the canyon itself dominates the prose.

"We watch the boatmen traverse one ledge with a rather indecent exposure, two hundred feet of vertical space full of nothing but gravity. The ledge is three inches wide. There are no handholds. Most of us choose the sole alternative route, a humiliating crawl on face and belly through a claustrophobic tunnel" [HC, 68], an effacing experience to be sure. "Desert images" prevail in the book of that title too, forcing Ed into the background even as he speaks. "I peer out from the shade of my hat brim into the white glare of the salt flats. Close by is a wilderness of jagged, cutting, nearly impenetrable salt formations, knee-high blades and swords and stalagmites built up over the years by capillary action. Walking a half mile over and through that crackling, crusted ulcerous terrain would be a laborious project" [DI, 181]. Ed has, in effect, stepped aside to allow the visual and photographic contexts to supersede his presence.

Abbey also mutes the polemics in four of the five books. Even though he makes certain that his attitude toward environmental ruin is heard, he couches it more gracefully than elsewhere. In *Appalachian Wilderness*, where he sounds a requiem for the shrinking expanses of the East, he jabs at the savagery rather than swinging roundhouse punches. He thinks of Sylva, a lovely town: it "must have been beautiful. Now it is something else, for the streets are grimy and noisy, jammed always with motor traffic, the river is a sewer, and the sky a pall of poisonous filth" [AW, 104]. He worries about the nearby national park too: "one can easily imagine the great steel crustacean traffic jams of spring, summer and fall when the encapsulated multitudes come, in their lemming-like masses, to follow one another's tail pipes along the asphalt trails" [AW, 42]. And he gasps with horror at the "vast crimes . . . being committed in this region, whole hillsides raped and robbed, life systems that required ages for their weaving ripped apart" [AW, 18]. But he neither assumes the strident tones heard in *The Journey Home* about the rape of the West, nor professes the urgency found in *Abbey's Road*. He only reminds us that if Eliot Porter's pictorial world is all too fragile, Edward Abbey's is all too fleeting.

Slickrock, of course, goes much further in its attacks on the mad machine of technocracy and the twentieth-century worship of Growth. June Viavant of Salt Lake City's Escalante Wilderness Committee describes the situation: "Much has been done to protect these wild, beautiful, lonely places," she writes. "Much remains to be done. We can win many successive steps of a conservation battle, but we can lose only once" [S, 14]. Abbey's prose then sounds the battle cry for Viavant's followers, and the book builds toward a climactic diatribe. It begins softly, though, with a reminiscence about Ed's first glimpses of the canyon country and his first timid, and then braver, explorations. Commenting on the expansive view from Comb Ridge, he remembers, "In the silence and the heat and the glare we gazed upon a seared wasteland, a sinister and savage desolation. And found it infinitely fascinating." But years later "the words seem too romantic . . ., now that I have seen what men and heavy equipment can do to even the most angular and singular of earthly landscapes" [S, 20].

He castigates, in particular, the creation of Lake Powell, the place he believes symbolic of the worst that can happen to wild country when developers and their engines of destruction transform the land at will. Pointing out the differences between "a wild and flowing river lined by boulder-strewn shores, exquisite sandy beaches, thickets of tamarisk and willow, and glades of cottonwood" and "the present reservoir with its silent sterile shores and debris-choked side canyons," he decides the two are like life and death. "Glen Canyon was alive. Lake Powell is a graveyard" [S, 65–66]. But it does not have to stay that way. In a quiet aside, he thinks about shutting down the power plant, opening the diversion tunnels, and draining the reservoir—possibilities, if "the nation establishes a way of life adapted to actual resources and basic needs." And he fancies, perhaps naively, the regenerative process that would then restore life to the canyon. "Within the lifetime of our children Glen Canyon and the living river, heart of the canyonlands, will be restored to us. The wilderness will again belong to God and the people" [S, 69], its energy unharnessed by artificial means. Thus Abbey's *Slickrock* essay bridges the polemical disparities between the three personal histories and the other volumes of nonfiction, combining his tempered fury at "the domination of an insane, expansionist economy and a brutal technology" that will destroy us—"unless we find a way to stop it" [S, 77]—with a controlled artistry that produces an attractive, accessible picture book.

More typical of the five, however, is *Cactus Country,* whose editorial policy was not dictated by a conservationist lobby. There the publishers kept Abbey reined in (although Abbey "reined in" is noisier than most writers "unleashed"). A telling example occurs when Ed and a friend trudge toward the Papago Indians' sacred mountain, "up the ridge, into more thickets of scrub oak, tangles of thorny acacia, open places mined with prickly pear and Schott's agave. The October heat was sickening—a fierce, sullen resistance—and the trail petered out into an unfollowable maze of cattle paths and deer runs, through thorny tunnels under the brush" [CC, 93]. After the chapter digresses into an extended examination of desert vegetation, some endangered, some proliferating, Ed pauses to chuckle at the ruins of a fire-lookout station, abandoned in mid-construction when "the government officials gazed out from the peak upon that lovely, forlorn, splendid and desolate wasteland" [CC, 104] and discovered there were no forests in view to protect from fire! Rather than dwell on such foolishness, Ed's understated observation leaves the reader to draw the inferences. And later, when he surveys both the view from the top of the peak and the smog obscuring it, he assumes the same quiet tone. "When the air is clear, I've been told, you can see the waters of the Gulf of California, some 150 miles away by line of sight. Unfortunately the air is seldom clear in Arizona any more and on that day I could not see the gulf" [CC, 104–5]. Personable, informative, restrained, *Cactus Country* disguises its environmentalist leanings but makes absolutely certain that Abbey's views are recognizable anyway. In *Hidden Canyon* and *Desert Images* too, despite their varying designs, the author subtly discloses his uneasiness about the landscape's future.

"After *Desert Solitaire*," Abbey remarked in a 1975 interview, "I had a lot of offers to do the text for landscape picture books. . . . I don't find it difficult to dredge up the appropriate emotions, but I do find it difficult making it sound different each time around."[2] His demurral is odd. An important characteristic and a major accomplishment of the five coffee-table volumes is that no two of them sound alike. There is a resemblance, of course, but each has a distinctive stamp that sets it apart from the others and from the three personal histories. Because Abbey's prose style is so fluid, so graphic, and so professional, he is able to mold it into a form suitable to the style of an individual photographer. That is, the writer's eye imitates and enhances the camera's. And as a result, his diction and syntax change from book to book.

In *Appalachian Wilderness*, Abbey's prose catches the intimate, close-up perspective that characterizes Eliot Porter's photography. Porter's art details the landscape, tracing the pattern of a single fern, limning orange lichen on a slate-gray rock, magnifying the blossoms of wood sorrel around a rotten log. Abbey, finding such close-ups stylistically compatible, also looks at the wintry land with a microscopic eye. The specificity of his prose replicates the specificity of the photographs, as when he characterizes the primeval forest, whose leafless branches "sketch bare, delicate traceries of line against the neutral gray of the sky, in the manner of ancient Chinese brush and ink drawings" [AW, 94]. Sometimes Abbey explains the connection. "It looks like a scene invented by Eliot Porter," Ed notes as he pauses on a wooden bridge to admire the view upstream.

Granite-like boulders lodged in the torrent and sheathed in ribbed, rippled layers of ice; spillways and plunge pools, the roil and rush and roar of the complicated waters; giant hemlocks leaning over the stream, fresh snow clinging to their bark; the stones and pebbles of the creek bed gleaming through the flawless clarity of the water; and over all, illuminating the scene and blending with its shadows, the soft gray light of the humid mountain air, filtered by cloud and by random reticulation of the commingled tree branches and pine needles overhead. [AW, 45–46]

Together, the two artists capture the secret stillness of snowy Appalachia, choosing, because of its metaphorical significance, an unusual season on which to focus, eying the aged, comatose land.

By contrast—bright, sunny, glaring—*Slickrock* separates divergent visions of essayist and photographer. Thus Abbey's style more closely resembles *Journey* or *Road*, reinforced by the Sierra Club's urgency to trumpet a battle call. And *Cactus Country*, less strident but no less characteristic, didactically matches pictures to prose and eliminates any artistic reason for the author to reshape his words. But in *The Hidden Canyon* he does so brilliantly, formulating a style completely unlike his normal mode. The impetus seems to have been twofold. John Blaustein's photographs, taken on thirty different river trips between 1971 and 1977, illustrate a world in constant motion. But the Colorado *is* a world in constant motion, a turbulence of water, rocks and sand. Storms, rapids, a host of animals arrested in midflight—Blaustein sees action more than stillness, power more than peace. In short, his vision contrasts enormously with Eliot Porter's quiet reveries. Yet Abbey's prose underscores Blaustein's sense of the natural milieu just as precisely. Whereas he wrote with a magnifying glass in *Appalachian Wilderness*, he borrows the movie camera's technique for *The Hidden Canyon*. Short, staccato, breathless sentences mimic the river's rush as well as the photographer's style.

Here they come. They disappear. They emerge, streaming with water. Dive and disappear again. Dark forms barely visible through the foam. The boat rears up into sunlight. Wally has crabbed an oar, lost an oarlock. He's in trouble. He's struggling with something. They vanish again, under the waves, to reappear not twenty feet from where I sit, bearing hard upon this immovable barrier. The dory yaws to port, Wally is standing up, he's only got one oar, looks like he's trying to climb right out of the boat onto my rock. I'm about to offer a futile hand when I realized he's climbing the high side, preventing the boat from capsizing. Cushioned by a roil of water, the boat and its three occupants rush past me, only inches from the iron rock. [HC, 109]

His prose roils from rapid to rapid down the river.

Water, on the other hand, barely moves in *Desert Images*, and the style there seems somnolent too. Instead of the rush of the river, Muench and Abbey picture an arid, silent land where visual mirages dominate, where, for example, crusts of salt repeat the flocked snow of a preceding photograph in a universal juxtaposition of barren forms. The immense, pictorial panels suit the languid, pontifical style that marks the accompanying essays. More descriptive than Abbey's other nonfiction, the adventures are framed moments, studied poses with Ed standing motionless. He looks toward "broad sun-baked near-level wastelands of small stones fitted to one another like the tiles on a bathhouse floor—'desert pavement,' it's called—with the surface tarnished by air and chemistry to the hue of rusted iron." He turns another way to see "the stone throats of wine-stem canyons polished by a million years of flashflooding to a finish slick as glass, inlaid with a mosaic of vari-colored jewels resembling garnets, jasper, amethysts, rubies, opals, ivory, crystal" [DI, 67–68]. But he does not move. Artistic magic may transform unattractive or even hostile images into stunning panoramas, but the end result is static, frozen, immobile.

Hills like melted elephants. Hills like crumbling castles. Buttes like skyscraper pipe organs. Cathedrals of stone, carved by wind and rain and frost and ice into an intricate tracery of lace and filigree, with gargoyles out of a gothic nightmare squatting on surreal pedestals of petrified mud. Moonlight scenes to horrify the innocent. Visions of eternity frozen in stone, hallucinations fixed in rock specters, enough to jolt the most hardened opium eater into permanent insanity—or back to earth. [DI, 68]

As a matter of fact, the entire scene is fixed in stone. By erecting a frame around each paragraph and by writing a series of stop-action essays, Abbey effectively captures David Muench's photographic spirit and, in turn, the tacit, majestic, omnipotent spirit of the desert.

Abbey does not, however, reject his own vision in favor of someone else's, in this or in any of the other nonfiction picture books. Indeed the opposite is true. Particularly in *Desert Images* his prose and Muench's photographs work together to evoke what we have seen in Abbey's other writing—the energy of the land, its intrinsic sacrality. Just as the essayist peers *into* the images he reconstructs, so the photographer focuses on the power *beneath* the landscape's surface. A chapter called "Wild Flowers," in particular, demonstrates this tangential arrangement. Preceding the essay is a full-page photograph of striated sand, dappled brown and streaked with gold. Near the picture's center, a single pale desert primrose, white with gold stamen, grows "in solitary splendor." But Abbey does not write about this particular phenomenon, a shocking bit of life in the midst of arid waste; instead he describes a second example,

a single Indian paintbrush lifting its cup of salmon-colored, petal-like bracts toward the sky. The paintbrush too is beautiful, with the special and extraordinary beauty of wild and lonely things. Every desert flower shares that quality. Anything that lives where it would seem that nothing could live, enduring extremes of heat and cold, sunlight and storm, parching aridity and sudden cloudbursts, among burnt rock and shifting sands, any such creature—beast, bird or flower—testifies to the grandeur and heroism inherent in all forms of life. Including the human. Even in us. [DI, 116]

Framing his picture as surely as Muench does, Abbey looks directly to the paintbrush's "cup of salmon-colored, petal-like bracts," to the core of the strength and sacrality of a lonely desert flower. After the writer's words have reinforced the photograph, Muench, in turn, vivifies the verbal description. A few pages later another full-page panel shows a cluster of paintbrush glowing red against a muted, rusty-orange sandstone facade with no visible means of support, no leaves, no soil, no water. While neither Abbey nor Muench names the life-source behind such flowers in their crannied walls, the source of strength is implicit. The rest of the essay "Wild Flowers," and the many other pictures accompanying it, substantiate the sacrality of the desert images felt, if not articulated, by both artists. So Abbey's vision is not diluted by Muench's presence, nor is Muench's controlled by Abbey's. Rather, the two embrace one another in a closely wedded whole.

All five picture books, in fact, employ a kind of sacred vision somewhat different from the one isolated in the three volumes of personal history. This characteristic results in part from Abbey's close association with the individual photographers—his affinity with Muench's grandiose style, for example—and in part from his awareness of his audience. People who buy $100 picture books, as opposed to people who buy paperback reprints of *Desert Solitaire*, do so because they want to display the works, not because they want to read them carefully. *Desert Images* simply weighs too much to hold on one's lap for any length of time, so the sacred images projected by Abbey and Muench in its pages necessarily take on an encapsulated Edgar Guest quality of easy philosophy that can be readily understood. A romanticized kind of sacrality, then, replaces the more substantive theory of Abbey's other prose. From *Appalachian Wilderness* to *Desert Images*, he transforms his serious ideas into simplistic versions, as the first two pages of *Desert Images* demonstrate. A woman wakes at dawn "On the Canyon Rim," playing a flute to the birds' song, to a coyote cry, to an armada of clouds, to the sun. The coyote's "barbaric yawp" responds: "A song of the self, of hunger, of loneliness hungering for an end to loneliness. A song of the desert" [DI, 13]. Candidly borrowing from Walt Whitman, Abbey sets a style for the rest of the book—celebratory, emotive, romantic, as well as pictorial. His final proclamation, "All deserts begin in the mind," implies that the following pages will likewise be filled with philosophic one-liners, as easy on the mind as the photographs are on the eye.

The Hidden Canyon, Cactus Country, and *Appalachian Wilderness*, while physically more manageable, suffer from the same lightweight pleasantries. The first, of course, captures a dynamic, rather than a static, energy, so its design speeds the reader rapidly through the canyon. The sense of sacrality derives from the river's turbulence, from "the unrelenting clamor of the cascading, clashing, tumbling, thundering, tormented waters" [HC, 66]. *Cactus Country* and *Appalachian Wilderness,* on the other hand, repeat the slower pace of *Desert Images,* with focused paragraphs that pay homage to the land but with shallow throw-away lines that detract from the celebration. "Which desert did I love the most? Which lady did I love the most? I loved them all. But one was lovelier than any other. One was richer, more complicated, more various. For all its harshness, loneliness, cruelty and cunning, one desert haunted me like a vision of paradise. Still does" [CC, 20], Abbey pontificates, leaving the reader amused, but unmoved, by his analogies. Characteristic, too, of his prose in these books are the simple sentences that pronounce the unpronounceable: "All deserts begin in the mind" [DI, 13]; "All the rest is mystery" [AW, 37]; "Which is enough" [CC, 113]. When Abbey sacrifices introspection to expedience, he sacrifices his own credibility as well.

Only *Slickrock* avoids the Sunday sermonizing that brands the other four. Because of its forthright purpose and tone calling for action, the book is meant to be read, considered, read again, and the pictures shared and valued. Here Abbey's prose invites contemplation, whether he is arguing for the cause or writing about why he loves the desert so. When he wonders, for example, "what would it be like to *live* in this place," a meandering canyon miles from the world of men, his answer makes the reader laugh, and then think. "Someday," Ed projects, "I shall make the experiment, become an ancient baldheaded troglodyte with a dirty white beard tucked in my belt, be a shaman, a wizard, a witch doctor crazy with solitude, starving on locusts and lizards, feasting from time to time upon lost straggler boy scout. Madness: of course a man would go mad from the beauty and the loneliness, both equally mysterious. But perhaps it would be—who can say?—a kind of *blessed* insanity, like the bliss of a snake in the winter sun, a buzzard on the summer air" [S, 62]. Abbey is at his best when he addresses the intangible through the tactile images of the natural world. The image of a basking snake (has anyone ever seen one in midwinter?) says more about "*blessed* insanity" [italics Abbey's] than a host of glittering generalities.

Unfortunately, the picture books too often resort to an easy popularization of the sacrality crucial to Abbey's vision, as if the format were a license to be glib. Because of the casual stance, however, the reader learns some things about Ed that might otherwise go unnoticed, intimate moments that previously have gone unmentioned. John Mitchell of Sierra Club Books describes "Abbey in a sandstone window overlooking a maze of canyons that wind off toward the deep gorge of the Colorado River. He was chewing on a blade of grass and the sombrero was low again in observance of sundown. . . . Time to return to camp. Abbey removed the hat and, holding it level, slowly extended his arm toward the big river." Mitchell calls the gesture unusual, then decides "it was at once natural and moving. Abbey, saluting the slickrock with that silly sombrero, reaching out to bless the stark chiseled bounties of that wild beyond" [S, 11]. While Abbey himself would consider such a gesture private, not public, another man can lightly give space to the episode.

Another example of how the coffee-table books overtly enshrine the land's subjective essence comes at the end of *Cactus Country*, after a dry desert hike in "Pinacate country, El Gran Desierto, this ultimate wasteland." Ed pauses to drink at a tiny water hole and to fill his one canteen. "We thought about the birds and bees and animals, the injustice of life, the general harshness of existence. I know, it's tough all over, but nowhere tougher than on the blackened slopes of Pinacate, under that pitiless Sonoran sun. All the water we had was in the one canteen. We emptied it back into the little stony basin. Not in charity but out of caution. It seemed, after all, no more than a prudent sacrifice to the spirit of the desert" [CC, 165]. Unlike Mitchell, Abbey refrains from calling the overt unction "natural and moving," but he articulates Ed's "prudent sacrifice" more explicitly than is usual in his writing. Books like *Cactus Country* relay an extrinsic respect for the land, whereas the personal histories show an intrinsic veneration instead. In *Desert Solitaire*'s world, the man sitting outside his trailer said simply, "I wait and watch, guarding the desert, the arches, the sand and barren rock, the isolated junipers and scattered clumps of sage surrounding me in the stillness and simplicity under the starlight" [DS, 14]. Knowing that Ed stands guard reassures the reader more than his prudent sacrifice, for the former act is a deep-seated ritual while the latter is a one-time gesture. Abbey's vision succeeds in clarity and impact when he integrates those rituals into his pilgrimage through the landscape; it sounds weaker when he overromanticizes the gesture, the word, and finally the dream.

The picture books do not necessarily cater to a shallow reading public or represent money-making ventures for a materialistic author. The five simply were conceived differently from the personal histories, and they should be evaluated differently too. As pictorial dialogues between writer and photographer, they succeed completely. It would be difficult to mistake the distinctive visions in picture and prose, as passages from each book indicate. Eliot Porter's: "An austere and ancient clapboarded farmhouse, taller than wide when seen from the road, it had filigreed porchwork, a steep-pitched roof and on the roof lightning rods pointing straight up at the sun or stars" [AW, 14]. The Sierra Club's: "Swimmers and boaters on the Glen Canyon Dam reservoir will plow through a film of soot; hikers will find a coating of the black dust on the ancient monoliths of Rainbow Bridge, the Arches, The Needles—everywhere, *hic et ubique*" [S, 75–76]. A Time-Life editorial board's:"It was a splendid shining golden-mahogany beast about 10 inches long, a bold handsome centipede, a warrior, with the concentrated sleek viciousness of an engine designed for destruction and nothing else" [CC, 74]. John Blaustein's: "Out there in the middle of the maelstrom the Eater waits, heaving and gulping, its mouth like a giant clam's, its roar like the 1896 Republican Convention, its mind a frenzy of beige-colored rabid foam" [HC, 66]. David Muench's: "I lie belly down on the cornice by the dune, looking over the edge. Fine grains of sand, backlit by the sun, shining like particles of light, are swirling in the air. I can hear them tinkling and chiming as they fall on the sand below. Like crystals of quartz; like tiny fragments of broken glass" [DI, 24]. If read as Abbey intended, each of his pictorial voices extends the boundaries of his world. Informative, wide-ranging, somewhat subdued, the coffee-table creations are exceptional more for their stylistic variations than for anything else. They measure the talent of the craftsman.

7

Hiking Companions

Although Edward Abbey rarely frets about either his literary reputation or his rapport with other writers, he nonetheless recognizes
that no one produces books in a vacuum. His introduction to *Abbey's Road* proffers a number of relevant touchstones that connect
him to past and present American essayists and novelists—the
weight of regionalism, the tradition of nature writers, and the influence of his personal favorites. While his subjective estimate of
those influences varies from utter condemnation of most editors
and reviewers to high praise for a novelist like Peter Matthiessen,
whose *At Play in the Fields of the Lord* he describes as "strange, green,
haunting, and lovely" [AR, xxi], Abbey makes additional provocative statements about the literary path followed by all writers. Repeatedly emphasizing that his course is a lonely one and advising
"take the other" road, he paradoxically counters with a historical
awareness of the company along the way. In *The Journey Home* he
dismissed his predecessors in a single breath: "So much for the
mantle and britches of Thoreau and Muir. Let Annie Dillard wear
them now" [JH, xiii]. But in *Abbey's Road* he modifies his expatria-
tion, acknowledging at least some tangential connection with his
peers, those "sons and daughters of Thoreau. . . . Like vacuum

cleaner salesmen, we scramble for exclusive territory on this over-sold, swarming, shriveling planet" [AR, xx].

Listing his fellow scramblers with tongue in cheek, Abbey names several sons and daughters who "abound in contemporary American writing, if we can believe the reviewers." He includes himself in the company of "nature writers" Edward Hoagland, Joseph Wood Krutch, Wendell Berry, John McPhee, Ann Zwinger, and again, Peter Matthiessen and Annie Dillard. It is Dillard, however, who to him seems "the true heir of the Master. Only she has earned the right to wear the Master's pants and this for the good reason that she alone has been able to compose, successfully, in Thoreau's extravagant and transcendentalist manner" [AR, xx]. Nevertheless, a good case can be made for Abbey's communion with Thoreau as well. While one never would accuse him of effusive transcendentalism or of the radiant religiosity of Annie Dillard, he still repeats and reaffirms many of Thoreau's strongest convictions.

Despite his frequent disclaimers,[1] Abbey shares more common interests with the author of *Walden* (1854) and of "Civil Disobedience" (1849) than he has admitted publically. Both believers in the joys of solitude, in the need for wilderness, in the enormity of big government, and in the efficacy of studied dissent, the two men march to the same drummer much of the time. In a paragraph from *Walden* that Abbey must have read, Thoreau writes,

We need the tonic of wildness,—to wade sometimes in marshes where the bittern and the meadow-hen lurk, and hear the booming of the snipe; to smell the whispering sedge where only some wilder and more solitary fowl builds her nest, and the mink crawls with its belly close to the ground. At the same time that we are earnest to explore and learn all things, we require that all things be mysterious and unexplorable, that land and sea be infinitely wild, unsurveyed and unfathomed by us because unfathomable. We can never have enough of Nature. We must be refreshed by the sight of inexhaustible vigor, vast and Titanic features, the sea-coast with its wrecks, the wilderness with its living and its decaying trees, the thunder cloud, and the rain which lasts three weeks and produces freshets. We need to witness our own limits transgressed, and some life pasturing freely where we never wander.[2]

Surely Abbey agrees. When he speaks of wilderness and freedom in *The Journey Home* and elsewhere, he echoes Thoreau almost point by point: the wilderness keeps us psychologically attuned, we cannot survive without it, the wilderness provides us a model, we can only hope to touch on its infinite powers. Thoreau writes, "We can never have enough of Nature"; Abbey says, "Wilderness is not a luxury but a necessity of the human spirit, and as vital to our lives as water and good bread" [DS, 192]. Thoreau says, "We need to witness our own limits transgressed, and some life pasturing freely where we never wander"; Abbey writes, "The finest quality of this stone, these plants and animals, this desert landscape is the indifference manifest to our presence, or absence, our coming, our staying or our going. Whether we live or die is a matter of no concern whatsoever to the desert" [DS, 300–301]. Each man, looking at the wilderness and luxuriating in the freedom that he feels, unabashedly celebrates the mysterious, the unexplorable, the unsurveyed, and the unfathomed. "Here you may yet find the elemental freedom," Ed writes as he gazes "through a hundred miles of untrammeled atmosphere" across canyons and mesas to the peaks beyond. "The elemental freedom . . . to make the discovery of the self in its proud sufficiency which is not isolation but an irreplaceable part of the mystery of the whole" [JH, 88].

The two men look at "the mystery of the whole" in much the same way too. Recognizing the sacred energy inherent in the natural world, each observes it as much through a microscope as through a wide-angle lens. They find sacrality's mystery in nature's minutiae. A battle between red and black ants intrigues Thoreau as thoroughly as a mating ritual between two gopher snakes fascinates Abbey. Both write at length about the creatures who visit them by night or day. Whippoorwills, owls, jays, chickadees, partridges, bullfrogs, fox, and squirrels abound in *Walden's* pages, just as Abbey's nonfiction includes a host of beasts and birds. His picture books, in particular, show us the infinite variety to be found in the wilderness, but his personal histories, too, introduce us to numerous wild creatures. "The bird list grows slowly," Ed notes in a lookout diary. "Add barn swallow, cliff swallow, water pipit, raven, blue grouse, white-tailed ptarmigan, rufous hummingbird, brown creeper, gray jay, evening grosbeak, red-shafted flicker, loon. *Loon!*— heard from the lake far below—that wild, lorn, romantic cry, one of the most thrilling sounds in all North America. Sound of the ancient wilderness, lakes, forest, moonlight, birchbark canoes" [JH, 41]. Sound of sacrality.

"I have travelled a good deal in Concord," Thoreau announces about the microcosmic world where he makes his observations. So, too, the solitary Arches ranger describes experiences in the park—the dance of the snakes' courtship, the pursuit of the moon-eyed horse, the search for the dead man at Grandview Point—that grow universal in his mind. Other canyonland ventures expand his imaginative realm even further—drifting down the Colorado, exploring Havasu, climbing Tukuhnikivats, dropping into the Maze. For three years, artistically fused into a single season as Thoreau condensed his time at Walden, the narrator returns because "I want to know it all, possess it all, embrace the entire scene intimately, deeply, totally" [DS, 6]. His words might have been written a hundred and twenty years before. "I went to the woods because I wished to live deliberately, to front only the essential facts of life, and see if I could not learn what it had to teach, and not, when I came to die, discover that I had not lived."[3]

To live as they wish, the two men discover they must be alone much of the time. Whenever he can, Ed wanders into the canyon country "very quietly and selfishly, all by my lonesome" [DS, 249] to taste the tonic of the landscape and to stir his imagination, for he finds it impossible to experience self without solitude. "I wait. Now the night flows back, the mighty stillness embraces and includes me; I can see the stars again and the world of starlight. I am twenty miles or more from the nearest fellow human, but instead of loneliness I feel loveliness. Loveliness and a quiet exultation" [DS, 15]. Thoreau would agree with Abbey's prescription for peace. "I find it wholesome to be alone the greater part of the time," he wrote definitively. "To be in company, even with the best, is soon wearisome and dissipating. I love to be alone. I never found the companion that was so companionable as solitude."[4] Nor did Abbey, who says "a man can never find or need better companionship than that of himself" [DS, 111]. Although less eremitic than the easterner, Ed finds solitude his most frequent comrade. "Most of my wandering in the desert I've done alone. Not so much from choice as from necessity—I generally prefer to go into places where no one else wants to go" [DS, 226]. Those places, philosophical as well as physical, metaphorical as well as tangible, stand at the end of Abbey's road. But Thoreau's road leads there too.

It is possible to turn page after page of *Walden* and discover lines that speak Abbey's deepest thoughts. Certainly *Desert Solitaire* is an original work of art, with its fresh vision of the wilderness and contemporary man, and no one would accuse Abbey of cheap imitation anywhere in his prose. But the thrust behind both imaginations is startlingly similar—both believe that "the mass of men lead lives of quiet desperation,"[5] acknowledge that "true magic inheres in the ordinary, the commonplace, the everyday, the mystery of the obvious" [AR, 195], and insist on the need for freedom and wilderness. Perhaps Annie Dillard wears Henry Thoreau's britches, but Edward Abbey wears his boots.

The author of the personal histories, *The Brave Cowboy, Fire on the Mountain,* and *The Monkey Wrench Gang* sounds like Thoreau in another way too. "Civil disobedience" is not a notion foreign to his imagination, nor is the idea that big government intrudes upon the lives of men strange to his ears. Thoreau bluntly calls the "authority of government . . . an impure one,"[6] and suggests that the American government seems "to be losing some of its integrity."[7] He writes at length about the impure power of an aggregate that overrides the needs of individuals that constitute its parts. Abbey instinctively agrees with Thoreau's expressions of distaste, although as a man of the twentieth century he goes even further in his pronouncements against any conglomerate that greedily usurps freedom and/or the land. In *Slickrock,* for example, he laments: "The tragedy of our national situation lies in the strange historical process by which the majority of us have acquiesced in the creation of a whole that is far worse than the sum of its parts." Isolating a class of men who believe "in growth for the sake of growth: a blind faith in blind progress," he supposes that "as individuals . . . they know better" [S, 76–77]. Abbey's point resembles Thoreau's— sometimes men create a megamonster, like the State or like a giant corporation, which becomes the master of the people instead of their slave.

Both men then ask what an individual should do. "Unjust laws exist: shall we be content to obey them, or shall we endeavor to amend them, and obey them until we have succeeded, or shall we transgress them at once?"[8] Thoreau answers his own question, citing his personal act of civil disobedience as an example of what a man may have to do. Jailed for refusing to pay his poll tax, Thoreau, at least in principle, confronted the State. The outcome, unlike the consequences of Paul Bondi's, Jack Burns's or John Vogelin's actions, was benign—a night in jail, a belief upheld, a debt paid by someone else. But Thoreau's point could easily be Abbey's. The

State "is not armed with superior wit or honesty, but with superior physical strength. I was not born to be forced. I will breathe after my own fashion. Let us see who is strongest,"[9] the one-time prisoner pronounces. Speaking not only for himself but for all the ironical anarchists who will follow, Thoreau draws a battleline where he holds his convictions. John Vogelin, standing up to all the forces the United States government can muster, would understand those convictions since he, too, "was not born to be forced."

And when Thoreau proclaims idealistically that, "If a man is thought-free, fancy-free, imagination free, . . . unwise rulers or reformers cannot fatally interrupt him,"[10] Paul Bondi would agree (we must remember, he and his buddy signed H. D. Thoreau's name to their document advocating civil disobedience to the Selective Service), and so would Bondi's creator, in principle. When Abbey writes of the sit-ins at the Rocky Flats Nuclear Facility, he affirms the ethical stand Thoreau outlines, but when he draws fictional characters who confront "superior physical strength," he lets them lose, fatally. Except in an ideological sense, neither Jack Burns nor John Vogelin survives. But perhaps that is enough. Their stories exemplify what Thoreau meant when he said a free man could not be interrupted, since the cowboy's and the rancher's beliefs in the freedom of self in the face of unjust force prevail, even after they die.

In a way, then, Thoreau's ideals live in Abbey's characters. Whether Ed is peering "down there in the rocks" or setting off on a dirt track alone, whether Jack Burns is clawing his way up a rough-hewn escarpment or John Vogelin is standing grimly on his porch, the characters, and thus their creator, act and speak in ways that would please Thoreau. "Nevertheless," Thoreau has said, "of all the characters I have known, perhaps Walden wears best, and best preserves its purity."[11] So perhaps he would understand best and prefer Abbey's desert to his fictional figures, for of all the characters the Southwesterner has given us, the desert wears best, and best preserves its purity.

The desert, however, or rather, the expanse of a continent, separates these two writers more than a hundred years have done. Despite their mutual affinities for the wilderness and man's place in it, Thoreau's New England is far removed from Abbey's Southwest. Geographically more attuned to the author of *Desert Solitaire* are the regional writers whose visions bring the western landscape into

focus. Too often the term *regionalism* has implied something infe-
rior, trite, and repetitious when attached to the literature of the
American West. Only a few writers have dared defy conventional
expectations; even fewer have done so successfully. Abbey explains
the lamentable connotations of "the West" that novelists like Walter Van Tilburg Clark, Wright Morris, William Eastlake, and Larry
McMurtry have had to overcome.

The great American *West,* that one-third of a nation which lies between
the West Coast and the central plains, from Canada to Mexico, remains
little more, in the literary world, than an old joke. A vast, grand but empty
stage whereon cavort, from time to time, the caricatures of myth and legend, noble cowboys and ecological Indians, sentimental gunfighters and
whores with vaginas of pure gold. Hollywood on location. Whores, bores,
and melodrama. Who can overcome such a curse? [AR, xix; italics Abbey's]

Fully committed to the West's frontiers, Abbey has fought the unfortunate curse to a virtual stand-off, drawing the battlelines, and
stepping across wherever and whenever he chooses. "It may turn
out in the long run," he adjudicates, that "the best writers on the
West were the scientists and explorers," those who stretched the
frontiers first physically and then imaginatively, "men like John
Wesley Powell and Clarence Dutton" [AR, xx]. The former, more
than the novelists mentioned previously, found a Southwest landscape akin to Abbey's.
   The first man to explore the length of the Colorado and the first
writer to capture its grandeur in words, John Wesley Powell epitomizes the skill and spirit Abbey respects. The twentieth-century
author refers to his nineteenth-century forerunner numerous times,
quoting him not only in *The Hidden Canyon* where Powell plays a
major role, but in *Desert Solitaire* and in *The Journey Home* as well.
Indeed, he explicitly announces that "my favorite [of those nineteenth-century souls who belong in a cult of the wild] is, of course,
Major J. Wesley Powell" [DS, 191], and affirms that *The Exploration
of the Colorado River* by the one-armed adventurer is a "classic, my
favorite western book" [JH, 189], an essential accompaniment on
any float trip. Characterizing Powell's prose "in panegyric accent,"
Abbey cites lines that have appealed to him as detailed reminders
of the sensuous complexity of the Grand Canyon—its "forms un-

rivaled even by the mountains, colors that vie with sunsets, and sounds that span the diapason from tempest to tinkling raindrop, from cataract to bubbling fountain" [JWP, in DS, 192]. Elsewhere, Abbey assesses the explorer's overall written accomplishment. "In page after page Powell strove to describe a kind of landscape neither he nor any of his men had ever seen before. He came closer than anyone else to evoking through words the character of the canyonlands. Yet the strangeness of it can barely be suggested through language. In fact, the land can hardly be understood through the eyes. The imagination cannot comprehend what is so remote from all previous experience—'rock forms that we do not understand' " [JH, 200–201]. But Abbey and Powell keep trying.

What the twentieth-century river-runner admires most in his predecessor, however, is not Powell's artistic merit but the man himself, his courage and fortitude, his probing and inquisitive spirit, his perceptual responses to the scenes unfolding before him. At the close of an essay called "Down the River with Major Powell," Ed salutes his mentor—"old comrade, one-armed vision seeker with your wooden boats, your moldy bacon and your silted flour, your gallant crew, and your never-dying romance with the world" [JH, 201–202]—and ends with a quotation from the major that could be voiced by Abbey too. "We have an unknown distance yet to run, an unknown river to explore" [JWP, in JH, 202]. Pervading the journeys of both men, the invincible essence they have in common leads them away from the beaten tracks and directs them toward roads not yet traveled by others, roads both physical and perceptual. While many now have explored the canyons of the Colorado and the surrounding desert environment, and others have written about the special Southwest beauty, few have done both as successfully as Abbey and Powell. Kindred souls, so to speak, the two are caught by their needs to investigate the unknown and to write about the experiences. When Ed suggests, "the century that divides in time our trip from Major Powell's has dwindled to nothing, a mere abstract point in the temporal" [JH, 196], he speaks metaphorically for Abbey too. What divides the major and his modern counterpart is more a matter of detail than of spirit.

In the twentieth century, the western essayist closest in spirit is Joseph Wood Krutch, as Abbey himself affirms. "I admired [him] because he was so gentle, rational, learned, and wise a man. He

abhorred the empty spaces of windy rhetoric and never indulged"
[AR, xx]. He also respects the land. Any one of Krutch's books
about the desert landscape—*The Desert Year* (1951), *The Voice of the
Desert* (1955), *Grand Canyon* (1958), for example—depicts a familiar
scene. When he announces his reaction to his first desert vista
("there was something so unexpected in the combination of brilliant sun and high, thin, dry air with a seemingly limitless expanse
of sky and earth"[12]), when he explains he is "trying somehow to
take possession"[13] of the country around him, when he ventures
through what he calls "Undiscovered Country" with perceptive
enthusiasm, or when he describes what he sees in loving detail
("a family of Gambel's quail strolling about like barnyard fowl—the
babies much like baby chicks, the mother with one coquettish plume
curled out from the top of her head and bobbing before her eyes"[14]),
Krutch reveals an awareness of his surroundings much like Abbey's.
Both men derive pleasure from naming and cataloguing the desert's
animals and plants because the process, for them, is a way of turning the alien into the familiar, and both men also derive pleasure
from a personal intimacy with those creatures. Krutch plays "Peep-
ing Tom to the wooing of two lizards"[15]; Abbey voyeuristically
watches his courting gopher snakes. Krutch rescues a drowning
bat from a neighbor's swimming pool; Abbey spends half a day
digging a cow out of canyon quicksand. And Krutch devotes a
lengthy discussion to a single plant, marveling at its color, its water-
storage capacity, its overall structure, just as Abbey frequently does.

To use the term *sacrality* for Krutch's vision of the landscape would
be a mistake, however, for when he writes of the desert's spirit he,
unlike Abbey, forthrightly accedes to a supreme omnipresent deity.
When he chooses a lone plant that expresses "the spirit of the
Sonoran Desert—one which combines oddness of form and habit
with the courage to flourish under seemingly impossible conditions,
and which combines also the defensive fierceness of thorns with
the spectacular, unexpected beauty of brilliant flowers"[16]—the oco-
tillo—he intends something quite different from Abbey's "hovering wings." He means the metaphorical, rather than the metaphysical, analogy.

Nevertheless, Krutch, a refugee from academic life, acknowledges
as Abbey does, the crucial role played by the land in teaching man
the source of his own energies. "Not to have known—as most men

have not—either the mountain or the desert is not to have known one's self. Not to have known one's self is to have known no one."[17] In fact, Krutch fancies that "deserts suggest and confirm a system of values,"[18] a system of which he approves. In the desert "the very fauna and flora proclaim that one can have a great deal of certain things while having very little of others." Using notions of abundance and satiety, Krutch then compares desert economy with human appetites, questioning, as he writes, "the assumption that endless progress implies the endless multiplication of goods and gadgets." Less angry than Abbey but no less distressed by man's worship of Growth, Krutch fashions his arguments persuasively and repeats them in Abbey's 1968 interview with him.

"Whenever I saw one of the billboards with the slogan 'Help Tucson Grow' I think, God forbid,"[19] Krutch begins his critique of the cities of the Southwest. Then he turns to the wilderness itself, and to the parks that are supposed to preserve it. "Too many people use their automobiles not as a means to get to the parks but rather use the parks as a place to take their automobiles. What our national parks need are not more good roads but more bad roads." "Bad roads?" the interviewer leads him on. "Yes," Krutch replies, "to act as a filtering device. There's nothing like a good bad dirt road to screen out the slightly interested and invite in the genuinely interested. And it's perfectly fair and democratic." One can almost hear Abbey chuckle. After that, he deftly steers Krutch toward affirmation of the many beliefs the two men hold in common—a thirst for solitude, a love for the desert scene, a distrust of mechanized growth, a need for the desert's space.

However, Abbey's radical solutions for dealing with environmental issues outdistance Krutch's conservative approach. Where the one would completely quash "industrial tourism," for example, the other would only curb its proliferation. The final chapter of Krutch's *Grand Canyon* advances his theory of national parks, using his analysis of the north and south rims to support contentions that while new "Tasty Teepees" should not be allowed, the current limited development of the two rims is acceptable, and that while nearby mining desecrates the environment, the park still proves a sanctuary for those who venture off its pavement. Although Abbey might partially agree, he advocates far stricter regulations, calling for the total elimination of cars where Krutch only wants their presence controlled, and chastizing the Park Service where Krutch praises them for doing a good job. "Grand Canyon is still what it should be," alleges Krutch in 1958,

one of the most accessible of the nature reserves. Merely as a spectacle it is popularly recognized as one of the "wonders of the world" and could not reasonably be denied even to those who desire no more than to look at it and go away, satisfied that another item on the list has been checked off. Yet despite the tremendous number of visitors, the inaccessibility of all but a very limited part has prevented it from being spoiled as Yellowstone has been—to the extent that at Yellowstone one is reminded of man and his works at least as often as of nature's.

At the canyon most of the visitors willingly confine themselves to a very restricted area, and if that area is by now almost a mere resort, there is a great deal left that is not.[20]

After listing places where men can still escape from man, Krutch concludes that "the Grand Canyon as it now stands and is now administered represents what is probably the best possible compromise between the desires and needs of the different classes of people who visit it and the limitations which have to be imposed if it is not to degenerate into a resort differing from other resorts only in being provided with a different backdrop."[21]

Surely Abbey would disagree with this summation. First, he would scoff at any notion that the Grand Canyon, or any other wilderness area, "could not reasonably be denied" to the people. In Abbey's world, it and all other pristine land could rightfully remain in splendid isolation forever. Second, he would never agree that the canyon remains unspoiled. In his eyes, every car diminishes its sanctum. Third, he would consider the Park Service's role neither well conceived nor well administered. Quite the contrary, as he proves by pointing to the South Rim's degeneration into a series of blacktop parking lots connected by a superhighway—"it is no longer easy . . . to get away from the roar of motor traffic" [DS, 52]. Finally, he distrusts the government's long-range vision. He not only ridicules the "Natural Money-Mints," suggesting that "with super-sensitive antennae these operatives from the C. of C. look into red canyons and see only green, stand among flowers snorting at the smell of money, and hear, while thunderstorms rumble over mountains, the fall of a dollar bill on motel carpeting" [DS, 57], but he questions governmental integrity too. "Toroweap Point in the remote northwest corner of the park, at present still unimpaired (though accessible), has not been forgotten; the plans are in the files for developing even that wild and lovely corner" [DS, 52]. In short, Abbey's words are angry ones, immoderate compared to Krutch's, at once more forceful and less credulous. Not only when he denounces the forces of industrial tourism but whenever he debates against environmental usurpers, the amiable anarchist sounds venomous if the landscape is endangered.

Here, then, is the major difference between Abbey and Krutch, between Abbey and the earlier essayists who wrote of America's open spaces. Although every one of them respected the land and supported its protection, no one was as outspoken, and explicitly irate and fanatical. Noisier by far than those predecessors, perhaps because he sees more damage done to the earth in the late twentieth century, Abbey advances a point of view consistent with his fears for the land's survival. He sounds more cynical too, because the passage of time has already substantiated many of his predictions. Although Abbey agrees with Thoreau, and even with Henry Adams, that technology has led America to a new perception of itself, to a new system of values distressingly removed from nature and art, he goes one step further. In tones of blasphemous irony, he turns on the culprits and demands that America set itself straight —dismantle the dynamo, as it were. Few literary essayists have sounded so noxiously antiestablishment.

Abbey's belligerence often dictates the direction of his road, but his affection for the land usually straightens out the track. Even though his rebellious tone separates him from the masses, his sense of sacrality, or at least his respect for nature's inherent energy, connects him to his fellows. Other writers have been equally committed to their environments, and while the degree of affinity, of mysticism, or of religiosity may differ from one to another, they have in common their sensitivity to the landscape's spirit. Joseph Wood Krutch, for example, approaches the subject on two levels, separating his semiscientific observations from a more abstract discussion of God and writing of the desert's spirit in metaphor or simile. Annie Dillard also writes from a dual position, despite a radiant, overriding transcendentalism that makes Abbey "nervous. It seems . . . the word 'mystery,' not capitalized, should suffice" [AR, xx], he mutters. *Pilgrim at Tinker Creek* (1974) concentrates on a microscopic biological world while *Holy the Firm* (1977) openly espouses her faith in a supreme being, so the reader must go from book to book to ascertain the full range of her spirituality. John Wesley Powell, on the other hand, acknowledges the mystery and the emotional pull of the canyons—"the Great Unknown"—without ever directing his focus far from a pointed observance of the rocks themselves. Several other examples come to mind—Wallace Stegner listening to his sounds of mountain water, Mary Austin describing her land of little rain, John Muir peering over the edge of Yosemite Falls. Each communicates a personalized response to nature's omnipotence and spirit that resembles Abbey's in general cognition of sacrality, yet differs in specific detail.

Of these writers, it is John Muir whose prose made the first effusive sounds of environmentalist nature writing. His every word articulates a vision of ecological energy. "Every clear, frosty morning loud sounds are heard booming and reverberating from side to side of the Valley at intervals of a few minutes, beginning soon after sunrise and continuing an hour or two," Muir explains. "The strange thunder is made by the fall of sections of ice formed of spray that is frozen on a face of the cliff along the sides of the Upper Yosemite Fall—a sort of crystal plaster, a foot or two thick, cracked off by the sunbeams, awakening all the Valley like cock-crowing, announcing the finest weather, shouting aloud Nature's infinite industry and love of hard work in creating beauty."[22] Muir cannot refrain from unleashing a spontaneous overflow of his own powerful emotions, so even when he gives factual information about what he sees or hears, he waxes poetic—"cracked off by the sunbeams," "shouting aloud Nature's infinite industry."

More than most essayists of his reputation, Muir resorts to the pathetic fallacy to make plants and animals come alive before the reader's eyes. After he measures and calculates the proportions of the California sequoias, he notes: "The giants become more and more irrepressibly exuberant, heaving their massive crowns into the sky from every ridge and slope, waving onward in graceful compliance with the complicated topography of the land."[23] After he compares them to architectural structures, he turns to their companions. "One soon becomes acquainted with a new species of pine and fir and spruce as with friendly people, shaking their outstretched branches like shaking hands and fondling their little ones, while the venerable aboriginal sequoia, ancient of other days, keeps you at a distance, looking as strange in aspect and behavior among its neighbor trees as would the mastodon among the homely bears and deer. Only the Sierra juniper is at all like it, standing rigid and unconquerable on glacier pavements for thousands of years, grim and silent, with an air of antiquity about as pronounced as that of the sequoia."[24] Animation and personification mark most of Muir's descriptions, just as reverence and awe characterize his vision of the landscape's powers.

Although Abbey can at times sound as euphuistic, he controls his prose more than the nineteenth-century ecologist did. A passage from *Desert Solitaire*, describing Ed's juniper, shows how.

My favorite juniper stands before me glittering shaggily in the sunrise, ragged roots clutching at the rock on which it feeds, rough dark boughs bedecked with a rash, with a shower of turquoise-colored berries. A female, this ancient grandmother of a tree may be three hundred years old; growing very slowly, the juniper seldom attains a height greater than fifteen or twenty feet even in favorable locations. My juniper, though still fruitful and full of vigor, is at the same time partly dead: one half of the divided trunk holds skyward a sapless claw, a branch without leaf or bark, baked by the sun and scoured by the wind to a silver finish, where magpies and ravens like to roost when I am not too close.

I've had this tree under surveillance ever since my arrival at Arches, hoping to learn something from it, to discover the significance in its form, to make a connection through its life with whatever falls beyond. Have failed. The essence of the juniper continues to elude me unless, as I presently suspect, its surface is also the essence. Two living things on the same earth, respiring in a common medium, we contact one another but without direct communication. Intuition, sympathy, empathy, all fail to guide me into the heart of this being—if it has a heart. [DS, 30–31]

We see Ed's juniper in more detail than we see Muir's trees. Its branch with "a sapless claw," its "silver finish," its "rough dark boughs bedecked with a rash"—even though such phrases personify the inanimate object—bring mind and eye together as Muir's descriptions do not. Whereas Muir *tells* us about the "venerable aboriginal sequoia," Abbey *shows* us the "ancient grandmother" standing before him; while Muir's juniper stands "rigid and unconquerable," Abbey's "glitter[s] shaggily." The author of *Desert Solitaire* uses concrete adjectives and lively verbs which shake his tree awake while the author of *The Yosemite* relies on pathetic fallacies, imprecise abstractions like "shaking hands" and "fondling their little ones," to convince the reader of animation. When Abbey writes about the ethereal qualities of his tree, he does so concretely. Ed's juniper breathes the common air, and it may or may not have a heart. Muir's trees, on the other hand, are more distant and remote, as if he were venerating their stature rather than touching them up close. A matter of degree, Abbey's sacrality comes alive because his prose comes alive, while Muir's more formal mysticism sounds stiff and more removed.

Nevertheless, each man reveals a curiosity about his environment that leads him to consider its essence deeply. When Muir leans over the edge of Yosemite Falls where "the view is perfectly free down into the heart of the bright irised throng of comet-like streamers into which the whole ponderous volume of the fall separates, two or three hundred feet below the brow,"[25] he does so in a spirit of inquiry like Abbey's. But Abbey looks "down there in the rocks," focusing on the sacred energy that he *sees:* "Down . . . and . . . down and . . . down, your mind falls to the green pool in a sandy basin far below. Perennial springs flow there, under this overhanging spout we lie upon; we can see the glaze and glitter of a stream snaking through jungles of willow, box elder, redbud, and Fremont poplar toward the Escalante River somewhere beyond, hidden in its profound meanders" [AR, 119–120]. Muir focuses on how he *feels:* "So glorious a display of pure wildness . . . is terribly impressive."[26] Abbey's view may be just as impressive, but instead of announcing its wildness he leads the reader to the same conclusion via a more precise description.

Nineteenth-century conventions may account for the qualities of Muir's prose—its flowery exuberance, its reliance on catchwords like "sublime," "awesome," or "venerable," its diction and syntax "cracked off by the sunbeams." Mary Austin, writing at approximately the same time and place, displays similar turns of phrase and philosophy when she looks at her environment. "It is a pity we have let the gift of lyric improvisation die out," she avows in *The Land of Little Rain* (1903). "Sitting islanded on some gray peak above the encompassing wood, the soul is lifted up to sing the Iliad of the pines."[27] Like Muir, Austin sings eloquently of nature, her own prose a melodic example of lyricism and hymn-making. Like Muir, too, she leans heavily on the pathetic fallacy to enliven her vision—"the young rivers swaying with the force of their running, they sing and shout and trumpet at the falls," while the trees "are home-dwellers, like the tender fluttered, sisterhood of quaking asps.''[28] Furthermore, she acknowledges her affinity with Muir's mode of spiritualizing the land. "Weather does not happen," she proclaims. "It is the visible manifestation of the Spirit moving itself in the void. It gathers itself together under the heavens; rains, snows, yearns mightily in wind, smiles; and the Weather Bureau, situated advantageously for that very business, taps the record on his instruments and going out on the streets denies his God, not having gathered the sense of what he has seen. Hardly anybody takes account of the fact that John Muir, who knows more of mountain storms than any other, is a devout man."[29] And Mary Austin is a devout woman.

She is different from Muir, though, and more like Edward Abbey, in the significance she gives to human beings in nature's scheme. T. M. Pearce's introduction to the Zia paperback edition of *The Land of Little Rain* places Austin in a group of writers that includes Thoreau and Muir but adds: "her world was 'peopled,' not empty. The farm lands near her home in Illinois not only called her attention to the sights and sounds of birds, the patterns of leaves and flowers, and the maze of forest pathways, but they also brought the mystery of forces sustaining all growth as a shelter and sustenance for the human race. The arid regions of the West, too, were not just a panorama of sand, bunchgrass, and wildlife, but an expression of energy to which both people and animals were related."[30] Pearce's final sentence is crucial. Abbey's personal histories look at the West's arid regions much as Austin's essays do, envisioning how the panorama before him expresses not only its own inherent energies but the energies of people and animals too. The dead man at Grandview Point is as important as the canyons themselves when Ed tries to grasp "the plow of mortality [that] drives through the stubble, turns over rocks and sod and weeds to cover the old, the worn-out, the husks, shells, empty seedpods and sapless roots, clearing the field for the next crop" [DS, 242]; Austin's pocket hunter and her basket maker, likewise, are two hardy souls who contribute as much to the desert's essence as the desert does to theirs. If "sacrality" can appropriately characterize her thoughts, then, it is as Pearce says "an expression of energy" to which people and animals and the panorama of the land itself are all related. Abbey, less inclined than either Austin or Muir to speak straightforwardly of God, would find her sacred sense at least partially compatible with his own.

More to the point, though, he would find her sense of the desert distinctly consonant. Like Powell, like Krutch, and like Abbey himself, Austin intuitively loves the arid vistas. "If one is inclined to wonder at first how so many dwellers came to be in the loneliest land that ever came out of God's hands, what they do there and why they stay, one does not wonder so much after having lived there. None other than this long brown land lays such a hold on the affections. The rainbow hills, the tender bluish mists, the luminous radiance of the spring, have the lotus charm. They trick the sense of time, so that once inhabiting there you always mean to go away without quite realizing that you have not done it."[31] Abbey, who first saw "the land of his deepest imaginings" in 1944, has never left the desert either; his spirit, along with Powell's, Austin's and Krutch's, never will. Abbey recognizes the desert's eternal magnetism and, like the author of *The Land of Little Rain*, knows he cannot escape its pull. "Even after years of intimate contact and search this quality of strangeness in the desert remains undiminished. Transparent and intangible as sunlight, yet always and everywhere present, it lures a man on and on, from the red-walled canyons to the smoke-blue ranges beyond, in a futile but fascinating quest for the great, unimaginable treasure which the desert seems to promise. Once caught by this golden lure you become a prospector for life, condemned, doomed, exalted" [DS, 272].

Many American essayists have been "caught by this golden lure" and have become life-long pocket hunters themselves. Everett Ruess, lost near the Escalante almost half a century ago, wrote in his last letter before he disappeared: "I have not tired of the wilderness; rather I enjoy its beauty and the vagrant life I lead more keenly all the time. I prefer the saddle to the street car, and the star-sprinkled sky to the roof, the obscure and difficult trail leading into the unknown to any paved highway, and the deep peace of the wild to the discontent bred by cities. Do you blame me then for staying here where I feel that I belong and am one with the world about me?"[32] Abbey, who admires Ruess, would never blame him—he knows instinctively why the young man wrote as he did and understands the paradox of his exaltation and consequent doom. Colin Fletcher, author of *The Man Who Walked Through Time* (1967), is another who has followed the desert's relentless tug, caught by the lure that has made him "a prospector for life" too. Yet it is safe to say that none of these writers has articulated his sense of the land quite as Edward Abbey has. Certain tenets characterize Abbey's thoughts as well as the other writers'—a belief in wilderness as a necessity for life, a dismay at inroads (in the name of progress) man has made against the land, a conviction that man must respect the earth's sacred energy and so must reverse the present trend toward growth at any cost, an unwavering love for what is wild. But two distinctive signs mark Abbey's road as his alone. One is the pictorial quality of his prose; the other is the direction of his vision. That is, his personal style and his created world of the romance set him apart from other American nature writers of the past one hundred fifty years.

The two, style and vision, are inseparable. Muir's reverent awe shines through aloof, deferential, sometimes bombastic sentences; Evert Ruess's romanticism reflects off its own glittering abstractions; and Austin's living landscape—its "hills, rounded, blunt, burned, squeezed up out of chaos, chrome and vermilion painted, aspiring to the snowline"[33]—almost breathes. A detailed look at their rhetorics reveals their characteristic visions too, because each writer's style leads to the figurative dimension of his thoughts.

Abbey, perhaps more than any of the others, lives comfortably within the raiment of his prose. Characteristically he writes in fluid sentences with refreshing images. Often he chooses combinations of words that invite us to look at our surroundings in such unexpected ways that, even when he describes a scene we have viewed a thousand times, we see the picture recast.

Off in the east an isolated storm is boiling over the desert, a mass of lavender clouds bombarding the earth with lightning and trailing curtains of rain. The distance is so great that I cannot hear the thunder. Between here and there and me and the mountains is the canyon wilderness, the hoodoo land of spire and pillar and pinnacle where no man lives, and where the river flows, unseen, through the blue-black trenches in the rock. [DS, 218]

A storm boils over a desert landscape, as it might in any other purple sage paragraph, yet Abbey achieves novelty. Lavender clouds "bombard," spires and pillars and pinnacles melt into a "hoodoo land," the river flows through "blue-black trenches in the rock," and thunder does not boom, echo, or reverberate. While such word choices may appear ordinary, the combination is not. Colors and shapes pictorially blend and clash to create the hoodoo land of Abbey's vision, the romancer's realm where Ed and the reader move in tandem between the red world and the green.

What Abbey creates, then, is not a pictorial imitation of the canyons before him, but a stylistic incantation of their spirit. "What I hope to evoke through words," he explains in *Cactus Country*, "is the way things *feel* [italics his] on a stormy desert afternoon, the exact shade of color in shadows on the warm rock, the brightness of October, the rust and silence and echoes of human history along dusty desert roads, the fragrance of burning mesquite, and a few other simple, ordinary, inexplicable things like that" [CC, 21]. When he first realized the enormity of the task he set for himself—"language makes a mighty loose net with which to go fishing for simple facts, when facts are infinite"—he also circumscribed his own ends. "Not imitation but evocation has been the goal" [DS, x]. Fortunately, Abbey has the means to achieve that evocation, the strength of his own skill. A writer equally at ease in many guises, he can change his style at will—to match a photographer, to suit an editor —he can move smoothly from descriptive to narrative to argumentative prose, he can switch back and forth between glib one-liners and extended pictorial paragraphs, he can capture in words the essence of what he feels.

He does so by means of a particularity that engages the reader's senses with his own. "Sand sage or old man sage, a lustrous wind-blown blend of silver and blue and aquamarine, gleams in the distance, the feathery stems flowing like hair" [DS, 31]; "the instant redneck" swallows "a sweet, green provincial brew mass-produced from reprocessed sewage water near Denver" [AR, 165]; "the solution to pollution is dilution," he quips sarcastically when corporate smokestacks spew their filth in an ever-widening circle [JH, 155]; "an hour later the outer world is gone; we float on the dream-like river down into a subterranean country of water and walls, with fluted gray limestone at the river's edge, tumbled boulders, banks of sand where the mesquite grows (leafing out in spring green), clusters of bamboo twenty feet tall, thorny acacia in golden bloom spicing the air with a fragrance like that of apple blossoms, everything illuminated by a soft, filtered, indirect, refracted light. A tunnel of love, while it lasts" [AR, 100]. Whether he means to be witty or wise, satiric or solemn, pictorially evocative or simply provocative, Abbey presents details that galvanize our responses. Feathery wind-blown aquamarine, a sweet green brew, or spicy acacia and fluted gray limestone—such perceptions, based on the senses, move the reader to internalize the evocation. Even a cheap slogan like "the solution to pollution is dilution" does the same. When Abbey's prose is at its best, it draws an audience toward his world as if they were prospectors following the "golden lure" of his words.

Unfortunately, his greatest strength turns, on occasion, into a debilitating weakness. Sometimes his tongue runs away with his thoughts, and even though he recognizes the loss of control, he is unwilling, or unable, to stop. A particularly egregious paragraph from *Abbey's Road* begins, "The train crept on," and then Ed leaps onto his own bandwagon. "Wheels roll, you say, they do not and cannot creep. What do you know, insolent reader? Eh, what do you know, you crass whelp of a dingo bitch, you foal of a hunchback camel, you sore-eyed, scab-covered noseless dropping of a syphilitic two-dollar Baton Rouge, Louisiana whore? I ask you. The train *crept* on, I say" [AR, 50–51]. The reader finds such treatment undeserved, although Abbey defends himself by rationalizing, "The purpose of the literary device illustrated above is to suggest to the reader a state of extreme boredom without at the time lulling the reader asleep." His alibi is weak, an apologia lost in a spate of verbiage.

This prolixity is the only one of *Jonathan Troy's* serious flaws that plagues Abbey's later writing. Occasionally, when describing a landscape, arguing a point, or just trying to be funny, he lets his own verbal energies take control. A problem encountered in the picture books is a result of this excessiveness too—the overly romanticized portions occur in effusive passages. When Abbey's words explode in all directions at once, or when he tries to quantify his emotions, his writing loses some of its natural power. Fortunately, this happens rarely; in fact, the lapses would not be so noticeable if the rest of his prose were not so strong and disciplined.

An excerpt from *Cactus Country* shows what Abbey can accomplish in a single paragraph when he enforces restraint. In six well-balanced sentences, he pictures a scene both graphically and imaginatively, communicates some factual information, makes an evaluative judgment, and touches on sacrality as well (or at least indicates a kind of vigor).

Scrub cattle ranging through the bush galloped off like gnus and wildebeests at our approach. I never saw such weird, scrawny, pied, mottled, humped, long-horned and camel-necked brutes trying to pass as domestic livestock. Most looked like a genetic hash of Hereford, Charolais, Brahman, Angus, moose, ibex, tapir and nightmare. Weaned on cactus, snakeweed and thistle, they showed the gleam of the sun through the translucent barrel of their rib cages. But they could run, they were alive, not only alive but vigorous. I was tempted to think, watching their angular hind ends jouncing away through the dust, that the meat on those critters, if you could find any, might just taste better than the aerated, water-injected, hormone-inflated beef we Americans get from today's semi-automated feed lots in the States. [CC, 143]

The reader can see those scruffy cattle, can smell, hear, almost feel them, can even taste a chewy steak, because the prose brings the cows to life, "their angular hind ends jouncing away through the dust." This paragraph is no different from thousands of others Abbey has written where lively words arrest the senses and a romancer's overlay tops the picture.

Of course the latter sets him apart even more than the quality of his prose. He looks at the contemporary West with the same optimism that drove the pioneers across the land—indeed, through the same rose-colored glasses worn by the Zane Greys of literature —seeing in the open spaces a place where unlimited opportunities exist for all. But unlike others of the "strike-it-rich" vision, he knows the frontier trail has changed directions in the twentieth century. Finite natural resources shape its twists and turns, and a need for freedom and wilderness greater than a need for growth and progress directs its course. Abbey insists, in strong language, on a renewed American dream of temperance and conservation. "Don't talk to me about other worlds, separate realities, lost continents, or invisible realms—I know where I belong," he maintains. "Heaven is home. Utopia is here. Nirvana is now" [AR, 129]. Modern man can still realize the dream, if only he will stop, and look, and listen, and see.

Walking up the trail to my lookout tower last night, I saw the new moon emerge from a shoal of clouds and hang for a time beyond the black silhouette of a shaggy, giant Douglas fir. I stopped to look. And what I saw was the moon—the moon itself, nothing else; and the tree, alive and conscious in its own spiral of time; and my hands, palms upward, raised toward the sky. We were there. We *are*. That is what we know. This is all we can know. And each such moment holds more magic and miracle and mystery than we—so long as we are less than gods—shall ever be able to understand. Holds all that we could possibly need—if only we could see. [AR, 129; italics Abbey's]

Speaking (to use Austin's words) "as one lover of it can give to another,"[34] Abbey reflects the affection of Austin for the land, the reverence of Muir, the respect of Thoreau, the enthusiasm of Krutch. But his design is his own, a careful crafting of landscape into art, a vision of the contemporary world transformed into a better one imagined. "If only we could see. . . ."

Abbey's road leads straight to the romancer's abode—"Heaven is home. Utopia is here. Nirvana is now." On its journey, the course tracks aggressively through the American West, tearing down the survey stakes that mark further desecration of the land and erecting signposts that point out damages already done. Ed makes sure the reader stays beside him. Even as he threads his way carefully between the green world and the red, he reminds us constantly of the place at the end of the trail. "Years ago a fellow ranger and I were exploring a canyon in what is now Arches National Park. I stepped right over a three-inch, elegantly chipped spearhead; the fellow behind me found it. I'd been looking at the sky and landscape; he kept his eyes on the ground, watching his step. He is now superintendent of an important national park" [DI, 204]. Ed is not, nor does he want to be. He is the reader's guide into the romancer's world where the landscape and sky show Abbey a sacred vision of the earth and of man's possibilities for happiness there. "Balance, that's the secret. Moderate extremism. The best of both worlds" [DS, 298], red and green. In the name of "moderate extremism," narrator and author steer an illusory course through a West of their own making, where "the tangible and the mythical become the same."

Part III

Cross Country

The Later Fiction

Although Edward Abbey published more nonfiction than fiction during the 1970s, he continued writing both kinds of narratives. Three novelistic tales have followed at intervals since the publication of *Desert Solitaire* in 1968, books that repeat and refine the themes, concerns, and designs of Abbey's previous books. Like the earlier fiction, the three introduce stylized individualists who both anachronistically and anarchistically rebel against an increasingly hostile twentieth century. More like the nonfiction, though, they resolve their protagonists' plights, although somewhat indirectly, as their author further defines his distinctive vision of past, present, and future in the American West.

The three books differ enormously in tone. The first, *Black Sun* (1971), comes closer to tragedy than any of Abbey's other writing. A pastoral love story that ends almost before it begins, this brief and cryptic tale follows the passions of a man who has opted out of the contemporary scene and out of relationships with his fellows. Even when a path to Abbey's world opens before him, his emotional paralysis holds him to a few tentative steps and then dooms him to an elegiac existence. The fact that ecstasy tantalizes him but cannot sustain him makes the story increasingly painful, until it ends in an excruciating hell from which there is no exit.

At the opposite end of an emotional continuum lies the rollicking comedy of *The Monkey Wrench Gang* (1975). Here Abbey tries another approach to his visionary world, a track marked by a joie de vivre that leads humorously past the Western conventions rebutted by his other writing. Whereas Will Gatlin, *Black Sun's* protagonist, retreats from the complications of twentieth-century life, the gang members rush pell-mell into the fray to deliver their own contemporary brand of frontier justice. Their boundless energy explodes into Abbey's most popular piece of fiction as the four eccentrics systematically attack any equipment or edifice they dislike. More than Abbey's other fictional characters, they appreciate the earth's sacrality and do their utmost to protect the land. Their battlecry—"Keep it like it was!"—rings through the pages of this propagandistic assault on all the mad machines that savage the twentieth-century scene.

While *Black Sun* casts a shadowed vision across the modern landscape, *The Monkey Wrench Gang* relights the way with an energetic and comic renewal. But Abbey's latest fiction, *Good News* (1980), expends a different wattage, a magic lantern of pain and laughter that subsumes both comedy and tragedy into a satiric construct. For the first time since his earliest writing days, Abbey moves away from the romance design toward a different kind of artistic universe. Dark, hostile, chaotic, the ironic milieu of *Good News* transfers Abbey's vision from the past and present into a bleak and devastated future, a fearful prophecy of what may lie ahead if modern man cannot control his appetites. It also transforms romantic desert scenery into naturalistic deserted scenes, as Abbey's imagination ranges into nether regions more rigidly conceived than any artistically malleable world. Despite its gloomy set, however, *Good News* does convey some "good news," a gospel of people helping people and a predilection for commitment.

Each of these three fictions advocates a defined vision of man's potential that fully complements Abbey's nonfiction exhortations. Notions of respect—for the land, for a sacred power, for oneself, and for others—are the cornerstones that support each tale. As divergent as the books appear to be, each finally stands in Abbey's world, that imaginary kingdom where Abbey's deepest beliefs find shape and substance. The three intrinsically suppose a sacred vision of the land. Will Gatlin lives in the wilderness, the Gang vows to preserve and protect what is left, and the survivors of *Good News* comment repeatedly on the mountain sentinels that guard a ruined city. The three fictions also articulate imaginatively the dismay, indeed the horror, Abbey feels as he watches his twentieth-century contemporaries. While the first tale indirectly condemns modernity, the second attacks it physically. Through a format of wish fulfillment, *The Monkey Wrench Gang* brings its author's dreams to fruition, blasting myth and machine together into the polluted Southwest skies. Then *Good News* turns that dream to nightmare. Parodying the romance, its ironic mode signals the demolition of Abbey's own best writing design and the devastation of the American West itself.

These three fictions steadily stretch nonfiction issues past their tangible limits. From the realm of the moon-eyed horse and the land of the techno-industrial complex, Abbey wanders farther into a twilight zone of his imagination, toward a universe where reality and romance meet head-to-head, and beyond that, to a place where red and green finally can fuse in some way. There, just possibly, contemporary man can escape the worst of present-day life and happily employ the best. There, for the first time in his fiction, Abbey gets close "to the West of [his] deepest imaginings—the place where the tangible and the mythical become the same" [JH, 5].

What makes these novelistic ventures different from Abbey's earlier attempts, in fact, is this philosophic assuredness, a quality best exemplified in their three denouements. Whereas both *The Brave Cowboy* and *Fire on the Mountain* ended precipitiously and unsatisfactorily, the later books, like the nonfiction, presume a final cohesiveness. Each does not necessarily end "happily-ever-after," but each closes with a definite sense of narrative management and philosophic control. The author, not some amorphous fate, draws explicable and justifiable conclusions. The truck that hit Jack Burns and the heart attack that killed John Vogelin were devices that effectively stopped the action but resolved few of the intellectual questions raised by the two stories. Such life-taking inventions do not mortally thwart Abbey's later protagonists. Instead, the author stymies his characters by natural, believable forces that cause them to make choices and to affirm their individual value systems. The Grand Canyon stops Will Gatlin, both physically and metaphorically, the Maze and Bishop Love arrest the Monkey Wrench Gang's extralegal activities, while the disintegration of the modern world halts the men and women of *Good News*.

None of these characters is permanently stymied, however, for

Abbey's cyclical view of history, of mankind, and of the earth itself now dominates his prose. Writing increasingly in the continuous present to indicate a constant flow from past to future, he alternates a look at man's apparent inability to learn from the past with a prayer that everyone do so. Sometimes literary devices point this out to the reader—*Black Sun's* repeated shifts of verb tense, for example, or the resurrections of Jack Burns' from book to book project tangible kinds of continuity. But more often Abbey uses intangibles, such as the consequences of individual failings or the results of offenses committed against the land, to show how past practices can compound present-day problems into future monstrosities. Thus his later fictions effectively reconstrue those personal and environmental issues that were important to the nonfiction.

A large measure, in fact, of the excellence found in *Black Sun*, *The Monkey Wrench Gang*, and *Good News* comes from their forceful tones. Beyond each fictional perspective lies a limitless mental purview which, because more down-to-earth than escapist, provokes an audience involvement more intellectual than emotional. One cannot read these last three fictions without looking past the stylized characters and their uncomplicated actions, past the intricate structural manipulations, to apprehend at last the defined vision so important to Abbey's world. "Everything in it is real and actually happened," the author joshes. "And it all began just one year from today" [MWG, vi]. There in the West of his deepest imaginings, any part of this modern romancer's vision—threat or promise, nightmare or dream—could come true.

8

The Descent

Black Sun

A quiet and sobering book, *Black Sun* (1971) is more poignant and deeply introspective than any of Abbey's others. While its characters and setting somewhat resemble those of *The Brave Cowboy* and *Fire on the Mountain*—with stylized although human figures and a shadowed although real milieu—its presentation differs. Abbey adroitly controls his prose in this fourth work of fiction, employing a comprehensive narrative vision that blends both the story and its author's point of view into a thematic whole. This romance considers carefully one man's sense of self, of love, of his relationships with others. Set in the past, the present, and the future, its narrative flows through a continuous present that twists the fragile tale from a dream into an allegorical nightmare and then releases it into a somnambulance where some incubus of fate apparently will haunt him forever. "We are deep in the wild now, deep in the lonely, sweet, remote, primeval world, far far from anywhere familiar to men and women" [DS, 189], Abbey wrote while floating down the Colorado in *Desert Solitaire*. He might have been foreshadowing *Black Sun's* descent.

The tale is a love story with an unlikely cast of characters and a heart-wrenching ending. It tells of a short-lived, passionate affair between Will Gatlin, an ex-college professor who has isolated himself in a fire-lookout tower, and the much younger Sandy MacKenzie, "a kind of wood nymph"[1] who flits into his life and out again. Their unusual but idyllic relationship brings peace and fulfillment to both, until reality intrudes in the shape of Lawrence J. Turner III, Sandy's fiancé from the Air Force Academy. The spell is broken; the girl disappears, whether accidentally on a solo hike into the Grand Canyon, or purposefully in flight from both men, remains unclear. Will is left alone, as he began, staring out into the forest.

Many readers have dismissed *Black Sun* lightly. A surprisingly obtuse review in *The New York Times Book Review* by Edward Hoagland categorizes the book as "wilderness writing"[2] and says it cannot be read as a novel, as a romance, or even as a statement. A somewhat friendlier assessment by Thomas J. Lyon concludes that *Black Sun* is "more profound than it looks,"[3] but Lyon does nothing to help the reader understand its depths. He questions the book's proportions—it "is short, the characters few, the structure chopped and seemingly evasive of long, deep, development"—even as he rightly decides the locus is "the author's mind looking back, arranging, adding dimensions missed, *seeing*." But Abbey is able to look back, to arrange, to add dimensions, to see, precisely because he has designed a structure that allows, and in fact encourages, him to do so. Thus, while *Black Sun* may seem cryptically abbreviated and even convoluted, it actually has been pieced together with skill, its threads carefully interwoven. The result is an allegorical tapestry, a modern man's ascent into heaven and descent into hell, his fictive journey there and back ending in an existential nothingness peculiarly Abbey's own.

For several reasons, the threads are difficult to untangle. Realistic men and women become metaphoric embodiments in this deceptively short tale, their personalities representational and their quests symbolic of individual desires and defeats. But Abbey not only presents scene and story in multiple layers, he blurs the time sequence as well. To enter *Black Sun's* romance world, then, the reader first must straighten out the time warp that distorts the chain of events.

Rather than organize Will's story chronologically, Abbey mixes past, present, and future. The chapters follow no perceptible order —some describe the progress of the love affair, some interrupt with anecdotes about peripheral characters, some connote Will's psychological state after his devastating loss, and some recall moments of remembered passion. The latter, in fact, are expressed so ambiguously that it is difficult to tell if scenes actually are occurring or if Will is only fantasizing about the past. But aside from the occasional confusion, it makes little difference that past, present, and future intertwine because a tonal continuity unites the action. A melancholia, extending from the first page of Will's tale to the last, overrides the passage of time. Using the continuous present to chant a threnody, Abbey turns the book into an elegy of love and loss, a celebration of joy and pain.

Even so, it is important for the reader to separate the moments of illusion from those of disillusion. A technical device simplifies that task. Those chapters which assess Will's psychological limbo after Sandy's disappearance are written in the present tense, while those which bring the lonely man together with the girl take place in the past. This plan results in a clarity of presentation and intent that was missing from Abbey's earlier fiction. Unlike *The Brave Cowboy*, *Black Sun* already has occurred, and the aftermath is perhaps more crucial than the story itself. That aftermath—emotionally frozen chapters of living death—takes place in the continuous present and thus seems more real than the love affair, more tangible than the intangible dream. "Each day begins like any other. Gently. Cautiously. The way he likes it. A dawn wind through the forest, the questioning calls of obscure birds" [11]. Chapter 1, the reader's first view of the lonely man, opens in medias res, after the affair has ended. Like our introduction to the brave cowboy and to *Desert Solitaire's* Ed, we join Will in the early morning as, sipping his first cup of coffee, he greets the sun. But unlike those of his predecessors, this man's greeting is a frozen, immutable one. "This world is very quiet. Almost silent" [12], as he "gazes out at the morning" [13]. The next several chapters alternate: Sandy's first visit to the tower (in the past tense), more morning ablutions (in the present), a scene of lovemaking (past and present combined in the slough of Will's imagination), a visit from an old friend, another passionate moment with Sandy, and then again the continuous presence of hell on earth.

He smokes, gazing out at the forest.

All is silent. The sky low, heavy, a gray still overcast. One bird sweeps down and across among the trees but disappears, making no sound.

Returning to the cabin . . . he is halted by a soft voice
> *Will*
>> calling his name
He stops, looks back and around, searches the depths of the forest.
But there is nothing. [34; italics Abbey's]

Nothing breaks the painful monotony of the continuous present except memories from the past.

Despite those myriad time shifts that move characters and reader between present and past, *Black Sun* easily can be realigned chronologically. To do so, of course, negates a measure of Abbey's artistry because part of the book's power comes from its modulations of ecstasy and despair. But perhaps even more of its success comes from its author's preconception of his tale. Undoubtedly Abbey drew the story line from personal experience. He wrote the book after the untimely death from leukemia of his wife, Judy, and after the disappearance early the next year of a young hiker at Organ Pipe Cactus National Monument, a girl who "probably fell or slipped, injured herself and crawled into one of the many small caves or brushy crevices in the cliffs for shelter from the cold and wind. Since searchers the next day heard no hint of a human cry for aid it also seems likely that she lost consciousness soon after her accident and died of shock, bleeding and exposure" [CC, 76]. No trace of her body was found. Transmuting those two losses to the romance world of *Black Sun*, Abbey designs a narrative that will focus on the man who is left behind. For the first time in his fiction, he brings together a structure, a vision, and a plan that will control his book from start to finish. This pattern, when unravelled chronologically, follows a traditional sequence.

"In the romance pattern everything leads to or follows from its primary action, the quest; the hero's advent and initiation mark its prologue, his descent and recognition its epilogue."[4] As surely as if he were a full-fledged, fighting member of the famous round table, Will embarks upon just such a quest. He follows a road of misdirection, lost paths, and dead ends in his relentless search, while concurrently undergoing a process of initiation. His descent and recognition, too, track a familiar pattern. The only difference between his venture and those of previous knights-errant is the difference between the modern age and the age of chivalry, an enormous gap of psychological perceptions and social changes. But the pursuit remains the same, one man's search for self amid the madness of his generation.

Abbey structures Will's story with the five parts that have constituted the backbone of romances for centuries: isolation, contact, ecstasy, a descent into hell, and a return to earth at the end. Beowulf, alone at first and then a part of the revelry at Heorot, must descend into the mere, the hell of Grendel's mother, before rejoining Hrothgar's thanes. Dorothy, alone in Oz, finds three helpful friends but must tackle the Wicked Witch of the West by herself before she can return to earth. While these two examples may lurch from the sublime to the ridiculous, they indicate the wide range of literature that follows the five-step progression, a range extending well beyond the purely fanciful. One of the finest examples is *Moby-Dick*, which moves Ishmael from his opening loneliness to a relationship with the other members of the Pequod's crew and on to the excitement of whaling. That excitement explodes into hell when Ahab irrationally pursues the white whale, until the final, climactic scene which leaves Ishmael the sole survivor. Such a synopsis is oversimplified, of course, but it outlines the essential five steps whereby an author flings his characters into a maelstrom and tests them through physical and emotional experiences that either strengthen, inure, or destroy. The pattern, useful in twentieth-century American literature to William Faulkner in "The Bear" and to Saul Bellow in *Henderson the Rain King*, is invaluable to Abbey, too, as a means to test the unhappy protagonist of *Black Sun*.

For Will, the trial begins in unmitigated, self-imposed isolation. "In the forest are deer, and coyote, and a few black bear, and the rare far-ranging mountain lion. And himself" [19]. A recluse, he has forsaken his career and his personal relationships to hide away from most social contact. "No calendar, no clock, no radio, no magazines, no newspapers. No telephone. No doorbell. No mailbox" [21] in his forest tower. Intrusions are few—an occasional letter or visit from his long-time friend Art Ballantine, a rare tryst with his sometime lover Rosalie. The latter's role drifts, undeveloped, in and out of the story, while the former's measures what Will has left behind—liquor, sex, superficiality. But neither embodiment of the external world touches the fire lookout deeply. The only person to break Will's intrapersonal barrier is Sandy MacKenzie, "slim and brown, smiling. The long hair framed her sunburned face, the clear gray-green steady eyes. . . . She wore what was called a minidress, a thin flimsy thing in psychedelic yellow, which left her arms bare to the shoulder, and the fine legs exposed high above the knee. She wore no makeup or jewelry, the small front teeth revealed by the smile appeared to be just a trace crooked, and her nose was peeling" [41]. Despite her particularized physical description, she seems more a dryad or wood nymph, an almost intangible vision from the green world of romance.

Sandy breaks into Will's isolation, makes contact, and softly touches him in ways he had believed impossible. "They stared at each other in silence for a prolonged moment, amazed by something wild and strange and sweet which seemed to have come suddenly into the space which both separated and united them" [45]. From the instant their eyes lock in visual awareness, the two very different individuals' fates twist irrevocably together and the contact explodes quickly into ecstasy. Although the physical relationship occurs later, they experience the joys of human communication during a long drive from one rim of the canyon to the other, as they swim in the river and share a picnic along the way. Their love grows; ecstasy builds. Graphically, Abbey charts the course of their affair, an almost pastoral, green-world idyll. Their interludes of love take place in an enchanted fairyland, where a kaleidoscope of color serves as the backdrop for powerful green-world magic.

They walked over the gray rock daubed with green, red, yellow, rust-brown lichens, past the twisted and silvery skeletons of long-dead trees, and along an icy cornice of snow which overhung the inner basin. Down in there, among the rock slides, snow fields and pinnacles, were islands of forest, and springs and running streams, deer and columbines and purple fields of lupine and larkspur. Above them was only the sun, the solitary star in a burning wine-dark sky. [115–116]

Moments earlier though, among the leaves, Will "had seen the face of a green god, goat-horned, smiling on their delirium" [112]. The presence of that face and, above it, the "burning wine-dark sky," intimates that the green world is not altogether safe from external intrusions. Each time the lovers come together, in fact, Abbey throws a shadow across them, an intimation that chaos surrounds their island of bliss. Part of that darkness comes from the aura cast by the alternating chapters of pain in the continuous present, but part of it also comes from the obvious forebodings in the otherwise romantic scenes. "She raced to the edge of the water, dove in and swam toward him. He caught and embraced her, kissed her, dragged her into the deep." Cavorting along the Colorado River, Will and Sandy playfully splash and chase each other without a care, but even as they laugh, the reader hears the rapids below the bend. "Constant in the air hung a low vibration, the sound of spray and thunder and madness, like the sea, like the roaring of a distant multitude." And beyond the sudden drop, "more rapids. Three hundred miles of wild river and a hundred rapids, each more terrible than the one before. All down there in the canyon, in that dark inner gorge. Where the river goes underground, into Hades" [73]. Abbey's description is literally true—although the river does not physically go underground, the walls on either side turn black in the depths of the Grand Canyon. To drop between them makes one feel very much as if he were descending beneath the surface of the earth. Abbey intends, however, to cast a metaphorical chill over Will and Sandy even before their relationship has developed. Despite the burgeoning happiness of the dream, a nightmare waits ahead. "The green-gold water of the river surged past their wet and shining bodies. A dazzling light streamed down and exploded in a million glints of fire on the roil and play of the waves." And yet, "from downriver" comes a warning, "the low roar, like an endless, tireless, fanatic applause, of the rapids. Under the listening sky" [74].

But Abbey is not ready to specify the nature of the nightmare. Still focusing on the dream, he lets Will and Sandy express their love physically, joyously, ecstatically. Although some readers have criticized the author for describing too explicitly, the details underscore the growth of the lovers' feelings for each other and the carefree, almost adolescent, quality of their time together. Softly, Abbey crafts Will's tenderness and Sandy's inexperience into a whole. "She trembled in his embrace, her vibrant body burning with an animal heat and freshness which astonished, delighted, amazed him; he had forgotten so much" [97]. Puns abound too in the author's emphasis on joy and laughter. Even as the couple dismisses the underworld beyond the river's bend, they playfully affirm their belief in "plutonic love." And when Sandy looks at the canyon's yawning abyss, reciting, "Yonder before us lie, Desert of vast eternity," Will's rejoinder is short and to the point—"Marvelous." Later, they contemplate "the cunning lingo of love," with Abbey's own marvelous sense of humor inflating theirs into a burst of affection. "But they, while the sun ran, became themselves a kind of flower and sank into a great white blue-veined flower that blinded thought and every sense with its dazzling, overwhelming, perfumed and momentary splendor. That is what they knew" [122]. Their pastoral bliss reflects their author's studied avowal elsewhere that, "Wherever two human beings are alive, together, and happy, there is the center of the world" [JH, 34].

Yet this particular ecstasy cannot last. Just as Ed cannot gaze too long over the abyss and just as he cannot follow the moon-eyed horse too far, so Abbey cannot rhapsodize forever under the summer sun. Ecstasy quickly turns to chaos, heaven to hell, when the red world intrudes on the green. This time, however, no county sheriff or United States marshal powers his way into the tale and no posse or troops drive the protagonist into a fictive corner. Instead, a single, innocuous young man, Sandy's boy friend in Colorado, begins to make demands. Stiltedly he writes to Will—"it seems apparent that you are taking advantage of her immaturity and lack of experience for ends of your own, which, under the circumstances, seem to be of questionable honor" [86]. He writes to Sandy too, calls her every night, and plans a visit, until the pressure forces her to choose between the two very different men. "I just have to get away by myself for a few days," she tells Will, "try to think things through and figure things out" [136]. And in a page she vanishes. "Well, God damn it, Will, her car is gone," a ranger argues when neither Gatlin nor Turner can find her. "She sure as hell didn't take the car down in the canyon. . . . She could be anywhere in the world now" [138]. But Will believes she is there, lost in the depths of the Grand Canyon, and he descends to try and find her under the hot August sun.

Chapter 37 describes his burning quest [BS, 137–151]. As with so many of Abbey's best extended prose passages, this one needs to be read in its entirety, not excerpted bit by bit. Its impact increases proportionately to its overlapping imagery, a pictorial profusion dominated by the burning sun that "rose out of the desert far beyond and glared through unclouded sky into the canyon. The heat intensified immediately." So, too, the quintessence of the book burns more intently page by page. Imperceptibly, as the temperature rises, the focus shifts from the physical heat of the desert to the metaphysical heat of hell, from the tangible search for Sandy to an intangible search for Will's soul.

What did he really expect to find? A footprint, a message in a log, a scrap of tartan plaid on a thornbush, a faded picture? A broken body draped on rock, a thin cry for help? He knew that the possibility of any of these things was too small to measure to make sense. His descent into this inferno was itself an act of insanity. Yet he could not have imagined doing anything else, any less. He trudged on under the cliff, under the blaze of the soaring sun.

He sees no trace of her passing.

The first day, although treacherous, is uneventful. Will rests during the hottest hours, searches along horizontal benches the rest of the time. During the next twenty-four hours, he drops closer to the inner gorge where the landscape turns from red to gray to black and where the heat so confuses him that he begins hallucinating. His dreams turn into nightmare, his nightmare into reality. "The long hair shining like burnished copper, fragrant as cliff rose, hung across her bare shoulders and trailed in his face. He could smell the perfume of her breasts, taste the sweetness of her arms. He opened his eyes. Strands of a cobweb tickled his face. A few inches from his nose a spider, gray as the dust, dangled from the overhanging rock, extruding from its abdomen a hairlike filament of spume." Will twitches in revulsion, thrusts the spider away from him, rolls from the shade toward the white-hot sun. He "felt the pang of loss, the bewildering pain of something precious, beautiful, irreplaceable swept away forever."

Under an indifferent existential sky, the narrative grows increasingly hostile. "His life melted into dreams," Abbey writes, but those dreams turn into an ordeal reminiscent of the author's own frightful LSD experience in Death Valley. The earth comes alive.

Tortured by thirst, he crawled toward the final resource he had prepared [to trap water] days before, the disc of silver gleaming under the fire of the sun. He neared the place, came upon it, eagerly removed the dirt and sand and lifted the transparent sheet. Instead of water he saw a nest of scorpions, a writhing mass which squirmed, piled, crawled upon itself, multiplying as he watched, there in the pit.

Will escapes to a second reservoir where he lifts the clear plastic and finds "not water but a giant rose" that changes before his eyes into a vision of his mother, father, brothers, the farmhouse haven of his youth. Losses he has suffered since boyhood tumble in front of him until, "waking once again, he was struck nerveless, drawn hollow by the horror of his deprivation. By the senseless sudden blackness of her vanishing." And so he plunges on to the depths of the canyon and of himself, his hell coming as much from within as without. "The sun, touching the horizon, burned for a few minutes directly into his face. He paused to rest, turning his back on the glare, and gazed with weary, aching, blood-flecked eyes at the world of the canyon. He was alone in one of the loneliest places on earth."

Like Jack Burns's flight up the escarpment, Will Gatlin's descent to the river grows more excruciating with every step. The reader can almost feel the heat physically, taste the dust, ache with the exhaustion. Equally powerful is the emotional prose, for some of Abbey's finest writing occurs in the description of Will's agony.

He was alone in one of the loneliest places on earth. Above him rose tier after tier of cliffs, the edge of the forest barely apparent on the rim of the uppermost wall; around him the gray desert platform where nothing grew but scrub brush and cactus sloped toward the brink of the inner gorge and the unseen river. From river to forest an ascent of over five thousand feet; from rim to rim ten miles by airline at the most narrow point; from canyon head to canyon mouth two hundred and eighty-five miles by the course of the river. In all this region was nothing human that he could see, no sign of man or of man's work. No sign, no trace, no path, no clue, no person but himself.

Alone. Was he alone?

"Sandy!" he howled. And waited for an answer.

As the sun etches the pain into his heart, only an echo breaks the silence of his despair.

> SANDY
>   Sandy
>   sandy . . .

Will's howls reach just to the canyon walls, but Abbey's reach far beyond. The author clearly intends that the entire search sequence be taken figuratively as well as literally. Will's is not merely an imprudent descent to the bottom of the earth's deepest canyon in August, but a psychological tailspin to the bottom of his soul. "No sign, no trace, no path, no clue, no person but himself"— Will must face a wrenching isolation, that of modern man in an indifferent, sometimes hostile, always alien, universe. Like the quests of so many of King Arthur's knights, his quest is doomed— the holy grail is out of reach. Like so many of our century's existential protagonists—Camus' stranger staring out between his prison bars, Sartre's three bleak souls squabbling from the confines of their exitless walls—Abbey's creation will not succeed in his search for human contact.

Will is neither a Sir Lancelot nor an existential man, however, for Abbey has offered him neither religious promise nor a Sisyphean fate. Indeed, the former college professor has no rock to push, and that is the point—nothing, not a single task, can ease the agony of his loneliness. Even his trek to the bottom of the canyon brings no relief—"What did he really expect to find?"—just unrelieved pain. Unlike Ed, who looks "down there in the rocks" to discover a sacred vision, Will sees only the creatures of nightmare, tangible replicas of the intangible horror: "dun-colored diamond backs lay coiled, regarding his passage with lidless eyes and black flickering tongues, their rattles whirring like choruses of locusts. The lizards darted out of his way—whiptails, geckos, collared lizards, fat chuckwallas that hissed and blinked and inflated themselves to grotesque proportions, meant as menace. He passed the tunnels of tarantulas; he saw now and then a centipede, a scorpion, a solpugid. He found nothing that could interest him." In fact, in all the world "there is nothing . . . each time he looks out upon [it], it seems to him more alien and dreamlike than before. And, all of it, utterly empty" [13].

A relentless encounter with nothing characterizes Will's return to earth. Apparently he stays in his tower for another year or two, but the passage of time remains as unclear as his consequent actions. He is doomed, after his descent into hell, to eternal loneliness; the hours, days, and weeks mean little to him. Unimportant, too, is how he spends his time. When the book drifts to a close a few pages after his empty cry at the canyon walls, he seems to be leaving his refuge for good, but with no clear destination in mind. "Coming back?" Art asks. "Never," comes the reply. Will closes the tower for winter, then drives away in his pickup truck, felling aspen behind him to block the road. His direction is unknown, his goals unnamed, although Art snidely remarks, "Somehow I gather from a certain 'aura' . . . that you have perhaps finally had about enough of solitude, the forest, reverie, and other forms of autoerotic madness. I trust that this means I may succeed in luring you with me back to the life of the world" [151]. The reader, however, cannot be sure Art will succeed at all. The tale ends as silently as it began, with Will staring "out the window, into the forest" [159].

On the bereft man, the images, the chapters, the meaning, and the essence of the book converge. His quest provides the five-part structural foundation that gives direction to the otherwise jumbled interplay of past, present, and future. While the chronology traces his story from isolation to ecstasy to hell on earth in a fairly balanced plot outline, the artistry of the book focuses on the final, and crucial, aspect of his quest, the recognition that comes when his search has ended. A Zane Grey novel or a *Wizard of Oz* stops short of this resolution—that the hero or heroine survives intact is enough—but a *Black Sun*, like a *Moby-Dick*, has more to say. In the pages of the continuous present, Abbey communicates his romancer's vision, the knowledge of what Abbey's world could be and the recognition of how Will Gatlin missed the road that leads there.

As we already know, neither *The Brave Cowboy* nor *Fire on the Mountain* projected that vision, for the two early narratives merely polarized their red and green alternatives. In Abbey's nonfiction, however, the author offers another choice, a plateau beyond the abyss where modern man might live in peace if he would respect himself and the earth's sacrality. Abbey argues specifically for man to reduce his reliance on material goods and to seek contentment from his personal relationships. "I want to wake at dawn with a woman in my arms," he claims in Ed's voice. "I want to share the day's beginning with her, while woodpeckers drum on hollow snags of yellow pine and the sun rises into the crimson clouds of morning. I want to share an orange, a pot of black cowboy coffee, the calm and commonsense of breakfast talk, the smiles, the touch of fingertips, the yearning of the flesh, the comradeship of man and woman, of one uncertain human for another" [AR, 190]. *Black Sun*, written after *Desert Solitaire* but before *The Journey Home* and *Abbey's Road*, first hypothesizes this personal dream.

Will and Sandy have a chance to find that kind of happiness, as the lonely lover recognizes at the time. "He wanted to see it all again with her, that world which he had thought he no longer needed or wanted. He even thought, in the heat of this strange enthusiasm, that he could enjoy coming back at evening through the catatonic crowds of Manhattan, under the river through the Tubes, to a cold-water flat in Hoboken, if she were there, waiting for him" [66]. Together they might have been able to overlay green on red, to reach that romancer's superstate where Reason—"fidelity to what alone we really know and really must love—this one life, this one earth on which we live" [AR, 127]—prevails. But Sandy could not make up her mind; and Will would not make it up for her. Evading a commitment to themselves, they miss the turn that might have led them to a sacred realm. Lacking "intelligence informed by sympathy, knowledge in the arms of love" [AR, 127], they lose their way to Abbey's world.

Will recognizes his mistake, but he cannot articulate the engagement that would reverse his misdirection. "He said nothing. The words he was meant to say remained locked in his head. *I love you,* and so forth. *Will you marry me, Miss MacKenzie,* and so on. *I am yours forever, beloved, through all eternity,* and what not. He could not quite get them out" [134; italics Abbey's]. He does not, cannot, speak. "Lost. Lost," Abbey emphasizes the prophetic recognition. Will says nothing,

although the words which he knew very well she needed to hear were right there, in his brain, resounding through the circuits of his nerves. *I too. Anything. Anything. Die for you. Go back to the schools again. Profess. Die. Live. Work for you, my love, my darling, my heart,* and so forth, in that vein. *Go back to the world again, back to the cities, emerge at last from this miserable pack rat's nest I've made in the forest.* Thusly, in that manner. The words were there, present. He had only to speak them. [134; italics Abbey's]

Still, he does not say what Sandy needs to hear. Like other characters of American fiction—Nick Carraway or Jake Barnes, for example—Will is unable to commit himself to anything. "He did not speak. In the air, surrounding, embracing, assuming them, floated a sweet, melancholy music. Sounds of a dying century, infinitely tender and subtle. Lost" [135].

Neither the life he left nor the love he feels can dissuade Will from his inherent reserve and his determination to remain uninvolved. In this respect, he is perhaps an odd protagonist for a romance since, unlike a typical knight, Will initiates nothing and promises nothing. Incidents happen *to* him. His own actions never set the story line in motion. Refusing to take responsibility for starting the affair with Sandy, he informs her bluntly, "I want you to come to me. You know where I live. . . . Bring your toothbrush"

[86]. If she wants Will, she must make the decision on her own. Likewise, the relationship is truncated through her volition, not his. "If only you could help me a little more," she pleads in the last note she writes. "But I guess what you want is that I settle this thing myself, on my own, and no doubt that is the best way and the only way to do it" [136–37]. Will, in turn, waits tacitly for her decision. Even when Lawrence J. Turner III accosts him in a parking lot, he refuses to move. " 'You bastard. Won't you fight?' The young man hesitated, his fists ready, his body balanced, waiting for Gatlin to make a move. 'Are you really a coward?' " [132]. Will remains silent.

Uncommitted to anything except the present because the past has been so painful and the future so unpredictable, he stands mute, unable to defend himself either verbally or physically. Only after Sandy disappears does he direct his own actions, and then the effort is both frustrating and futile. His descent into hell catapults him into a catatonic and emotionally frozen limbo. There, even though he acknowledges his human need for commitment, he realizes the discovery comes too late:

—back and back into time more remote than human memory. But thinking of her voice, the gentleness of her hands, her wild hair, her eyes in firelight . . .

Now he would welcome fire, the crash of a bolt spiraling down a tree trunk, the rip of a fireball through the forest carpet, even the hurricane roar and onrush of a great crown fire. Anything, anything, to smash his idleness and reverie, to drag him into the midst of trouble and terror. [128]

Anything, to drive him out of his senseless ennui. Isolated, now, from either green world or red, Will has no direction; he has lost irrevocably the way to Abbey's world.

That special place, in fact, does not exist in *Black Sun*, at least not in a tangible state, for in this tale Abbey's world remains a dream, not a reality. Will and Sandy's love takes place in a green world wholly isolated from red, not in the third possibility affirmed by Abbey's nonfiction. "Human bodies and human wit," he insists in *The Journey Home*, "united in purpose, independent in action, can still face that machine [Abbey's metaphor for red world constructs] and stop it and take it apart and reassemble it . . . on lines completely new. There is, after all, a better way to live" [JH, 226].

While the characters in *Black Sun* intuit that via media and recognize a realm of possibilities, they cannot find the way because they do not know how to take their own world apart and reassemble it on lines completely new. A single impotent intrusion by a foolish young man sends them both devastatingly astray. Nevertheless, since Sandy and Will potentially touched happiness, the two lovers are better off than either the brave cowboy longing for an unreachable future or the grizzled rancher remembering a long-gone past. Ed, of course, is better off still. In the personal histories Abbey creates a character who can look steadily at the mad machine, who can suggest ways to redirect the "whore of industry," who can articulate his own human needs. Since the 1968 publication of *Desert Solitaire*, Abbey has communicated a real sense of the possibilities that exist for reconciling man and his sacred landscape.

So even though *Black Sun's* characters cannot hold to the track down Abbey's road, the quest is not a failure. Will Gatlin's mistakes suggest a plausible course of action to his audience; his recognition of those mistakes, and the price he has to pay for that recognition, speaks profoundly to the reader who will hear. His story, then, is a twentieth-century romance communicating a modern romancer's vision. No simple shepherd in an Arcadian forest and no bold knight on a snow-white steed, Will nevertheless quests through a wilderness of self, a man-made forest where Abbey's via media lies buried in the trees. That Will's recognition does not lead back to charted lands is no flaw, for this time both reader and author hold the master plan in their hands. Where *The Brave Cowboy* and *Fire on the Mountain* failed, *Black Sun* succeeds, its potential "a blinding and terrible beauty which obliterated everything but the image of itself" [153]. Thus Will sees his love; thus Abbey sees his world.

Just as the man and his maid never achieve their pastoral dream, so the book that tells their tale cannot be categorized a pastoral romance. But the word "pastoral" is helpful when discussing this surprisingly complex tale because it suggests still another dimension of Abbey's accomplishment. To understand that dimension, we need to look at characteristics of the pastoral novel, specifically, at the fiction of George Eliot, Thomas Hardy, and D. H. Lawrence.

Each of these writers used rural life "to reveal an integrated culture whose values are more essential and significant than those of urban life."[5] Successfully weaving realism and the pastoral scene together, novels such as *Middlemarch, Far From the Madding Crowd,* and *Sons and Lovers* contrast country with city, simplicity with complexity, nature with machine in juxtapositions that make elements of each world attractive. Ostensibly, *Black Sun* does the same. While it borrows many pastoral conventions—idealizing the simple life, criticizing the modern treadmill, and implying a Golden Age of peace and satisfaction—Abbey's vision ranges far past the idyllic green world. Yet his book cannot be called a pastoral *novel* for it is too brief, too abstractly rustic, and wholly allegorical, with characters and plot that move in ways beyond the boundaries of reality. The forest tower, for example, is an emblem of rural isolation, not a tangible locale like the Poysers' farm in *Adam Bede;* Lawrence J. Turner III is a symbolic figure of the red world, not a concrete manifestation like Casterbridge's Donald Farfrae; the ecstasy between Will and Sandy is more esoteric than the passion of D. H. Lawrence's men and women in love. Systematically ignoring the principles of novelistic realism and keeping cities and their mad machines at arm's length throughout the tale, Abbey has written something that bears only surface resemblance to those sprawling British novels of a hundred years ago.

The author of *The Pastoral Novel* would argue that he had no choice. Indeed, Michael Squires summarizes his fine study with the regretful conclusion that the pastoral novel is "no longer a truly viable mode of literary expression for major writers"[6]; no wonder Abbey has not found the novelistic form compatible. Another critic, Leo Marx, concurs that most American writers never have been able to effect a meaningful integration of the rural ideal with its realistic counterforce as the English did in the late nineteenth century. The two remain separate forever in the best of our literary tradition. "The outcome of *Walden, Moby-Dick,* and *Huckleberry Finn* is repeated . . .; in the end the American hero is either dead or totally alienated from society, alone and powerless, like the evicted shepherd of Virgil's eclogue. And if, at the same time, he pays a tribute to the image of a green landscape, it is likely to be ironic and bitter."[7] Will Gatlin certainly is such a man—"totally alienated from society, alone and powerless" as he paces around and around his isolated tower, staring ironically at the forest clearing and the canyon abyss beyond, "looking out upon this world . . . more alien and dreamlike than before. And, all of it, utterly empty." Marx, who assumes that the notion of reconciliation is obsolete, adds that all we can expect of our artists today is their acknowledgment of the impossibility of resolution. In Marx's mind, society—not art—

must predicate the union first, and society has not yet done so. It follows, then, that Abbey cannot allow Will Gatlin to yoke green world with red because no one in contemporary life or fiction can.

But *Black Sun* contradicts Marx's pessimistic conclusion in that this modern version of pastoral does offer an artistic reconciliation of sorts. While Will personally fails to reconcile himself with the world around him, Abbey nonetheless projects a vision beyond the chaos. That is, the romancer refuses to dismiss his belief that some day, in some way, a third possibility can surpass the present options of red world and green. Pointing out the causes of Will's failure and projecting a range of possibilities for success, Abbey at least envisions a harmonious mode. He communicates that vision in a way wholly different from the one chosen by the pastoral novelists or even by his predecessors in American literature, turning back to the distant past for a suitable form. He designed *Black Sun* like a tapestry in black and white. We neither look at a medieval wall-hanging and see in-depth psychology nor gaze at an allegorical panel and see complex philosophy; rather, we examine the threads and colors, then step back and perceive the impact overall. In the same way, we must judge *Black Sun*.

The layering, of course, comes from the careful blend of past, present, and future. The subtle time shifts, in turn, are indicative of the shadowed distinctions between what is real and what is illusion. Like the brave cowboy's mountain and the Box V Ranch, this book's physical environment exists, but, as before, an ambience of the romance cloaks the reality. Abbey describes each setting —the tower, the forest, the river, the canyon—not only as the eye sees it but also as his own vision transforms it.

> The tower is surrounded by the forest. In all directions lies the sea of treetops, a seemingly unbroken canopy of aspen and conifer rolling toward deserts in the dawn, toward snow-covered mountains far to the south and west, and on the remaining side toward something strange, a great cleft dividing the plateau from end to end, an abyss where the pale limestone walls of the rim fall off into a haze of shadows, and the shadows down into a deeper darkness.
>
> There is nothing out there which is new to him, nothing which is wholly unknown. [13]

The world of *Black Sun*, "alien and dreamlike," suggests a new romance world with countours more profound and dimensions less predictable than found in Abbey's earlier fiction. With its "haze of shadows," its "abyss," and its "deeper darkness," it becomes a backdrop for allegory.

This book more closely resembles allegory because a one-to-one correspondence exists between many of its figures and many of its author's key concerns. The names of the characters, for example, suggest their roles: Will—of the will, the willfulness of self; Sandy—of the earth, dust to dust. Even Art Ballantine's name—artifice and scotch whisky blended together—indicates his contrived role. Specifically, Will and Art represent opposite ways that modern man can cope with the madness he sees in the twentieth century. Will chooses isolation, an eremitic retreat that separates him from his fellows. "You're becoming a freak," Art tells him. "A fanatic. A weird kind of anchorite. You're dreaming your life away" [24]. Will, however, ignores his friend's recriminations. While it is true that his relationship with Sandy counteracted his instinctive avoidance of humankind for a time, as with most fractures the healing makes the reflex stronger. Will prefers to be alone, eternally. Art, a man who flings himself into the melee of society, responds assertively.

Don't give me that Thoreauvian bullshit, man. Listen, leave this Smokey Bear stuff for the local jokels. They can hack it, they've got nothing to begin with anyway. But outside there's a world, Will. The great world. All yours. Full of fruit, wine, beautiful ideas, lovely and lascivious ladies, enchanted cities, gardens of electricity and light. [26]

A list of women loved and discarded, a series of decadent nights, a set of superficial experiences characterize the man's carpe diem creed.

Although Will's and Art's options might appeal individually to some readers, neither wholly satisfies Abbey. Twice he displays a distrust of Will's perceptions. The most obvious occurs when the reticent character cannot acknowledge his need for Sandy and the author repeats, "Lost. Lost" [135]. A more subtle instance comes when Will admits both his uneasiness about the desert—"There's something about [it] I don't understand. Something out there, in that emptiness, frightens me"—and about "the canyon. The underworld. The Hopis think it's the home of evil spirits. They may be right" [118–19]. To miss the earth's sacrality, in Abbey's world, is tantamount to failure as a human being, so Will's misstatements about the landscape correspond to his mistakes as a man. But if he is uneasy about Will's perceptions, the author treats Art with even more irony. "His arm on Gatlin's shoulders, Ballantine speaks of love. A two-time loser, he speaks of marriage. A doctor of philosophy, he speaks of duty, honor, obligation and the world. He speaks of choice, of decision, of creation and significance. Of purpose and meaning. Of happiness. Of joy" [30]. Obviously Abbey knows there is little joy in Ballantine's self-serving flirtations or in his biting self-degradation. While Art's friendship for Will makes him somewhat admirable, the aging Don Juan otherwise seems utterly superficial. Neither man, then, embraces a satisfactory life-style for the twentieth century, but, in a stylized way, they represent two plausible options.

Equally representational in this black-and-white romance milieu is the extended imagery that weaves the book together. Abbey transforms the canyon below the rapids, for example, into hell, with countless allusions to its alien state. When the couple flies over it, Will muses to himself about "that dungeon labyrinth of rock and cactus and rattlesnakes" [64], an obvious foreshadowing of what he and Sandy will find there. His appraisal is reiterated later that day by the author, as the two lovers cavort above the rapids that lead to "that dark inner gorge. Where the river goes underground, into Hades" [73]. The strongest premonition of the book's final descent, however, comes in a section written in the continuous present. The scene postdates Will's descent into hell, but predates the reader's knowledge of the book's climactic passages. Alone, Will cruises up and down the Colorado in an outboard motor boat, "over a waterway that gleams under the sun like polished brass, golden and dazzling, under the red cliffs of the canyon" [87]. After spending a lazy afternoon fishing, swimming, floating, dreaming, until "the heat becomes oppressive," he suddenly decides to plunge "deeper into the gorge." Through the first set of rapids he drops, then steers toward "the beginning of the wilderness."

Around a bend. Not far ahead he can now see what looks like the end of the river. The water seems to come to a sudden fall or dropping-off place beyond which the river cannot be seen. Along this edge hovers a mist of spray, pale against the darkness beyond, and into the mist, at irregular intervals, curling waves leap from below.

Down there. Gatlin stares into the chaos before him. Down there. . . .
[89–90]

Beaching his boat, he climbs onto a huge boulder where he sits and watches the river tumble past.

"Gatlin is tempted. Why not, he thinks. Go on. Into it. Keep going. All the way into the underworld." He stares; he dreams Sandy might still be alive. "No. There is no remedy." He jerks his thoughts back to reality, where Abbey cements the hellish dichotomy. "A diamondback, six feet long and thick as [a] forearm" startles Will, until his fear changes to recognition. "Cousin," he speaks directly to the coiled rattler. "Cousin," he cries, transforming the snake into a kin of self and of Satan. "What have you done with her?" he begs. "Where is she? . . . Where is she?" [91]. On that desperate note, the black-tongued reptile glides away and the chapter ends without an answer. Despite Abbey's silence about Sandy's actual fate, his choice of snake imagery implies two important things: the edenic, idyllic, short-lived quality of the love between the two lost souls, and the tangential presence of a nearby hell into which they will be cast, a labyrinth guarded by creatures of the devil.

Such imagery abounds in *Black Sun;* its fabric is embroidered with birds and beasts. Some, such as the snake and the soaring buzzards, are harbingers of the underlying horror of the tale—"far above, against the blue, a single vulture gyred through space, black wings motionless, and scanned the desert below with magnetic vision—those protruding eyes socketed in the red raw naked flesh of the beaked head" [144]. Others, such as the deer grazing near the tower, carry more subtle connotations. Appearing throughout, these gentle creatures remind the reader of Sandy, "like a startled doe, quick with life" [31], with "her half-wild eyes. The eyes of a doe" [66]. Will, in fact, sees one or more deer whenever he stares out at apparent nothingness—"a single yearling doe, its head up and alert, facing him, listening" [34], a tiny herd lowering "their heads and . . . feeding in the silent gathering pool of darkness in the clearing at the foot of the tower" [78]. Like a trusting doe, Sandy glides into Will's life; like a startled doe, she darts from him when he cannot say he needs her; like a ravaged doe, she is destroyed. Near the conclusion of Will's debilitating trek into the canyon, Abbey combines his imagery of vulture and doe to underscore the chasm between her innocence and the anguish of Will's loss. The bereft man spots three buzzards "gradually descending, in cautious spirals, toward some attraction on the ground" [149]. Even as he watches, more scavangers appear. He slides, stumbles, gasps, cries his way toward their prey. "Halfway down the slope Gatlin stopped. The quarry was only a deer, a small doe battered and partly dismembered by a long fall from the cliff above. He turned aside" [150]. Neither Will nor the reader mistakes the implied analogy.

Abbey not only characterizes Sandy by comparing her to a swift-running doe, he also haunts Will with a continual presence that reminds him of his lost love. Chapter 25, two pages of stream-of-consciousness pain, indicates the symbolic torment. "Around and around on this tower. . . . What is this thing that haunts my soul night after night and day after day, week after month after year?" [97–98]. He continues to pace, pondering his heartache. "Oh my love, I see thee everywhere. In the wild eyes of a doe. In the dove's song. In the secret places of the forest. Sun gleaming on grass" [98]. Everywhere. Suddenly the incantation shifts its focus from his memories of the girl—"Where could she have gone?"—to the deer grazing in the clearing below.

Where could she have gone? Look at them, licking my salt. When October comes I'll murder you, my darlings, and carry you away. You think your days are numberless, they are not. You think you will live forever, you will not. Even the forest will die. Lightning from my rifle will strike you dead. There is death in my glance, death in my love. What is it that slides invisible among my thoughts? What transparent thread weaves my days together? Always at the corner of my eye, just beyond the focus of my vision, something moves, disappears when I turn toward it. Day after day. Kill your deer and get out of here. My ax will fell the slender aspens down the way. Close that road for the winter. What did I say? Close that road. [99]

Will's musings directly foreshadow the final chapter of the book, in which he hunts the deer across the clearing and closes the road behind him when he leaves. But neither task purges his pain. First of all, he cannot shoot. Aligning the sights of his rifle on that autumn day, he "shifts his bead from the spine to the forehead of his target, not more than fifty feet away. Between the eyes. Relaxed, not breathing, he begins to squeeze the trigger. The doe gazes back at him, straight across the blackened open sights, into his face. Intensely alert, posed for instant flight, she seems nevertheless not afraid" [155], just like Sandy. The vision, too reminiscent of the doe he already has destroyed, keeps him from shooting. He "lets out the trigger, draws the rifle back across the sill. The deer spring away and vanish. For awhile he sits there, idle" [155], haunted.

Across the chasm of time and an inconsolable loss he sees the soft glow of her hair, her timid smile.
"Sandy?"
The deer lift their heads at the sound of his voice, stare up at him not in surprise, not in fear, but with a calm, unruffled, almost complacent consideration. . . . [78]

The repetition of this image from one chapter to another indicates still another way Abbey spins his tale into a unified work of art. The book's simple threads are woven together in a complexity of vision not found in his fiction before. In *The Brave Cowboy*, for example, he apparently had no comprehensive perspective, and consequently he was unable to control his symbols—the mountain shifted back and forth from haven to hell, the truck driver from nemesis to victim. In *Fire on the Mountain*, too, he took the easy way out. But the composition of *Black Sun* differs. Now Abbey has arranged both his thoughts and his methods, using an artistic technique that blends form and content in a seamless whole. *Black Sun*, indeed, to use Sir Walter Scott's comparison of his own novels with those of Jane Austen, is his "finely-wrought cameo," vastly different from the "big bow-wow strain" of Abbey's other fiction.

Of the images and ideas holding it together, the sun is at once the most significant and the most complex. Radiating on nearly every page, "floating down through plane on plane of heat and color and form, under the wide wild candescent sky" [71], its rays cast a Lawrentian vigor on Sandy and Will. But when the sacred relationship is lost, the sun changes into an emblem of hostility, of that which destroys rather than of that which energizes, an enemy to be outlasted—"the glare of the sunlight made his eyes ache" [149] —not a sacred fount. Earlier in his career, Abbey waffled about the implied meanings of the symbols he chose. Now, however, he controls his presentation so that shifts in interpretation smoothly reflect shifts in mood, in values, in point of view. Whereas Jack Burns's mountain shimmered before his very eyes, Will Gatlin's sun accurately predicts the course of his quest. As he ascends, it glorifies his love; as he descends, it burns and torments him endlessly. As he recognizes his own failure and as Abbey projects a vision beyond that human frailty, it becomes the black sun of the title.

The words "black sun" should not be unfamiliar to Abbey's readers. They first appeared in *Fire on the Mountain*, when young Billy "sketched a picture of myself on horseback riding across the White Sands with two buzzards circling above me and a black sun circling above the buzzards" [FM, 83]. In context, these lines follow the discovery of the boy's favorite horse, old Rascal, shot by persons unknown, so the implication of the sun's blackness is strongly negative. In *The Journey Home*, however, its powers seem more benign. "No matter where my head and feet may go," Ed acknowledges there, "my heart and my entrails stay behind, here on the clean, true, comfortable rock, under the black sun of God's forsaken country" [JH, 12]. Later in that same book, the sun's sacrality turns somewhat alien—"in the spring and summer the black grass; in fall and winter the black snow. Overhead and in our hearts a black sun" [JH, 90–91]—but the pronouncement refers to a city sun and so is much weaker than a dark desert pessimism.

By 1979, the black sun's image exploded. Its white-hot heat now has the power to purify, its searing energy the strength to change Ed's pessimism to optimism and his depression into a revelation of self worth. *Abbey's Road* ends with Ed poised on edge of the abyss, taking pleasure from "the rock's abrasiveness, its staunch solidity," and simultaneously preparing to pray toward the illusiveness of dawn. The book's final lines, set off from the rest of the text, chant:

> Black sun
> Heart's sun
> Black raging sun of my heart
> Burn me pure as the flame
> Burn me and take me
> And let me sleep
> Down by a river I know
> In the land of stone and sky
> Until we wake again
> In a new and bolder dawn. [AR, 198]

Praying to the black sun of his heart, Ed asks it to burn with a hard and gemlike flame that will transform self into selflessness, reality into art. "Black sun/Heart's sun" leads Abbey to "wake again/In a new and bolder dawn" that shines on the landscape of romance, an interchange between the sun's power and the author's that energizes him to write with more strength of his own. While these words appeared in print nearly a decade after *Black Sun* was published, they pronounce an epitaph for the fiction whose name they invoke as surely as they image the considered impact of *Abbey's Road*.

The author of *Black Sun* and the voice of the poem assume an affinity between the black sun's alien force and a personal humanness—"Black raging sun of *my* heart" [italics mine]. Will makes no such connection. An early chapter of *Black Sun*, a barroom conversation between the lookout and three Indian drinking buddies, reveals his limited view. The Indians declare, with some mockery, "That's the trouble with you white men. You're not Indians." Then they announce, "The sun will eat the earth." Its energy, its hunger, greater than all others, will prevail. "No," responds Will.

> "Why not?"
> "Because we shall eat the sun."
> "You white men. You'll eat anything."
> "We're hungry." [56]

Revealing in those two lines his social bonding with Art Ballantine, a man of enormous appetites, Will affirms an attitude Abbey sees as all too prevalent in the twentieth century. Modern man rarely comprehends how he can live in harmony with the earth's sacrality, whereas "the Indian does not have to rationalize. He knows the truth intuitively: that one cannot conquer or control the sun, one can only co-exist with it in the actual world."[8] William T. Pilkington's analysis, the only perceptive criticism of *Black Sun* to date, optimistically assumes that Will jokes about being hungry to eat anything, even the sun, and that he is headed down the right track, "to blend his being with nature and attain [an] instinctual level of awareness." However, the evidence shows that Will already has stumbled off Abbey's path and that *Black Sun* was written to retrace the lookout's missteps along the way.

His errant quest culminates, not in lucid resolution, but in lonely cogitation. "What in God's name do you think you're doing here?" Ballantine asks him one day while visiting the tower.

"What do you *really* want to do anyway?"
"Really want to do," Gatlin repeats softly, still gazing out over the forest. Toward the desert. A pause. "Stare at the sun," he says.

"What?"

"Stare it down."

Ballantine sighs. "Will, you're crazy."

"Stare it out," says Gatlin, smiling. "Stand on this tower and stare at the sun until the sun goes . . . black." [29–30; italics Abbey's]

In short, cryptic sentences, Abbey keynotes the title of his book and his protagonist's clouded vision. To stare at the sun until it goes black would blind a man forever, because the human eye simply is not designed to tolerate the sun's direct rays. So Will's literal description of what he really wants to do indicates a figurative will to blindness, a yearning for an eclipse of his endless pain. "The senseless sudden blackness of her vanishing" has disoriented him permanently, sending him "trudg[ing] toward the sun." After Sandy disappears, he loses the grasp of sacrality that was gradually developing in his heart, loses the energy gleaned from the relationship and from the earth. Because he could not fully commit his life, he doomed himself and his love under the black sun's malevolent rays. The sun no longer energizes, it enervates.

For the rest of his days, Will is fated to stare endlessly—looking for Sandy, for self, for an eclipsing blindness that will nullify his agony.

Ballantine sags over the rail and stares down at the ground far below where the deer are now moving slowly through the clearing, heads lowered, nuzzling the earth. . . . All does and fawns. Thin gray shapes, silent as shadows. Tiring of them, he looks where Gatlin is looking.

"What do you see?"

"Nothing."

"What are you looking at then?"

Gatlin does not answer. [28]

In fact there is no answer. "What do you see, Will?" Art asks again and again. "Saw her smiling reflection rise beside his. The sunlight shone through her hair. He felt her hands move up his back, onto his shoulders, into his hair" [31]. Saw himself. Saw the does and fawns and Sandy's image. Saw their mutual damnation because of his own blindness. Saw, in the black sun, a way to manifest his agony. For Will, then, the black sun burns over his personal hell. By refusing love's sacrality, he has cut himself off from happiness, from peace, from the vital force of the earth itself. And so he is cast out, back into the grasp of Art and the red world of the twentieth century where no redemption exists in the present and no prayer will be answered for the future. Unlike Ed, he will not "wake again/In a new and bolder dawn."

Abbey, in contrast, lets the black sun "burn . . . pure as the flame." Conceiving a set of characters and their attendant fates from the beginning, layering them carefully on a tapestry of time and space, he has, in *Black Sun*, written his finest piece of fiction to date. "Did they ever find that girl who was supposed to have disappeared a couple of years ago?" Art asks at one point in the story. "Did she even exist?" [153]. It makes no difference under the black sun of this twentieth-century version of a pastoral romance, a book that even Abbey himself calls "a romance" [JH, xii].

9

Bushwhacking

The Monkey Wrench Gang

"Freedom, not safety, is the highest good," rejoices George Washington Hayduke as he wheels down a narrow Arizona highway at seventy miles per hour, "scarfing up more beer" and "bellowing some incoherent song into the face of the wind."[1] No protagonist could less resemble *Black Sun's* Will Gatlin, who countered twentieth-century pressures by opting for static safety, than ex–Green Beret Hayduke, the genial maniac of *The Monkey Wrench Gang* (1975) who makes freedom the driving force behind his dynamic modus operandi. No piece of fiction, in fact, could less resemble Abbey's quiet pastoral romance about the pain inherent in a retreat from life than the wildly rollicking adventure story that assaults the modern age. Ignoring safety and plunging hell-bent into the fray, the Monkey Wrench Gang faces the mad machine and tries to destroy it. In so doing, its members come closest among Abbey's fictional creations to successfully reaching Abbey's world.

Doc Sarvis, an Albuquerque surgeon who excises billboards in his spare time, and Bonnie Abbzug, his receptionist, lover, chauffeur, and confidante, combine with the madcap Hayduke and a jack Mormon river-runner called Seldom Seen Smith to form the merry band of marauders. Together and separately, the four set out to rid the redrock country of unwanted techno-industrial intrusions. Roads, railroads, bridges, dams, mining operations, and any sort of large machine are fair game for their destructive talents. *"Keep it like it was"* [77; italics Abbey's] is their motto; nonviolent assault is their trademark. Their ground rules are fairly simple, as Abbey explains in Chapter 6. Limiting their projected field of operations, they settle on "the canyon country, southeast Utah and northern Arizona" [67]. Outvoting Hayduke's unbridled enthusiasms, they agree to avoid bloodshed. At first they avoid munitions and explosives too—"it became a question of subtle, sophisticated harassment techniques versus blatant and outrageous industrial sabotage" [70]—but gradually they compound their activities. In the name of deicide, "the murder of a machine" [81], they advance upon Abbey's symbolic villain of the twentieth century, meting out a vigilante justice on those that would desecrate the land.

The great golden light of the setting sun streamed across the sky, glowing upon the clouds and the mountains. Almost all the country within their view was roadless, uninhabited, a wilderness. They meant to keep it that way. They sure meant to try. *Keep it like it was.* [77]

Tacitly, they recognize the earth's sacrality and, although individual gang members rarely pause to consider its implications, they do everything in their power to protect the land. "Because somebody has to do it. That's why" [176]. Their efforts may fall short, but their spirit prevails.

Boisterous, witty, and full of life, *The Monkey Wrench Gang* charges past the bounds of conventional western fiction and proposes a new doctrine of frontier behavior. "I think of it primarily as an adventure story with an environmental theme," Abbey said in an interview given shortly after the book's publication. Then he added, "I guess you could say there is also a strong element of wishfulfillment. Everyone will read it in their own way, but I intended it to be mock-heroic, or perhaps a little more than that. But above all I wanted it to be entertaining."[2] Entertaining it is, from the first paragraph of Chapter 1—

Dr. Sarvis with his bald mottled dome and savage visage, grim and noble as Sibelius, was out night-riding on a routine neighborhood beautification project, burning billboards along the highway—U.S. 66, later to be devoured by the superstate's interstate autobahn. His procedure was simple, surgically deft. With a five-gallon can of gasoline he sloshed about the legs and support members of the selected target, then applied a match. Everyone should have a hobby. [9]

—to the final word on the final page. Because of the book's tone, reviewers and critics have tried repeatedly to categorize its outrageous language and monstrous deeds. "It's a sad, hilarious, exuberant, vulgar fairy tale—part adventure story, part melodrama, part tragedy," *The National Observer* informs the reader on the cover of the paperback edition. *New West* thinks it defines a new fictional genre, "the ecological caper," and C. L. Sonnichsen has called it a "propaganda novel." A more accurate label would be simply another Edward Abbey romance.

Such distinctions are immaterial, except as they lead the reader to a fuller understanding of the intent of the work itself. *The Monkey Wrench Gang* has more ambition than an ordinary propaganda novel of eco-raiders and environmental protest and speaks more profoundly than a vulgar little fairy tale. Specifically, its new heroics broaden the dimensions of the romance in even more directions than Abbey has extended them before. Designed to project Abbey's increasingly complex vision of what man can do to stop the twentieth century from cannibalizing its land and its humanity, this fanciful story continues to introduce stylized yet real figures who move across a mythic yet real landscape. Its proportions, however, are different. Two elements set *The Monkey Wrench Gang* decidedly apart from *Black Sun* and Abbey's other romances. Its extraordinary sense of humor sounds nothing like the somber, almost wistful air that lowers over his first fictions, and its picaresque structure sprawls its rampaging characters all across the countryside. Abbey's own term "mock-heroic" suggests the nature of the deeds performed, as well as the satirical spirit in which they are described, while his additional remark, "perhaps a little more than that," acknowledges his serious commitment to the book's designs. *The Monkey Wrench Gang* means not only to explode those structures that are changing the face of the West, but also to detonate the reader's innocent regard for them. No one who reads of the crusade can ever look at superfluous superhighways, at smog-producing and land-consuming mining operations, or at impenetrable concrete dams in quite the same light again, because Abbey questions their very existence. This book's romantic quest would eliminate them forever.

To bring his revelations up to date, Abbey borrows from the old-fashioned Western. First delineated at the beginning of the twentieth century by Owen Wister and then codified by Zane Grey, the Western, with its purple-sage conflicts between good and evil, has been a popular subgenre for generations. Some writers follow the strictures seriously, while others combine the elements in new and imaginative ways. Abbey himself twisted many of the conventions in his first Western book, *The Brave Cowboy,* where he pointed to the inevitable disappearance of the heroic, self-sufficient breed. *Fire on the Mountain,* too, contemplates the passing of a frontier way of life. *The Monkey Wrench Gang,* on the other hand, rides the Western myth right into the twentieth century. Abbey stretches its proportions—rather than send a single man into a circumscribed area to fight against a distinguishable ill, he unleashes a foursome of Lone Ranger types across two states to battle an omnipresent techno-industrial foe. He inverts the conventional tone, dropping romantic seriousness in favor of comic hilarity, and he rejects the traditional emotional bases too, substituting simple lust for virginal love and simple destruction for real violence. The anarchistic escapades of the gang differ immensely from by-gone confrontations like the shoot-out in the middle of a saloon filled with applauding townsfolk, for such midnight tasks as machine murder and bridge blasting bring little heroic stature to "the band of four idealists" [75].

Yet the Monkey Wrench Gang performs a necessary function in an indifferent twentieth-century world. Recognizing the irony of modern machinery—"they had to build a whole new power plant to supply energy to the power plant which was the same power plant the power plant supplied—the wizardry of reclamation engineers!" [161]—Sarvis and company focus attention on the problems and the inevitable destruction caused by man's worship of the God of Growth. In other words, the book projects a fictive version of Edward Abbey's wildest nonfiction dreams. The Western formula circumscribes his exuberant imagination, inducing him to impose a nineteenth-century brand of frontier justice on the modern atrocities he sees everywhere. The resulting concatenation of past, present, and future not only collapses the generation gap between centuries, it also argues the author's cyclical view of history. "This book, though fictional in form, is based strictly on historical fact. Everything in it is real and actually happened. And it all began just one year from today" [vi].

It all takes place in Zane Grey country—"sunward, downward,

riverward, upwind, into the redrock rimrock country of the Colorado River, heart of the heart of the American West" [111]. Driving into that heart, expecting "nothing but skeleton rock, the skin of sand and dust, the silence, the space, the mountains beyond," Hayduke and Smith suddenly find paradox. The red desert literally has turned to green; the idyllic green-world milieu metaphorically has turned into nightmarish red.

Somebody had removed the Colorado River. . . . Instead of a river he [Hayduke] looked down on a motionless body of murky green effluent, dead, stagnant, dull, a scum of oil floating on the surface. On the canyon walls a coating of dried silt and mineral salts, like a bathtub ring, recorded high-water mark. Lake Powell: storage pond, silt trap, evaporation tank and lagoon. [112]

The old romantic Western scene is dead, replaced by a contemporary version that replicates what Abbey sees when he looks four hundred and fifty feet down from the same bridge over Narrow Canyon. He smells the same stench of decay and imagines the same old rocks deep under the water, waiting "for the promised resurrection. Promised by whom? Promised by Capt. Joseph 'Seldom Seen' Smith; by Sgt. George Washington Hayduke; by Dr. Sarvis and Ms. Bonnie Abbzug, that's whom" [112–113]. Promised, too, by the romancer who plans to turn the contemporary scene upside down in his imagination.

In a conventional Western, the power of the landscape, which stems from "its simultaneous beauty and cruelty,"[3] overshadows the power of individuals who would tame it. In Abbey's world, the same would be true although, unlike a hack writer, he projects a landscape vision more sacred than profane. But in Abbey's book, powerful forces have cruelly transformed the land's beauty, changing Glen Canyon to a silt reservoir, for example, "obscuring the morning sun behind an immense smudge of coal-gray and soil-brown particulates" [157] so that the earth's energy pollutes the sky. In order to reverse that process, not necessarily to bring back the specific beauty of the past but at least to promise a future harmony of some kind, the Monkey Wrench Gang must promulgate their own brand of cruelty. Violent methods are imperative if the land is to be resurrected.

The implications trouble Doc Sarvis, who insists, "We are a law-abiding people." His cohort, a veteran of jungle warfare, disagrees.

"What's more American than violence?" Hayduke wanted to know. "Violence, it's as American as pizza pie."
  "Chop suey," said Bonnie.
  "Chile con carne."
  "Bagels and lox." [163]

Abbey's double entendres clarify Hayduke's point. To the extent that violence presently characterizes much of the American scene, America has borrowed from others the tactics of cruelty and made those tactics its own. [As I was writing this page on March 30, 1981, a would-be assassin was shooting the president of the United States.] Long since, the mode has moved from battlefields across the oceans into this country's urban areas and is spreading rapidly now, into the silent desert. There, Abbey points out, not society's outcasts but the so-called establishment perpetrates the devastation. "Their view from the knoll would be difficult to describe in any known terrestrial language. Bonnie thought of something like a Martian invasion, the War of the Worlds. Captain Smith was reminded of Kennecott's open pit mine . . . Dr. Sarvis thought of the plain of fire and of the oligarchs and oligopoly beyond . . . But George Washington Hayduke, his thought was the clearest and simplest: Hayduke thought of Vietnam" [159]. Because a twentieth-century holocaust has altered the West's scenery from primeval beauty to a veritable backdrop of war, it is fitting that Abbey replace the fictive landscape of the romantic past with monstrous descriptions of the all-too-real present. And because violence begets violence, it is fitting that the gang make the enemy's tactics its own.
  It is fitting, too, that Abbey introduce "young George, all fire and passion, a good healthy psychopath" [167], as his surrogate western hero, the invincible figure who metes out justice with his own hands. Of course the gang itself, all four members together, functions as the Lassiter or Shane figure who rides mysteriously into a troubled land, but it is Hayduke, "warped but warped in the right way" [166], who dominates the forays. "A short, broad, burly fellow, well-muscled, built like a wrestler" [17], with a shaggy black beard, the unlikely protagonist resembles a hippie more than a hero. However, at least one observer, Jenni Calder, actually has described the Western hero as "the hippie of the nineteenth century."[4] Calder sees in the mountain man or the lonesome cowboy a profoundly romantic soul who epitomized anticulture, who ig-

nored the trappings of civilization even as he helped bring it to the West. The only native hero America has ever had, he permits his idolators to keep their rose-colored glasses firmly in place, even as they note the irony of his passing. Abbey's portrayal of Hayduke, except in its satiric overstatement, differs little from Calder's overview of the legendary prototype.

Several irresistible traits characterize the western hero. He is a man of independence; his spirit is one of freedom tinged with loneliness (as Shane reveals when he rides away at the end of Jack Schaefer's novel). He is self-reliant, but vulnerability tinges the edges of his sensitive soul (as Lassiter reveals when he deals with his love for Jane in the purple sage). Above all, the western hero is a survivor. He endures, beating impossible odds to achieve victory and honor. So, too, Hayduke functions in *The Monkey Wrench Gang*. A survivor not only of the Vietnam war but of Vietcong capture, Abbey's antihero revels in his freedom and outlasts his foes, turning certain defeat into stunning victory in the book's final scenes. Hayduke shows human weaknesses too—a nagging fear of loneliness down in the Maze and a vulnerability that grows with his love for Bonnie. Abbey characterizes his hirsute protagonist in ways reminiscent of many other heroic figures but does so satirically, simultaneously undercutting western heroism and elevating his man to just that pedestal.

Hayduke is like a child, "a hotheaded brain-damaged overemotional child. Hyperactive type" [258]. His comrades doubt his maturity, while his creator openly agrees he is "more destructive than bright" [98]. Boyishly, he "love[s] guns, the touch of oil, the acrid smell of burnt powder, the taste of brass, bright copper alloys, good cutlery, all things well made and deadly" [19]. But with a straightforward dig at the macho model, Abbey admits that "George Hayduke had never killed a man. Not even a Vietnamese man. Not even a Vietnamese woman. Not even a Vietnamese child. At least, not to the best of his knowledge" [243]. A most unlikely hero, Hayduke is a Lone Ranger of comically pseudomythic proportions. In this respect he differs enormously from Abbey's first cowboy figure, the anachronistic Jack Burns, who elicited more pathos than laughter and caused more sorrow than celebration. The brave cowboy signaled the end of an era; Hayduke marks a beginning.

Permanently scarred by twentieth-century warfare, a psychological misfit whose reflexes have long since replaced his reflections,

George Washington Hayduke is as much a hero of his time as his namesake of two centuries ago. He deals directly with the issues. His first escapade, for example, brings retribution to a Flagstaff cop who had arrested him several years before. "Of course I can't kill him," the modern Nemesis realizes. "Ruin his evening; nothing drastic or irreparable" [19–20], just make him miserable. So Hayduke steals the man's patrol car and, after a riotous ride through downtown Flagstaff, abandons it on a railroad crossing. "As he hustled away from the scene of his crime, arms full and heart beating with joy, he heard—beneath the screech of brakes, the bellow of klaxons —one solid metallic crash, deeply satisfying, richly prolonged" [23]. In retribution, Hayduke ruins the officer's peace of mind, just as the officer had ruined his. For this unmasked marauder, the retaliation fits the crime.

"Amuse me, I'm bored," Bonnie announces one evening to her new lover and partner and friend.

"Okay. Here's one for you. A real conundrum. What is the difference between the Lone Ranger and God?"

Bonnie thought about it as they rattled through the woods. She rolled a little cigarette and thought and thought. At last she said, "What a stupid conundrum. I give up."

Hayduke said, "There really is a Lone Ranger." [225]

In this case, Hayduke, Abbey, and a critic, Jenni Calder, agree. The twentieth century needs a Lone Ranger as desperately as the past did, but it requires a new breed of avenger, men (and women) who develop creative tactics for exposing the villains, the unscrupulous cheating cowards and the overbearing bullies of the modern age. The Monkey Wrench Gang answers that need.

All four of its members are societal misfits, egocentric souls who march to different drummers. In a romancer's fashion, Abbey stylizes their character traits in the service of truth, using exaggeration to overstate his message. Doc Sarvis, an environmental purist and philanthropist, singlemindedly pursues a cause most unlike his surgeon's calling. His nurse's aide also is "learning anew the solid satisfaction of good work properly done" [43]—burning billboards pleases her liberated woman's brain with its "intelligence too fine to be violated by ideas" [40]. The mores of Seldom Seen Smith, equally paradoxical, are stated with similar tongue-in-cheek humor. "On a lifetime sabbatical from his religion" [29], Smith happily practices plural marriage and, like the mountain man of yesteryear who materialistically piloted settlers into the very wilderness he wanted to preserve, operates Back of Beyond Expeditions to carry tourists down the Colorado River. Along with their explosive friend, these three comic figures prove Calder's adage that "there must be a Lone Ranger," and Hayduke's that "there really is a Lone Ranger." Abbey pondered, in his nonfiction, the efficacy of civil disobedience, and he rendered ineffective such ironical anarchists as Paul Bondi, but now he has found that the best defense is a good offense. So the gang strikes, protecting the defenseless earth.

They start on Comb Ridge, pulling up survey stakes ("That's the first goddamned general order in the monkey wrench business" [80], Hayduke avows), pouring sand into crankcases and Karo syrup into fuel tanks, doing all they can "to sand, jam, gum, mutiliate and humiliate" [85] the heavy equipment. They work together through the night. "Teamwork, that's what made America great: teamwork and initiative, that's what made America what it is today" [87]. Satirizing the modern businessman's code, Abbey turns the nineteenth-century ideal of a lonely cowboy avenger into a twentieth-century composite—the company team replaces the masked rider, and its prowess as a unit sharpens with every task it completes. From Comb Ridge it graduates to Black Mesa, where "lay the ever-growing strip mines of the Peabody Coal Company. Four thousand acres, prime grazing land for sheep and cattle, had been eviscerated already; another forty thousand was under lease" [154]. The crew sets about "Working on the Railroad," blowing up the company's shuttle system when it discovers the effectiveness of explosives over the avenging six-guns of old. It takes a team of two, Doc and Bonnie, to shove the plunger down.

At that moment the charges went off. The train rose up from the rails, great balls of fire mushrooming under its belly. Hayduke dropped again as pieces of steel, cement, rock, coal and wire hurtled past his ears and soared into the sky. At the same time loaded coal cars, completing their jump, came back down on the broken bridge. The girders gave, the bridge sank like molten plastic and one by one the coal cars—linked like sausages —trundled over the brink, disappearing into the roar the dust the chaos of the gorge. [187]

Several subsequent paragraphs document the damage more fully. Indeed, no saloon brawl could cause such widespread destruction. But the twentieth century is an age of violence, and this is a twentieth-century Western, Abbey-style, so the extensive demolition is appropriate.

Some readers, however, may feel victimized by overkill on the part of both the ecoraiders and their creator. If *The Monkey Wrench Gang* has a flaw, it is one of excess. Adjectives piled on top of lively nouns and adverb-laden action verbs describe each activity— "Gobs and gouts of burning slag fall through space, flaring hotter as their descent accelerates, and splash with a steaming sizzle into the water. Fragments of red-hot welded steel and broiled concrete follow" [297]—and the activities are many. A few representative attacks would suffice to characterize the gang's methods and purpose, but those would never be enough to satisfy Abbey's imaginative yearning. In his mind, he undoubtedly has destroyed every heavy-duty machine and leveled every structure at least a dozen times, so he has been unable to resist the onslaught on paper. One might argue that the picaresque structure invites a sprawling episodic story, but this book contains an overload of rather similar scenes. Hayduke converges on countless big machines, alone or with Seldom Seen or Bonnie, and he sets innumerable explosive charges that do and do not go off; the group together advances and retreats on various fields of battle, and sometimes the forays sound just too similar. But "somebody has to do it," Hayduke and Abbey would argue, defending the plethora of needed tasks, while only the most devoted Abbeyphile would concur that the book itself benefits from the episodic stockpile.

But "somebody has to do it" because the "mad machine . . . will end up by destroying not only itself but everything remaining that is clean, whole, beautiful and good in our America. Unless we find a way to stop it" [S, 77]. After defining the mad machine in *Slickrock*, Abbey proposes one particularized way to stop it in *The Monkey Wrench Gang*. To read the two books together casts a sharper light on the real-life contemporary western villains defined in the former who provide a motivation for the fictional forays described in the latter. Abbey replaces cattle rustlers with land-grabbers and outlaws with conglomerates in his twentieth-century examination of the old West revisited. The gang debates the nature of the foe. Early in the book Smith assumes, "They're people too, like us. We got to remember that, George. If we forget we'll get just like them and then where are we?" [90]. But after a series of confrontations, each more violent than the last, the jack Mormon changes his mind. "It ain't people," he decides. "It's a mechanical animal." Doc agrees wholeheartedly. "Now you've got it. . . . We're not dealing with human beings. We're up against the megamachine. A megalomaniacal megamachine" [155]. Substituting a mechanical monster for the traditional black-hatted bad guy, Abbey uses another device to maneuver his Western into the modern age. Just as the open range has blossomed into spoil banks and the Lone Ranger has turned into a fanatical foursome, so the enemy has changed from a discernible band of avaricious thieves into a much wider-ranging, interlocking set of corporations and even governments. "Peabody Coal only one arm of Anaconda Copper; Anaconda only a limb of United States Steel; U. S. Steel interwined [sic] in incestuous embrace with the Pentagon, TVA, Standard Oil, General Dynamics, Dutch Shell, I. G. Fargen-industrie; the whole conglomerated cartel spread out upon half the planet Earth like a global kraken, pan-tentacled, wall-eyed and parrot-beaked, its brain a bank of computer data centers, its blood the flow of money, its heart a radioactive dynamo, its language the technetronic monologue of number imprinted on magnetic tape" [159]. The ear-splitting description probably understates Abbey's revulsion for the monster.

The Monkey Wrench Gang, then, is an old-fashioned Western redesigned to eradicate a new-fangled foe. Using the techniques of a romancer and the structural underpinnings of a conventional cowboy novel, the author has fashioned a provocative myth for the modern age; using methods and tactics of modern warfare, the gang brings that myth to life.

Abbey's accomplishment is an impressive one. Whereas the traditional Western looks to the past, Abbey looks to the future. Whereas the traditional Western rehashes certain physical conflicts irrelevant to the twentieth century, Abbey redefines those conflicts in contemporary terms, replacing black-hatted villains with greedy conglomerates and range wars with environmental confrontations. Whereas the traditional Western makes heroes of those who would tame the land, Abbey elevates those who respect it, putting white hats on men and women who go one step further to risk their lives to protect their natural environment. Most impressively, whereas the traditional Western draws its frontier optimism from the infinite resources of the land, Abbey gains his from the infinite resourcefulness of individual human beings. *The Monkey Wrench Gang*

answers a contemporary need for heroism, just as epics and sagas
filled that void long ago and just as Western novels have done for
the century following the frontier's close, but its gang members
are a new breed of hero. Both romanticized and caricatured by their
author, they earn the reader's respect because of their unwavering commitment to their goals. Paradoxes remain, of course; the
Western thrives on paradox, as does Abbey. The best novelists
using its formula send forth conflicting sets of values to battle
on a moral landscape, and Abbey does the same, selecting contemporary issues to project on his red and green imaginative field.
Like all good novels, Abbey's fiction raises more questions than
it answers.

A consideration of the Western problems given a modern twist
in *The Monkey Wrench Gang* begins with the most obvious and the
most concrete. The issue of land use fascinates him. As it appears
in past Westerns, the conflict typically has been one of cattleman
versus homesteader. Conrad Richter's 1937 novel, *The Sea of Grass*,
for example, exposes the relative strengths and weaknesses of both
sides with propagandistic clarity, pitting a stalwart rancher in a losing battle against an army of encroaching nesters led by a self-
serving lawyer-politician. While that specific disagreement over the
open range seems to have been resolved several generations ago,
similar incompatibilities still plague the twentieth-century West.
Ranchers, miners, conservationists, and the United States government feud regularly over jurisdiction in dozens of states, and now
giant corporations have joined the fight too, expanding the scope
of the disputes into a multisided tug-of-war with the landscape
caught in the middle. Where once a single valley was the issue,
the future of the entire West is at stake today.

Abbey makes his position absolutely clear. Satirizing those who
devalue the land—"The engineer's dream is a model of perfect
sphericity, the planet Earth with all irregularities removed, highways merely painted on a surface smooth as glass" [75]—he fully
supports anyone who will protect it. Even Hayduke, "a saboteur
of much wrath but little brain" [211], earns Abbey's admiration because the man has his priorities straight. "My job is to save the
fucking wilderness," Hayduke insists. "I don't know anything else
worth saving. That's simple, right?" [211]. To emphasize his point,
Abbey purposely overstates personalities, procedures, and premises. Hayduke's modest proposal

I'd like to knock down some of them power lines they're stringing across the desert. And those new tin bridges up by Hite. And the goddamned road-building they're doing all over the canyon country. We could put in a good year just taking the fucking goddamned bulldozers apart. [64]

grows to comic proportions.

The grandeur of his reflections gave him solace as he bent to his lonely and ill-rewarded labors . . . George W. Hayduke tramped forward—a staunch and unplacated force—toward the clanking apparatus the tough red eyes the armored jaws the tall floodlit and brazen towers of . . . The Enemy. [252]

If passive resistance has no measurable impact, perhaps the swift sword of the satirist will.

Even so, Abbey recognizes the irony of his presentation. It takes brutal methods to stop the brutalization. Like the western lawman of old (and rather like this particular satirist himself), the gang must use excessive force to accomplish its goals, and even though it never hurts another human being, it inadvertently wreaks havoc on the land. In effect, it shows itself to be as primitive as those it would destroy. Here, then, is another dichotomy often debated in Western novels. Appraisal of the relative worth of frontier values, as embodied by primitive and civilized forces, becomes a crucial ingredient. *The Sea of Grass* includes the conflict as a psychological aspect of the physical battle for the land, while other novels, like A. B. Guthrie, Jr.'s *The Big Sky* (1947), focus wholly on the unresolvable question. Inevitably, it seems the primitive gives way to the civilized, both in Western history and in Western fiction, even though the values of the former may be preferable to the manipulations of the latter. Fifteen years ago, in his article, "The Primitive and the Civilized in Western Fiction,"[5] Levi Peterson contended that the conflict between the primitive and the civilized has been settled on the physical, but not the mythic, level. While this appears true in the novels Peterson discusses, *The Monkey Wrench Gang* deploys some different ideas.

First of all, Abbey would divide Peterson's notion of what is civilized into two separate parts: civilization and culture. In *Desert Solitaire* he showed us the difference between the former, a "vital force in human history," and the latter, which "thickens and coagulates, like tired, sick, stifled blood" [DS, 276–277]. For Abbey, then, the primitive and the civilized go hand in hand, and it is culture that intervenes. "Civilization is a youth with a Molotov cocktail in his hand," he anarchistically insists; culture, "the L. A. cop that guns him down" [DS, 277]. Civilization is the primitive Hayduke, saving "the fucking wilderness"; culture, the Bishop and his men and all their paraphernalia from the so-called civilized world. After redefining civilization, Abbey shows the ostensibly civilized twentieth century—or twentieth-century culture—cannibalizing the land in more primitive ways than any ostensibly uncivilized aborigine could conceive.

> He [the good doctor] watched the news. Same as yesterday's. The General Crisis coming along nicely. Nothing new except the commercials full of sly art and eco-porn. Scenes of the Louisiana bayous, strange birds in slow-motion flight, cypress trees bearded with Spanish moss. Above the primeval scene the voice of Power spoke, reeking with sincerity, in praise of itself, the Exxon Oil Company—its tidiness, its fastidious care for all things wild, its concern for human needs. [217]

Thus the author sarcastically maligns corporate savagery in the modern age. Indeed, his conglomerate descriptions belie the idea that primitivism on the physical level is no longer at issue, for the debasement of the bayous, of Black Mesa, of a thousand other American settings, indicates how far culture in the name of civilization has retrogressed. Taking the poles of primitivism and civilization, Abbey tumbles them end over end to show how confused the current generation's thinking has become. A century ago, violence and primitivism were considered synonymous; now, in his romances as well as in the world around him, Peterson's civilization/Abbey's culture has subsumed the characteristic aggression. The reader can no longer presume that Peterson's dichotomy has been resolved on a physical level. Mankind can no longer presume that violence belongs in the wilderness while the cities dwell in peace because, ironically, violence today follows wherever culture intrudes.

Abbey plays on that paradox, and on a subservient one. "A significant feature of the Western is that it compresses degrees of violence,"[6] Jenni Calder observes in *There Must Be a Lone Ranger*, adding that such writing willingly telescopes the distance between death and a black eye. Abbey, seeing the applicability of such compression to his theme, and "choking with laughter all the way to the top of the mesa" [128], diminishes the distance even more. When

Hayduke rolls "a herd of rocks" down to meet the Search and Rescue Team, the final blow exemplifies the way the author constantly parodies the reader's expectations.

There was an anguished crunch of steel as the Blazer, squirting vital internal juices in all directions—oil, gas, grease, coolants, battery acids, brake fluids, windshield wash—sank and disappeared beneath the unspeakable impact, wheels spread-eagled, body crushed like a bug. The precious fluids seeped outward from the squashed remains, staining the roadway. The boulder remained in place, pinning down the carcass. At repose. [128]

Hayduke's boulder comes to rest on the flattened carcass of a Blazer rather than on mortally injured men, spewing car innards instead of blood and guts in every direction. The "unspeakable impact" comically eases both the physical and emotional onslaught. Like children who have only been playing, Hayduke and Seldom Seen sleep peacefully that night, "the sleep of the just. The just plain satisfied" [128]. The reader relaxes too, content to see such forays end happily, telescoped by laughter in a romancer's world.

Abbey seriously intends, however, to turn conventional notions of violence topsy-turvy. If so-called civilization can violate the land, as it did in Glen Canyon, for example, then so-called violence can be used to stop it. Indeed, the gang's methods are more benign than society's. Word plays giving life to inanimate objects—the Blazer's "vital internal juices," its "body crushed," its "precious fluids" seeping out—connote a euphemistic kind of death. After all, only a vehicle has been ravaged. Far more murderous than a boulder falling on a Blazer is today's culture, which can transform aspen, pine, spruce, and fir into "a scene of devastation. Within an area of half a square mile the forest had been stripped of every tree, big or small, healthy or diseased, seedling or ancient snag. Everything gone but the stumps. . . . A network of truck, skidder and bulldozer tracks wound among the total amputees" [209]. By making the trees sound more human than the ruptured vehicle, and by leaving them maimed rather than putting them out of their misery, Abbey suggests that society's short-term methods and long-term results are more brutal than the gang's. That explains why Hayduke's primitive instincts finally are more civilized than society's determined violation of the land.

Most formula Westerns, while thriving on bloodshed and aggres-

sion, clearly indicate which deeds the reader should admire. In
Zane Grey's world, villainous acts are apparent. In the more complex Westerns, however, like *The Sea of Grass*, or *The Big Sky*, or *Shane*,
shades of good and evil color the motivations. Certainly the authors
of these novels take sides, but they also show the intricate value
systems that sway men's choices. Abbey combines both designs.
Borrowing from the formula, he clearly marks his characters good
and evil, but, like those who have advanced beyond the formula's
confines, he still turns his readers' expectations around. He makes
the bad guys good and the good guys bad, so we end up respecting the anarchists and hating the pillars of society.

Like Robin Hood's men, the gang operates from the purest of
motives, or so Abbey would have us believe. Its opponents, on
the other hand, he mires in mud. Since governments and conglomerates would be too abstractly gigantic to satirize effectively, he
isolates Bishop Love and his Search and Rescue Team as a worthy
Sheriff of Nottingham and his posse. The Team, then, he portrays
as aggressive and violent, more so than the lawless Monkey Wrench
Gang, and he pictures its fearless leader as more animalistic than
Hayduke. Bishop Love, with "a mouthful of powerful, horse-like
yellow teeth" [107], acts like a greedy one-man conglomerate,
"neck deep in real estate, uranium, cattle, oil, gas, tourism, most
anything that smells like money. That man can hear a dollar bill
drop on a shag rug" [109]. Abbey ridicules the crew throughout
the book, undercutting the Bishop's religious hypocrisy and un-
derscoring the Team's uniform incompetence at every turn. "One
man alone can be pretty dumb sometimes, but for real bona fide
stupidity there ain't nothing can beat teamwork" [338]. Abbey plainly
intends the Bishop and his followers to be a microcosmic manifestation of the larger predatory group—culture—that rampages
thoughtlessly through the canyon country. The Team causes less
damage than culture only because of its smaller size.

To best the Team on a small scale and to thwart corporations on
a large, Abbey delivers a monkey-wrench brand of justice, adjust-
ing the gang's jaws whenever appropriate. No machine is too unimportant to leave incapacitated, no structure too gigantic to leave
unscathed. The gang takes its license from another two-fisted creed
of Western novels, creating its own laws and delivering its own pun-
ishments against the apparent lawbreakers. Historically, frontier
justice meant different things in different places, which has led to

a fictional confusion of fact and fantasy that must delight the author of *The Monkey Wrench Gang*. Many Western novels would have us believe that sheriffs' posses, vigilante groups, and avenging gunmen regularly sidestepped the law to deal violent death to men who fled their force. Relying predominantly on the six-shooter or on the hangman's noose for authorization, they defined justice in their own terms. While the cowboy caricature of fair play was more a figment of the imagination than a reality of life, the fine line between justice and vengeance suggests some provocative paradoxes. Walter Van Tilburg Clark addresses this subject in *The Ox-Bow Incident*. In that novel's fine study of mob rule, a self-appointed posse hangs innocent men, an irrevocable act that later reverberates psychologically on everyone involved. No such horror awaits the Monkey Wrench Gang because, unlike Clark's more sobering story, Abbey's tale caricatures conventional notions of justice and vengeance. It shifts the traditional roles of lawman and lawbreaker, switches white hats and black among the characters, reiterates its author's contention that corporate horrors merit swift retribution, and makes the reader laugh.

"Somebody had to do it" [43], the avengers decide at the outset. Any and all methods of opposition to the "giant machines, road networks, strip mines, conveyor belt, pipelines, slurry lines, loading towers, railway and electric train, hundred-million-dollar coal-burning power plant; ten thousand miles of high-tension towers and high-voltage power lines; the devastation of the landscape . . .; the poisoning of the last big clean-air reservoir in the forty-eight contiguous United States, the exhaustion of precious water supplies. . . . All that for what?" [160]—any kind of opposition to "all that" is perfectly, morally acceptable. In the world of *The Monkey Wrench Gang*, anarchy rules because, in Abbey's world, the ends justify the means. The proceedings are a joke, however. Unlike Clark, who uses the Western's traditional distinction between proper justice and vengeance in order to create a tragic tension, Abbey uses the same dichotomy to disarm the issue. Both writers, of course, advance a serious problem well beyond the confines of a formula presentation, speaking not only about vigilante action in the mode of the nineteenth-century West but about mob (or gang) anarchy in the twentieth century too. It is Abbey, though, who somersaults even further, completely overturning his presentation. Apparently the megamachine of the techno-industrial society responds only to powers greater than its own, so those who would abort it must use a certain amount of force. "Back to work . . . We got three bridges, a railroad, a strip mine, a power plant, two dams, a nuclear reactor, one computer data center, six highway projects and a BLM scenic overlook to take care of this week" [228].

While the gang takes care of the tactical details, Abbey takes care of the propaganda, which, after all, is the point of *The Monkey Wrench Gang*. Designed to do "a little more" than just entertain, Abbey's 1975 "mock-heroic" romance manipulates as many conventions of the Western formula as it can in order to make its statement about the modern-day conglomerate westward movement. Such traditional issues as free range versus fenced, primitive versus civilized, violence versus pacifism, good versus evil, or justice versus vengeance appear among its pages in disarray because Abbey is writing not an old-fashioned Western but a singular vision of his contemporary world. "And it all began just one year from today."

The events of the book, appropriate for a romance, are fabricated. At least no anarchistic group has rampaged through the canyon country yet. But by covering his pseudo-Western with a make-believe disguise, even though concrete details still abound, Abbey avoids one of the traps that snare too many Western writers. Jay Gurian explains the difficulty. "If he is interested in 'reality,' the writer in our time must use what really happened a century ago, not as it really happened, but as his readers can make sense of it. A crucial weakness of serious western writers is that, ignoring the sense of their own time, they cannot make the necessary myth of earlier times."[7] Abbey, of course, makes the necessary myth, not by using what really happened a century ago but by projecting a sympathetic exposé of it onto an overlay of present and future. That is, he "makes sense of his own time" by subsuming "the necessary myth." He borrows the ingredients of the classic Western novel about the past, applies them in a realistic present-day setting, and so propels his reader to a future of his own making. There, where the red and green worlds come together, Abbey articulates his vision.

"To save the fucking wilderness," sounds Hayduke's cry, and he means to accomplish this end by physical force while his designer works with less tangible tools. A passage from *The Journey Home* explains again how the double-edged technique works for Abbey. "Human bodies and human wit, active here, there, everywhere, united in purpose, independent in action, can still face that machine and stop it and take it apart and reassemble it—if we wish—on lines entirely new. There is, after all, a better way to live" [JH, 226], so Hayduke and his friends, "united in purpose, independent in action," try radical methods to dismantle the mad machine. Abbey, on the other hand, uses the creative mode. "The poets and prophets have been trying to tell us about it for three thousand years" [JH, 226], he reports; he has been on the job for a quarter century. In *The Monkey Wrench Gang*, the most popular of all his fictive works, Abbey unleashes his comic imagination to try and "tell us about it," to show the awful devastation faced by the modern-day West. The reader can mistake neither his propagandistic intent nor the rollicking glee with which he pronounces his sobering message.

Although "rollicking glee" and "sobering message" may sound contradictory, the two phrases literally describe concurrent elements of the book. Underlying the escapades and the laughter is, to Abbey's mind, the most critical problem the West faces today. As far as he can see, and for entirely unacceptable reasons, developers are devouring the sacred landscape

to light the lamps of Phoenix suburbs not yet built, to run the air conditioners of San Diego and Los Angeles, to illuminate shopping center parking lots at two in the morning, to power aluminum plants, magnesium plants, vinyl-chloride factories and copper smelters, to charge the neon tubing that makes the meaning (all the meaning there is) of Las Vegas, Albuquerque, Tucson, Salt Lake City, the amalgamated *metropoli* of southern California, to keep alive that phosphorescent putrefying glory (all the glory there is left) called Down Town, Night Time, Wonderville, U.S.A. [161]

Unfortunately Abbey inadvertently loses part of his effectiveness when he writes like this, spitting propaganda staccato-style. When his inner rage overrides his control, his prose rhythm accelerates so quickly that the result, like the preceding extract, pounds cacophonously on the reader's ear. Similar passages appear in all his writing—the "incredible shit" section of *Desert Solitaire* or the "whore of industry" chapter of *Abbey's Road*, for example—with the effect, each time, of distracting the reader from the issue at hand. In other words, when he shouts his message, it is least likely to be taken seriously. When he disguises the propaganda, however, as he does in the more controlled parts of his nonfiction and in certain portions of *The Monkey Wrench Gang*, he is both powerful and persuasive. In the latter romance he chooses to do so comically, using his sense of humor to pronounce a sobering message. By cloaking the seriousness of his concerns in laughter, he makes his point most trenchantly. The prose, in fact, so entertains that one almost forgets the wisdom behind the modest proposal.

Numerous forms and degrees of humor pervade the book. One example shows a trim rangerette who, after spotting Seldom Seen praying for a "*pre*-cision-type earthquake" right in the middle of the bridge across Glen Canyon Dam, says "I'm sorry, sir, but you can't pray here. This is a public place" [33]. Another flashes a bird's-eye view of Lee's Ferry:

In order to administrate, protect and make the charm, beauty and history of Lee's Ferry easily accessible to the motorized public, the Park Service had established not only a new paved road and the gravel quarry but also a ranger station, a paved campground, a hundred-foot-high pink water tower, a power line, a paved picnic area, a motor pool with cyclone fence, an official garbage dump and a boat-launching ramp covered with steel matting. The area had been turned over to the administration of the National Park Service in order to protect it from vandalism and commercial exploitation. [35]

Abbey, of course, seizes upon such obvious inconsistency. Nothing, in fact, is too sacred for him to joke about. "He looked as a park ranger should look: tall, slim, able, not too bright" [189]; his burnished nameplate announces his affinity with the author, "Edwin P. Abbott, Jr." [190]; his statements reflect the inane park lingo—"It's not a people's park, it's a national park" [193]—spoken by innocent official protectors of the wilderness; his presence is a fine example of the author laughing at his own caricature.

Some of Abbey's humor sounds ironic and even bitter, but, for the most part, he fills *The Monkey Wrench Gang* with verbal feints and jabs meant to lighten the scene. Even whole episodes may take on a comic tone when he decides to ease the solemnity of the impossible mission. Discovering an unattended Caterpillar D-7 bulldozer one day, Hayduke cannot resist driving it wildly across an airstrip and dumping it off a cliff. A single line suggests the tone of the interlude—"At once the tractor began to move—thirty five tons of iron bearing east toward St. Louis, Mo., via Lake Powell and Narrow Canyon" [117]—but the entire escapade is hilarious, with Hayduke crouching ferociously over the controls, Seldom Seen shouting instructions, and the mad machine itself ricocheting from one impediment to another. The portrayal is only slightly less broad than slapstick, and just as humorous. Here Abbey has disguised his serious intent—to dismantle the mad machine—in an uproarious garb of good humor that itself dismantles the mad machine.

Much of the pleasure in reading *The Monkey Wrench Gang* comes from the vicarious thrills of tasting the forbidden. Like all effective escape fiction and like Abbey's nonfiction romances, this book invites armchair participation, but it adds a bonus of laughter that extends the reader's enjoyment of Hayduke's adolescent machinations. The author seems to relish the vicarious fun as much as his audience does, for the book contains a number of incidents that surely reflect Abbey's own fantasies. Chapter 16 of *Abbey's Road*, "In Defense of the Redneck," describes an adventure of Ed's in an Arizona bar where he asked some silly questions, struck up a foolish conversation, and nearly got beaten as a result. The fictional version lets Hayduke open his mouth wider and then closes it more forcefully. "Hi . . . I'm a hippie," the jester with "three shooters of Beam and a quart of Coors gurgling in his gut" announces, just before punching a cowboy in the stomach. "Well. Shit. Wrong cowboys this time" [202], and a full-fledged brawl ensues. Many such semiviolent scenes occur in *The Monkey Wrench Gang*, scenes that release physical tension without permanent damage, that realize actions a reader might secretly like to try, that execute stunts Abbey himself might like to perform. Not all of them are perpetrated by Hayduke.

Too much for Doc. All of a sudden it was all too much. He drew back his big booted right foot and kicked the picture tube square in the eye. It imploded-exploded with a sound like the popping of a grandiose light bulb. A blue glare filled the kitchen and then died in the instant of its birth; shards and flakes of fluorescent glass slid down the walls.

Doc paused to contemplate the awful thing he had done. "Thus I refute McLuhan," he muttered. [217]

Another example of Abbey's secondary presence in his fictional world comes with the consumption of beer. "Out in the open Southwest, he and his friends measured highway distances in per-capita six-packs of beer. L. A. to Phoenix, four six-packs; Tucson to Flag-staff, three six-packs; Phoenix to New York, thirty-five six-packs" [17]. "He," in this case, is Hayduke, but he could just as well be Ed. In fact, Abbey's fictive characters sound remarkably alike, and like their creator, when they speak out on the subject of what to do with all those empties. "I throw beer cans along the fucking highways," Hayduke affirms in his foul-mouthed fashion. "Why the fuck shouldn't I throw fucking beer cans along the fucking highways?" Seldom Seen gives Abbey's answer. "Hell, . . . I do it too. Any road I wasn't consulted about that I don't like, I litter. It's my religion" [65]. It is Ed's religion as well. In *The Journey Home* he explains, "Of course I litter the public highway. Every chance I get. After all, it's not the beer cans that are ugly; it's the highway that is ugly" [JH, 158–159]. Obviously Hayduke, Seldom Seen, and Ed all speak with Abbey's tongue, rationalizing a free-spirited moral-ity that considers every unwanted construct fair game for vandal-ism. At least in the fictive worlds of the romancer's imagination this is true.

The fertility of his imagination is obvious from the number of episodes which, repeated from book to book, not only offer spe-cial pleasure to those who sit safely at home but suggest that Abbey constantly refines his destructive technique as he writes. The de-tails of *The Monkey Wrench Gang* were figments of *Desert Solitaire's* fancy. We recall that a so-called nonfiction chapter, "Down the River," pictured a single "unknown hero" descending into the bowels of Glen Canyon Dam to hide explosives and attach blasting caps that will be ignited at the moment of the grand opening ceremony. "Idle, foolish, futile daydreams" [DS, 188], Ed decides, but eight years of imaginative work refine the notion. Apparently Abbey has decided that bridges blow up better at dedication ceremonies, while dams are best destroyed by more creative sabotage. The opening pages of *The Monkey Wrench Gang* outline a preferable scene—desert sun glaring on a hot July afternoon, travelers waiting restlessly, Indi-ans gazing from a nearby hillside, a workman scurrying to a last-minute task. The ritual begins with speeches, followed by the cutting of the ribbon.

Suddenly the center of the bridge rose up, as if punched from beneath, and broke in two along a jagged zigzag line. Through this absurd fissure, crooked as lightning, a sheet of red flame streamed skyward, followed at once by the sound of a great cough, a thunderous shuddering high-explosive cough that shook the monolithic sandstone of the canyon walls. The bridge parted like a flower, its separate divisions no longer joined by any physical bond. Fragments and sections began to fold, sag, sink and fall, relaxing into the abyss. [5]

Thus, the destruction of a bridge becomes an accomplished imaginative fact, a scenario Abbey has, over the years, refined pictorially.

But what about the dam? Obviously he wants it obliterated too. Not only did he fantasize such an act in *Desert Solitaire*, but he pursued the notion even further in *Slickrock*, when he reconceived Glen Canyon after the dam's removal. The Monkey Wrench Gang understands his wishes. " 'You know what we ought to do,' the doctor said. 'We ought to blow that dam to shitaree.' " Hayduke hesitates. "I can take out a bridge for you, . . . if you get me enough dynamite. But I don't know about Glen Canyon Dam. We'd need an atom bomb for that one." Seldom Seen jumps into the discussion. " 'I been thinking about that dam for a long time,' Smith said. 'And I got a plan. We get three jumbo-size houseboats and some dolphins—' " [63–64]. Dolphins? In soberer moments the marauders review the ultimate quest and, while dolphins may be absurd, houseboats filled with explosives sound increasingly plausible. Seldom Seen elaborates: "four jumbo-size houseboats, the kind millionaires use, them sixty-five footers. We pack them full of fertilizer and diesel fuel. Then we head down the lake toward the dam, slow and easy . . ." [147]. Back in Albuquerque by himself, Doc remembers the daydreams. "The devil finds work for idle hands. Dr. Sarvis reached for the newspaper. Saw the full-page ad on the back. Boat Show, Duke City Ice Arena. He thought he might go and have a look at the new houseboats. Tomorrow, or the next day. Soon" [217]. But Hayduke, a different breed of anarchist, prefers a single heroic gesture: "If I got a haircut and a shave and put on a suit and necktie and a slide rule and a shiny new yellow hard hat like all the Reclamation engineers wear, why maybe—just maybe—I could get right down into the control center with a satchel full of good shit, TNT or something . . ." [147].

Abbey persists, until he saturates *The Monkey Wrench Gang* with the pleasing notion. Not only does he energize his tale with fanciful deeds the reader may enjoy vicariously, but he repeats them so often that they almost sound believable. Furthermore, he projects these events into a properly continuous present where, even if they have not yet happened, they might occur tomorrow. The final chase sequence toward Land's End, for example, begins with the futile attempt to destroy the White Canyon bridge, concludes with the surrender of Doc and Bonnie, the capture of Seldom Seen, and the apparent liquidation of Hayduke, alias Rudolph the Red, and takes place in the present tense. Like Abbey's technique elsewhere, this makes the action seem ongoing, as if the gang were immortal and their raids on the establishment everlasting. Too, the author frames his story with a prologue entitled "The Aftermath" and an epilogue called "The New Beginning," both written in the present tense to heighten the timelessness of the tale. The prologue describes that explosive demise of the Glen Canyon bridge, while the epilogue traces the quieter dissolution of the gang. In those final pages, Abbey stresses both his cyclical sense of history and his prophecy of continuity. Bonnie and Doc are married, expecting a child, living quietly on a houseboat ten miles from Green River, Utah, near Mr. and Mrs. Seldom Smith. The jack Mormon, now living with only one wife, is otherwise "the same as ever. Still working on the dam plan" [336]. Hayduke, apparently undamaged by the fusillade of bullets on the edge of The Maze, certainly has not forgotten his vows. The fourth member of the defunct gang has, in fact, a new job as a night watchman, presumably at Glen Canyon Dam, where he plans to begin "work" next week. Meanwhile, he has nothing but praise for his friends' latest activities.

> Hayduke chuckles. "Good old Doc. Say, that was a nice job you and Seldom did on that bridge."
> "What are you talking about?"
> "No? I mean the Glen Canyon bridge."
> "That wasn't us." [386]

If Doc and Seldom Seen were not responsible for blowing up the bridge, and Hayduke had no part in the action—who did it? Abbey's vicarious anarchism must be at work, drawing other Lone Ranger types into the contemporary western scene. "You think we're alone?" Hayduke asked earlier in the story.

"I'll bet—listen, I'll bet this very minute there's guys out in the dark doing the same kind of work we're doing. All over the country, little bunches of guys in twos and threes, fighting back."

"You're talking about a well-organized national movement."

"No I'm not. No organization at all. None of us knowing anything about any other little bunch. That's why they can't stop us."

"Why don't we ever hear about it?"

"Because it's *suppressed*, that's why; they don't want the word to get around." [169; italics Abbey's]

But Abbey does want the word to get around. That is why he wrote *The Monkey Wrench Gang* and why he so carefully structured its retributive deeds into a continuous present of cyclical time.

That is also why he introduces another anarchistic surrogate. Late one night a mysterious stranger catches Hayduke draining the crankcase of an Allis-Chalmers HD-41. While the Gang member freezes at the sound of a "voice, deep and low, not twenty feet away," the anonymous tones tell him to "go ahead and finish what you're a-doin' under there" and continue: " 'I can see you do a good job. Thorough. I like that.' The man spat on the ground. 'Not like some of them half-assed dudes I seen up on the Powder River. Or them kids down around Tucson. Or them nuts that derailed—' " [220]. By implication, a wide network of amateur anarchists spreads across the West, and Hayduke's strange new friend is only one of many envisioned by the romancer.

Yet this vigilante differs from the others.

The stranger was wearing a mask. Not a black mask over the eyes but simply a big bandanna draped outlaw-style over the nose, mouth and chin. Above the mask one dark right eye, vaguely shining, peered at him from under the droopy brim of a black hat. The other eye stayed closed in what appeared to be a permanent wink. Hayduke finally realized that the man's left eyeball was gone, long gone, lost and forgotten no doubt in some ancient barroom quarrel, some legendary war. [221]

Riding a horse named "Rosie," the anonymous masked man helps Hayduke finish his tasks that night and then rides away. "Call him Kemosabe," Hayduke tells Bonnie when she asks, deliberately reminding her and the reader of the mythical Lone Ranger who "must" still exist. "Kemosabe" does not reappear until the last pages of the book where, teamed up with Hayduke, the two comrades establish contact with the retired gang members. But Abbey still keeps the stranger's identity secret. Not until *Good News* does the reader learn that the one-eyed man is Jack Burns, the brave cowboy resuscitated in order to breathe new energy into a hideously profaned environment. Abbey's belief in a rhythm of life leads him to reintroduce characters from book to book. They live in a kind of imaginative continuous present that carries their author's cyclical vision continuously forward.

A full discussion of Jack Burns's role as he projects that vision belongs elsewhere, but it is important to pause and recognize that to enter Abbey's world at any time is to reencounter a number of old friends and foes—whether characters or themes—reshaped and redefined. The earth itself—its sacrality and the profanation that destroys it—recurs most often as the focus, yet man's proper place in the earth's scheme is crucial too. In his nonfiction, especially in the three personal histories, Abbey places Ed in compatible juxtaposition with his natural environment, thus showing the potential for man's contentment in a world beyond the green and red. The fiction, however, usually depicts protagonists like Jack Burns who, for some reason, finally fail to reach that goal. *The Monkey Wrench Gang* is the happy exception.

Unlike their predecessors, the gang members emerge satisfactorily at their story's close, and the tale itself ends on an up-beat. Several pages describe the resolution—intricate legal maneuverings have resulted in short jail sentences followed by probation for the felons, while personal readjustments have led them to peaceful co-existences. Divorced by wives one and two, Seldom Seen lives with number three on a hay and melon ranch, as content as Doc and Bonnie who dwell nearby. The three marauders have achieved what Jonathan Troy, Jack Burns, John Vogelin, and Will Gatlin could not. An excerpt from *Abbey's Road* explains how they managed:

Aliens on this planet? Us? Who said so? Not me. And if I did, that was yesterday. Tonight I know better. We are not foreigners; we were born and we belong here. We are not aliens, but rather like children, barely beginning here and now in the childhood of this race to discover the marvel, the magic, the mystery of this gracious planet that is our inheritance. [AR, 189–190]

Because they vowed to preserve and protect their inheritance no matter what the cost, the Monkey Wrench Gang intuitively discovers "the marvel, the magic, the mystery." Even after their green-world idyll runs head-on into red-world reality—"Half in shade and half in sun they hustle up the bare sliprock, shuffle through more of the dragging nightmarish sand, clamber over spalled-off slabs and struggle on, straggle upward, into the barren tributary canyon. . . . The trap within the trap" [338]—they survive intact. Thus, at the close of their story, Doc and Bonnie and Seldom Seen exist in Abbey's world.

"It is not a question merely of preserving forests and rivers, wildlife and wilderness, but also of keeping alive a certain way of human life, a wholesome and reasonable balance between industrialism and agrarianism, between cities and small towns, between private property and public property . . . [where] it is still possible to enjoy the advantages of contemporary technological culture without having to endure the overcrowding and stress characteristic of this culture in less fortunate regions" [AR, 137]. *The Monkey Wrench Gang's* denouement, by showing the efficacy of a simple life and respect for the land, gives fictive life to Abbey's cherished doctrine. Furthermore, the gang members have earned their happiness. Because they committed themselves to champion the earth's sacrality, their creator rewards them with a long-lasting personal energy all their own. How different this is from Will Gatlin's fate, or John Vogelin's. The one must pace and stare because he could make no commitment; the other unfortunately committed himself to the past. Neither tactic sufficed, nor led to Abbey's world. Yet Hayduke, a misfit more damaged by society than either Gatlin or Vogelin as his story begins, and thus less likely to find the proper way, finds a via media untravelled by Abbey's more somber characters.

Hayduke's heroic creed, "to save the fucking wilderness," precedes his affection for Bonnie, but the two commitments together consecrate him for entry into Abbey's world. First, however, he must outwit the enemy. In a pursuit reminiscent of Jonathan Troy's race through the night, of the brave cowboy's flight up the escarpment, of Billy Starr's return to the ranch, and of Will Gatlin's descent, Hayduke clambers toward the Maze. "He had only a mile and a half to go, rounding the heads of a branchwork of ravines in the slickrock, dark little canyons deeper than wide, all of them starting to run with water now, red-brown silt-laden stuff, a foamy spongy bubbling liquid too thick to drink, too thin to walk on" [365]. But a great gray helicopter plus a team of men have him cornered.

They pin him to the edge of an abyss where "he teeters on the edge, arms flailing for balance." Then they close in, blasting him "with a storm of bullets" as the reader sees "the body ripped and fragmented, chips, rags, splinters, slivers flying off, the arms flopping as if broken, the rifle dropped, the head itself shattered into bits and pieces—the collapsing wreckage of what *could* have been, seconds earlier, a living, laughing, loving, red-blooded *American boy*" [374; italics Abbey's]. The hero's remains fall "like a sack of garbage into the foaming gulf of the canyon, vanishing forever from men's eyes. And women's too. (For indeed, the body was never found.)" [374]. Thus Abbey injects humor into what should be a morbid scene. Breaking off the tension of the chase and keeping the tone of the book uniform, the preposterous descriptions and the quick asides alleviate the mood. They also set up the final resurrection.

> "Is that you, George?"
> "Fuck yes. Who the hell else?"
> Doc sighs again. "They shot you to pieces at Lizard Rock."
> "Not me. Rudolf."
> "Rudolf?"
> "A scarecrow. A fucking dummy."
> "I don't understand." [385]

George Washington Hayduke lives (as Fred Goodsell this time) to father a new fight against the mad machine, achieving the immortality of a character who lives in Abbey's world. There, ribaldry reigns, bringing red and green together in a combination not found elsewhere in the author's fiction.

Although some readers object to the playful resolution because it again takes an easy way out of a structural box, it succeeds where the deus ex machina ending of *The Brave Cowboy* did not. The tone of Abbey's other major Western did not lead naturally to its conclusion, for Art Hinton's truck seemed too mechanistic and Jack Burns's death (or temporary incapacitation) too contrived. In contrast, *The Monkey Wrench Gang* ends as it began, in laughter and in the continuous present of a happy crew still committed to protecting the sacred earth. The climax and the aftermath fit their author's original conception. For that reason, the major characters belong, ensconced as they are, in Abbey's world. Although three-fourths of the crew has domesticated its anarchistic mode, they continue to lead a life Abbey respects. So does the fourth vigilante, who has joined the masked rider to make a dynamic duo and who seems as determined as ever to safeguard the precious environment. It would seem that Hayduke's creator is saving him and his friends for future appearances. After all, there is still Glen Canyon Dam.

10

About, Face

Good News

With *Good News* (1980), in some ways, Abbey leaves the world of romance behind. He departs from the strictures of that form neither because he has changed his attitudes toward the contemporary milieu, nor because he has redefined his own envisioned world. Rather, he moves away from the romance because he has discovered a new way of pronouncing his beliefs. That is, *Good News* communicates the same vision as before, but with one sweeping difference. Whereas his earlier prose contained ironic passages, now the entire shape of his vision is ironic, heavily so, as he comes face to face with the attendant horror of a future that has not recognized the mistakes of past and present. A parody of his previous writing, *Good News* spouts a prophetic frustration at modernity. It does so by using a form that builds upon the design of Abbey's other books. Romance becomes irony.

Northrop Frye explains the progression in a single sentence. "As structure, the central principle of ironic myth is best approached as a parody of romance: the application of romantic mythical forms to a more realistic content which fits them in unexpected ways."[1] This, then, is Abbey's new mode—to parody his own works, to reform and restate his own artistic vision of a failing twentieth century. *Good News*, an irony, turns his own romances upside down. The hero is an antihero—Jack Burns, a lifetime later; his quest, an antiquest—one doomed before its start; the time, in this world and yet not of it, is just a few years from today.

Set in an Arizona of the future, *Good News* pictures a world that succeeds the disintegration of modern society. "Not a nightmare of horror but a nightmare of dreariness"[2] has brought not a holocaust but a gradual dysfunction. Frayed planetary economy, small yet continuous wars, excessive exploitation of natural resources, overcrowding, overbuilding, overconsumption have all led, in Abbey's brave new world, to a breakdown both personal and international. Into the ruins, and into the civil war still waged by the survivors, rides the brave cowboy. Jack Burns "might be a ghost." A parody of his former self,

he is clearly old, well advanced in his mortality—the sunburned beak of nose projects above a narrow, pointed, cadaverous jaw that bristles like cactus, with stiff frosty stubble. Under the shadow of his broad-brimmed hat the eyes, set deep and wide in cavernous sockets, look out on the world with asymmetric intensity: one eye clear, bright, lifeless, the other old and dark and tired but alive, all the same, with a melancholy passion. The left eye is glass but the other—his shooting eye—is living plasm, wired to the circuits of the mind and soul. [6–7]

Together with an Indian friend, Sam, the aging cowboy seeks his long-lost son amid the southwestern ruins. The task, even more pointless than Jack's attempt to free Paul Bondi so many fictive years before, gives impetus to the plot of *Good News*.

The searchers experience various adventures along the way and encounter various prototypical characters. Those whom they meet are the survivors, men and women who will perpetuate and/or outlive society's decay. Exaggerated and stylized, these typical Abbey creations provide both human interest and philosophical depth to the course of the narrative. Often they take over, since both Jack and Sam disappear for long periods of time. Art Dekker, a young orphan from rural parts, loses his innocence in the embattled streets and alleys of the city. Professor Rodack and his idealistic followers lead the insurrections that Art joins. Their opponents, those in military control of the devastated territory, are dominated by the Chief, "a small man—slim, fit, beautiful, with a well-toned tension, under perfect control, in each movement, each gesture" [34], a megalomaniac who commands fear, if not respect, from his subordinates. The cast of *Good News* also includes such sympathetic characters as Dixie, the friendly barmaid, for example, and such notorious ones as the Chief's many satellites—Sergeant Brock and Mangus Colorado, the Apache, Major Roland, Corporal Buckley, the Inspectors Wolfe and Fox, and Captain Charles Barnes.

Linking these diverse characters is the episodic narrative. Although it loosely follows Jack Burns's quest, peripheral incidents continually interrupt the flow. Episodes and individuals enter and depart in staccato fashion, their stories reflective of the disintegration of the world in which they live. When the book ends, the reader finds he never really knew these people, nor can he be sure of their fates or their futures. Apparently Rodack, Art, Sam, and Dixie will continue fighting the oppressors; apparently the Chief and his mounted troops will press eastward to conquer new lands; apparently Jack Burns is dead, stabbed by a medieval lance in an oddly futuristic world. But that resolution is as indeterminate as his previous fate in *The Brave Cowboy,* for the final two pages of *Good News* pose the following conundrum:

> "Colonel, the men couldn't find the body."
> The colonel looks cross. "That's absurd."
> "Yes sir."
> "Did they really look? Couldn't they find our tracks?"
> "Yes sir, they followed the tracks and they found where the old man was. Found the lance. Dried blood all over the place. But no body."
> "Absurd. What about the horse?"
> "The horse was gone too."
> "Ridiculous."
> "Yes sir. Maybe coyotes dragged the body away."
> "That's really absurd."
> "I know, sir. But no body."
> "Absurd."
> "Yes sir."
> *"Absurd."*
> "You're right, Colonel." [241–242; italics Abbey's]

Absurdity is just the point of this imagined world, for Abbey intends scenes of abject chaos. *Good News,* then, is unconventional. A disappointment, perhaps, by traditional standards, with its abrupt tonal shifts, its disconnected scenes, and its one-dimensional characters, the book nevertheless accomplishes its author's goal successfully. As irony, as parody, as Abbey's vision distorted by the power of its magnification, this sixth fiction absurdly recapitulates the intellectual content of the preceding five.

The keystone of *Good News* is its form. By choosing irony for his organizing principle, Abbey gives himself full artistic latitude because, quite simply, irony has no organizing principle. Unlike the romance, or tragedy or comedy, irony possesses no consistent set of characteristics and follows no discernible mythic pattern. Instead, it thrives on the absence of norms, reaching its greatest achievements when chaotically turned loose.

Fragmentary, incongruous, indirect—terms like these point to the eclectic nature of irony and the paradoxical fact that the ironist, assuming the most independent of roles, is in fact the most dependent on the conventions of literature. Indeed, irony seems somehow parasitical, living on the other narrative patterns and drawing its sustenance from another value system, for there is nothing in its abstract and negative vision that can, in itself, generate anything like a conventional pattern of action.[3]

It seems that irony's only real constant is an imaginative and provocative inversion of the reader's preconceptions and expectations. Ironists do not write from a structure of their own design, they subsume and negate elements taken from other forms. Foulke and Smith explain further: "From romance irony borrows the ordered elements of the quest and dislocates them in the haphazard events and loose ends of the picaresque form. From tragedy it takes the sense of an arbitrary fate but refuses to lessen its nagging incongruities with a redeeming moral order. From comedy it draws out the conflict between the new and old societies but turns it to more corrosive satiric purposes."[4] Inverting selected parts from these other patterns, irony adopts a convention only to destroy it, points toward a conclusion only to reverse it. Such a malleable genre suits particularly well a contentious author like Abbey whose vision tells him that change is of the essence if the modern world is to be saved. *Good News*, in fact, is a textbook version of an irony that systematically —ergo, unsystematically—upends customs of form as well as proprieties of thought.

Like a comedy, the book pits a new society against an old, but with a surprising dichotomy. The new is old; the old, new. The Chief, his men, and the ideas they represent comprise an order which, in its energetic attempt to rule the new world, perpetuates the worst features of the old. Their glorious aim—"the unification of mankind into a planetary organism" [187]—encourages them to run roughshod over individuals and across the land. Opposing these soldiers are the new rebels, citizens and their agrarian cousins who themselves represent the oldest order of all. The Chief disdains their origins—"your Proudhonian libertarianism, your shopkeeper's anarchism, your Jeffersonian mediocrity" [187]—but they remain stolidly emblematic of age-old individualism. In this book, the old and new resemble players in an ancient comedy, ones thoroughly masked in paradox. Abbey sends the groups to battle one another, not to engender laughter, as the heroes and villains of *The Monkey Wrench Gang* do, but for "corrosive satiric purposes" instead.

A sample shoot-out takes place in the now-deserted El Con shopping center, "through corridors of this commercial labyrinth." The roar of motorcycles, the crackle of small-arms fire, the falling crash of glass and a scream of pain punctuate the dereliction of the stores. "A young man lurches . . ., black silhouette against the light. . . . He reels through the doorway and into Frederick's [of Hollywood], stumbles, falls, lies still on the floor amid the broken glass, shattered cabinets, fallen plaster, the headless, legless, pink torsos of plastic females" [62]. Jack Burns watches. Then, listening to the motorcycle sounds diminish—"lions of steel thundering up and down the courses of a maze"—and "tying his horse to a cash register," he aids the victim, the boy who turns out to be a young woman. Generating only cold, calculated, and corrosive laughter, Abbey's description calls both the skirmish and its participants into question. The horse tied to the cash register of a once-elegant store, the military charging its motorized steeds up and down an empty mall, "the barking of guns [and] the yells of frightened men," the mistaken identity—all these details implicate the author's sardonic attitude toward his creation. "Ruins. Ruins. All in ruins," he characterizes the scene in ironic, not comic, terms.

> Ruins. Ruins. All in ruins. Coyotes slink among the blackened walls, hunting rats. Anthills rise, Soleri-like, from the arid fountains of the covered mall. Young paloverde trees, acid green, and globemallow, and sun-

flowers, and tumbleweed, and the bright fuzzy cactus known as teddy bear cholla (cuddly and deadly) grow from cracks in the asphalt of the endless parking lots. [60]

As in tragedy, an arbitrary fate has indifferently cast its dice. So where shopping centers, golf courses, and airports once stretched as far as the eye could see, the desert now repossesses the horizon. "Stray horses browse among the sand dunes that are drifting fifty feet a year out of the southwest toward the mountains" [60]. From the ashes of the apocalypse, however, rise the very men whose mentalities caused it.

TIRED OF ARSON? MURDER? WAR?
READY FOR ORDER? LAW? PROGRESS?
SUPPORT OUR CHIEF! [60; italics Abbey's]

A billboard calls for moral support of the individual who relishes daily executions and whose army roams the streets in search of human prey. The Chief himself professes a virtuous certitude of order, law, and progress that his actions belie. He explains to a prisoner, for example, that "what we do is for causes even higher than honor, glory, heroism, patriotism. Even higher than the nation. What we do . . . is for God" [47]. Charismatically and persuasively, the Chief argues the incontrovertible morality of his army's means and ends. "Our purpose is to follow—the light. The light that leads us to God, my friend. And by that light, if we do not rebel against it like fools, or betray it like cowards, by that light, . . . we will meet God. We will become one in union with God. Forever. Beyond time. Through all eternity" [47–48]. He preaches an ethical sermon of brotherly love, even as his army brings more prisoners to be hanged and even as he hisses an aside about his one-man audience—"Now get the wretch out of my sight. I'm sick of the smell of him. And if he gives you one bit of trouble, shoot him instantly. Instantly" [48].

Abbey clearly recognizes the incongruities of the Chief's words and the absurdities of his successes, but just as clearly he refuses to reduce the impact of the man's triumphs. Because there is no redeeming moral order in this newly crafted and wholly ironic universe, there is no reason to punish the Chief and his followers, or even to question his arguments. In a world such as this, no extant code prevails. "Forward! Advance! Onward! *Onward*" [235; italics Abbey's] steps the grand parade of color guard, officers, cavalrymen, motorized equipment, and brass band. "An army, not a raiding party. A force, not a reconnoiter. A state, not a camp" [42]. In the name, ironically, of Coronado—the first great conqueror to sweep through the Southwest—the troops depart for the East. Nothing stems their progress.

Apparently victorious, they nevertheless leave their anarchistic opponents free. Major Roland, leading a rear guard in defense of the Chief's dark tower, will probably lose out to the "barbarians and infidels" because "Charles will never get there" [242] and because Abbey cannot resist the triple entendre that alludes to *King Lear*, "Childe Roland to the Dark Tower Came," and *Song of Roland* simultaneously. But whether or not the rabble will overthrow the Tower guarding Phoenix's corpse makes little difference to the narrative's close. Abbey purposely leaves the aftermath unclear, for in this ironic universe, mastery by any moral order is philosophically inappropriate. *Good News*, written completely in the continuous present to convey the cyclical endlessness of the frays, finishes as it began, perpetuating an oscillating and inconclusive amorality. Both the Chief's side and the infidels can appear triumphant because, in an irony, the outcome makes no difference.

Obviously neither comic nor tragic in its outlook, *Good News* simply ignores the strictures of those forms. It discards such presumptions as "the good guys always win" into a philosophic limbo from which there is no exit, disregarding the ethos of tragedy and disjointing the spirit of comedy. Like all effective irony, however, it draws sustenance from those forms, relishing its inversions of the reader's expectations. Most particularly, it draws life from Abbey's favorite mythos, the romance. Using the quest formula as its narrative base, a crafted nether world as its setting, and an olio of stylized characters as its population, *Good News* parodies its author's best writing in an effort "to give form to the shifting ambiguities and complexities of unidealized existence."[5] That is, Abbey's ironic 1980 vision most nearly echoes, then subverts, the expectations of romance.

One of those expectations involves the course of the plot—the quest. When a knight-errant, or in this case a cowboy hero, goes forth to right a wrong, the reader expects certain events in a certain sequence. A chivalrous horseman will slay dragons, best other knightly foes, and win the hand of a fair lady; a Zane Grey protagonist will battle hostile elements, stand up to rustlers or outlaws, and emerge victoriously from the ordeal. Jack Burns, however, follows no such predetermined trail. In fact, his quest strikes both his sidekick and the reader as absurd:

> The Indian points toward the smoldering city, the scatter of fires and lights spread across ten miles of the horizon. "How do you think we're going to find him? In that dying mess? All those frightened people? You don't even know what he looks like now."
> "I know his name. . . . I'll know him when I see him."
> "You think so? You last saw him twenty years ago." [9]

Looking for someone who must have changed enormously over the course of two decades, the questing father heads for the rubble of the smoldering city. Once there, he chooses to believe that Captain—now Colonel—Barnes is his son, Charlie Burns. No one can dissuade him, not those who point out the difference in names, not even the colonel himself who insists, "I don't know you, sir. . . . And my father is dead" [152]. When it finally becomes obvious to Jack that the colonel will never acknowledge a kinship, the brave cowboy transforms his quest into a new crusade. "Okay then, Charlie, I got to ask one more favor of you. Stand aside here, let me ride in and kill that other son-of-a-bitch" [230], the Chief.

Two incongruities dominate this narrative line: a traditional quest is neither so flimsily motivated nor so abruptly redirected. But an ironic quest operates differently, developing more by chance than causality, following no logical sequence or development, obeying no higher order. This accounts, then, both for the haphazard nature of Jack's adventures along the way and for the capriciousness of the outcome.

> The colonel sits slumped in his saddle and stares for a long time at the man on the ground. The sun glares from low in the west, under an armada of motionless clouds. The wind dies out as evening quiets the world. . . . The colonel watches the body of his father, and what he thinks he feels is not sorrow, nor regret, nor pride, nor anger, but instead a sense of ever-growing wonder. [233]

Ironically, the colonel and the reader discover the truth of the relationship only after Jack's death, only after the officer finds "the bleached-out photographs of a woman and a boy" [232] on the old man's body. The quest ends, not with a fortuitous reunion but with pointless bloodshed and an even more pointless recognition that postdates the action. The denouement merely affirms the futility of the search.

Two incompatible elements, combined in tragedy but kept separate in irony, characterize the tale. It is incongruous that Jack actually finds his son, and it is inevitable that he succeeds without knowing it. Like all ironists, Abbey twists these two polarities, the incongruous and the inevitable, to give shape to his narrative line. Each stage of Jack Burns's progression through the ashes of Phoenix mimics a traditional quest but, finally, misdirects the reader's expectations. When Jack confronts a hostile environment, it turns out to be a gigantic deserted shopping center; when he confounds the enemy, he does so by impotently emptying his gun at the sky. Even his final joust is incongruous because his pseudodeath is so arbitrary and unnecessary. That ending is inevitable, however, the final ironic completion of a senseless meandering quest.

In keeping with the disintegration of Jack's adventure, the entire narrative line of *Good News* disintegrates. Characters wander in and out of chapters, while episodes begin in medias res and stop before they are finished. A chapter-by-chapter breakdown shows the sporadic discontinuity, as scenes shift from desert to Tower to barroom to shopping center to underground hideaway and back to the streets. As soon as one plight attracts the reader's attention, another takes its place. Furthermore, a single event may itself be fragmented, told piecemeal, and fraught with surprises. The author interrupts Dixie's escape from the Tower, for example, with three separate incidents—the underground attack on Art and his revolutionary friends, the promotion of Colonel Barnes, and the first meeting between that soldier and his questing father. Distorting the normal passage of time and elongating Dixie's intrepid flight, Abbey once more skews the reader's expectations. His arbitrary design intentionally perverts the norm. And even the escape includes elements of surprise:

Corporal Buckley (always a bridesmaid) bends over the bed in the center of the room to straighten the black coverlet. A golden eagle, life-size, looks down from the ceiling with sheaf of arrows clutched in right talons, lightning bolt in the left: Nobility. Dominance. Penetration. Speed.

The andiron makes a soft but solid noise—*clunk!*—on the side of the corporal's skull. He utters a little, quiet cry as he sprawls across the bed. Dixie reopens her eyes, drops the weapon, gets quickly to work. [126–127]

Substituting the corporal's body for her own, she flees the Chief's domain, leaving that ignoble leader to take "his place on the chair, letting his robe fall open, looking down at his pride. All is well. Passive, docile, and waiting. With a smile meant to be stern but not cruel, he lifts his gaze to the pale odalisque [now Corporal Buckley, unbeknownst to the Chief] displayed on velvet" [127]. But Abbey sets up this incongruous situation only to drop it. He never describes the Chief's discovery, and inevitable fury at the switch, and thus once more twists our novelistic expectations, entangling more of *Good News's* plot than he unravels.

That an episode rarely resolves itself is due, in part, to the field of battle on which the action takes place. Jack's denatured quest and the escapades of the other characters occur in an environment hostile to their adventures. Inhospitable, harsh, indifferent—a string of adjectives carrying negative connotations describes the crafted Arizona wasteland where the action occurs. While the city obviously holds few pleasures in any form, the desert is equally unfriendly in this ironic landscape. Jack, for example, finds little sacrality in the Superstition Mountains:

On their right, to the north, stands a mountain shaped like a flatiron, or like a battleship, with near-vertical walls of volcanic rock, on its horizontal decks a crenellation of eroded towers, pinnacles, balanced rocks on pedestals—a voodoo landscape. Nothing seems to grow up there, in that waterless waste, but throne and spine and claw and needle and spear. Under the evening light, streaming in amber columns through a mass of clouds, the ancient rock of the mountain takes on a sullen glow, a mass of mangled iron heated from within by deep, infernal, other-worldly fires. Old Burns, glancing at it from time to time, cannot repress his feelings of discomfort.

"Good Christ," he mutters, "what a godawful place. Who could ever live up there?" [24–25]

Ed, by comparison, interprets the same scene quite differently: "A much eroded remnant of old volcanic structures, this range looks something like an antique Assyrian fortification, a mirage in the desert, a specter of olden times, abandoned by mankind" [CC, 42].

The romancer sees the energy of a rock formation that, despite its inhuman stature, emits a sacred glow, while the ironist notes only the mountain's "sullen," "infernal" qualities. In the nether world of *Good News*, even Jack mistakes the earth's powers.

But if towering landforms no longer give sanctuary in Abbey's new universe, human constructs certainly offer nothing better. "Like the face of a mountain wall, the Tower seems to lean back against the sky, to soar among the clouds, to rise—to be rising, with a grandeur both real and unreal—toward the noon sun. . . . Burns lowers his head, feeling dizzy" [145–146]. The Tower, phallic emblem of the Chief's control, dominates a city equally destitute of life-giving energy.

[The Chief] paces to the parapet and looks down into the dark streets, the whispering city, fifteen stories below. A few lights move about down there, not many—vehicular lights, electric torches, a few small campfires on the sidewalks. Three blocks south a building burns, unattended; the glow illuminates a vacant street, a glass wall opposite, the metal shells, like dead insects, of a mass of abandoned automobiles. One company of soldiers, commanded by an officer on horseback, approach the broad esplanade of the headquarters building, marching through the floodlit emptiness of Unity Square. Three dark bodies dangle on the gallows. From the bowels of the Tower, discernible from this height only as a steady, comforting, feline purr, rises the sound of the diesel generators. [94]

The Phoenix of *Good News*, an artificial facade, exemplifies the kind of ironic setting that inevitably occurs when writers imagine a chaotic world. T. S. Eliot's *Wasteland*, for example, conceptualizes a locale that appears dark, dirty, labyrinthine, and mysterious. Abbey's city, representing his own futuristic vision of contemporary America, resonates with the same tones. Eviscerated and sterile, both Eliot's London and Abbey's Southwestern urban sprawl pictorially render modern man's dereliction, there "in rats' alley/Where the dead men lost their bones." Furthermore, "the endless ruins, toward the smoking city and the dark towers" [58], depict Abbey's evaluation of modern technocracy's self-destructiveness.

The wasteland of *Good News* is, in fact, not far removed from the strip mines and desecrated canyons of *The Monkey Wrench Gang* or from the open pits and overdeveloped rural towns of *The Journey Home*. Abbey's writing has led steadily toward this latest nightmare, where "dangling [neon] signs, dead for a decade" keep watch over a "broad avenue littered with fragments of paper and glass, flanked now with dehydrated palm trees, abandoned automobiles, decaying office buildings with sagging walls of lathing, chicken wire, stucco, crumbling bastions of cinderblock" [59]. Riding away from the remains, the Chief ironically concludes, "You know, Colonel, poor Phoenix—it never was a real city"[235]. Instead, it was just a savage condition, a world crafted here by an artist who wishes to show, graphically, the incoherence of modern existence.

Into that abstraction he places a strange and unlikely assortment of characters. The oddest of all, perhaps, is the antihero. While *The Brave Cowboy*, a quarter-century earlier, presented Jack Burns as a peculiar kind of protagonist, one who even then reversed the reader's expectations, *Good News* portrays him today in an even bolder anachronistic guise. He rides a "mare, a gray-skinned, rack-ribbed, broom-tailed, towering specter of a horse seventeen hands high" [11] that reminds us of Ed's moon-eyed horse, a green world emblem from the past. Jack neither looks like a hero nor acts like one.

The old man grins his yellow-toothed grin. "It's me, Charlie." His mismatched eyes shine in the western light; bare-headed, his tangled shock of white hair tosses in the breeze. Tobacco juice dribbles down his beard. Senile, thinks the colonel, and a madman, riding that scarecrow horse. [229]

Part rebel and part victim, he, like other ironic protagonists, both invites his fate and stumbles beneath its blows. He might be any twentieth-century man—when asked his name he replies, "They tell me it's Jack Burns. . . . But that's only hearsay" [52]—or he might just be a ghost, "a single, shadowy figure, . . . illusory" [135]. Like the protagonist of *The Brave Cowboy*, he carries no identification —"Nothing at all. No driver's license, no draft card, no SS card, no credit card, no Internal Security card, nothing" [147]—and like the masked rider of *The Monkey Wrench Gang*, he once lived a more anarchistic life. "My father was a lunatic," Colonel Barnes insists. "Killed himself trying to blow up a dam. Thirty years ago" [150]. In other words, the Jack Burns of *Good News* is a parody of himself, an antiheroic catalyst who tracks through a hostile, futuristic ambience on an absurdly disjointed quest.

Other men and women in this book also parody the stock characters of romance. Sam, Jack's sidekick, resembles the Lone Ranger's Tonto, but the Indian in *Good News* is memorable more for his magic than for his role as the faithful follower. A shaman, he can change knives to rattlesnakes and Apaches to soaring birds; an ironic Sancho Panza, he can temporarily ease the pain of those around him. Dixie Dalton, his lover, tends bar. More like Dulcinea than Amanda Blake, she inverts the reader's expectations by her quick wit and genial manner. Women in ironic tales tend to be unattractive, but Dixie is an ironic exception who exudes a street-wise intelligence as well as a street-wary sex appeal. Also in the foreground of the book is Art Dekker, still another likable character. An ironic inversion of Billy Vogelin Starr, who lost his innocence by watching chaos around him, Art loses his naiveté by actively participating in murder, in torture, in outright warfare. He, along with other young rebels who follow Professor Rodack, undergoes a futuristic kind of initiation, learning about life from the massacres and mayhem of the present.

But if these would-be anarchists seem bluntly drawn, their foes behave even more like caricatures. Flatter, more stylized, and less personable, the Chief's legions function very like dragons or evil knights in a medieval romance, although they must carry the heavy armor of irony as they move in and out of the story. Some, like Sergeant Brock and Corporal Mangus Colorado, Jr., represent the most animalistic, and most sadistic, perpetrators of military force while others, like Major Roland, Captain Fannin, and Corporal Buckley, stand for the automatically obedient, and thus more masochistic, kind of followers. Each of these men and women might be more at home in a comic strip than in a novel, but through their presence Abbey communicates a serious portion of *Good News*'s irony. By exaggerating their foibles and flaws, he turns these demons into spokesmen for his nightmare. Sergeant Brock, for example, is a Gutierrez of the future, complexly redrawn to stress his ironic affinities. This military motorcyclist, who "holds his silver helmet, like a football, in the crook of one arm" [72], epitomizes a reactionary macho mentality, one that steadfastly perverts the sane enforcement of the law. The scene where he and Mangus Colorado torture Art and his girl friend, while the Royal Canadians sing romantically in the background, makes Gutierrez's brutality pale by comparison. And meanwhile, the malevolent presence of Brock's Indian henchman gives one more twist—a sadistic one—to the Tonto legend already turned askew.

Less physically gruesome, but no less psychologically frighten-ing, is the role of Captain Fannin. From her the reader hears eu-phuistic praise of "the golden age," of past glories, of all America has lost. "What we had then," she begins, "oh, it's nearly inde-scribable" [120]. For several pages, then, she describes the inde-scribable, sometimes emoting about tangible goods she no longer possesses, sometimes remembering sensuous pleasures, sometimes sounding almost philosophic about her regrets.

Dear Dixie, it was wonderful, you'll never understand how good and sweet and beautiful our lives seemed then. How can I explain it? And the great cities over the land, growing greater all the time. Our Pentagon, inspir-ing fear and dread throughout the world. Our thriving industries: the steel mills! the copper smelters! the power plants belching their great plumes into the air! Everywhere! The big laboratories where every day somebody was discovering some wonderful new miracle cure for can-cer, for the common cold, for lead poisoning, for emphysema, for heart disease. [122]

Captain Fannin's enthusiasms typify Abbey's ironic texture; even as she speaks in apparent honesty, the author undercuts her words. At times he does so directly, by selecting diction that connotes his own point of view—power plants "belch" great plumes, for exam-ple. More often he covertly destroys the speaker's veracity—the big laboratories find miracle cures for diseases which, without mod-ern technology, might never exist. Abbey and the reader know, if Captain Fannin does not, that cancer, lead poisoning, emphysema, and heart disease are byproducts of the industrial age, incubated by the very steel mills and copper smelters proclaimed in the same breath. To read *Good News* correctly, then, we must not take any-one's words at face value. And while it is easy enough to see through Captain Fannin's benediction of the past, other speeches are uttered with far more subtlety. The reader must beware.

It should be clear, by now, that any discussion of characteriza-tion in this book rapidly evolves into a discussion of ideas. Each stick-figure futuristically represents an attitude or a guise of mod-ern man. Those with savage proclivities carry most of Abbey's bur-den. An Art Dekker, for example, says little of significance and represents little beyond the pattern inversion already discussed, while characters like the sergeant and the captain have meatier parts to play. And more crucial still are the distinctive and stylized indi-viduals who keynote their author's ironic vision.

Foremost is the Chief, "a man once an Air Force general, then some kind of professor at the state university, who has made himself the master of the dying city. . . . Ruler of the condemned. Boss of the survivors. Commander, with imperial ambitions, of a mercenary army" [29]. In a romance this man would be the obvious villain, like an Ian Fleming evildoer—"The Chief's eyes are a pale recessive blue, large, sensitive, slightly protruding, the eyelids pink and delicate. A permanent frown creases the skin between his blond eyebrows" [33]—and like an ideological monster. But in this world of irony and indirection, he functions more subtly. A dictator, a sadist, a pseudophilosopher, Abbey's embodiment of the militaristic-technocratic mind nevertheless speaks and acts in ways that almost echo real voices of the 1980s. The reader must listen closely when the Chief fallaciously describes a new America: "We want a strong, centralized State, capable of dealing quickly and mercilessly with enemies, whether foreign or domestic. It will also be, out of necessity, a thoroughly technological State. The conquest of Nature, once far advanced, now temporarily interrupted, will be resumed and completed. Not a single square foot of soil, nor a single living creature, will ever again be allowed to escape the service of humankind, society, and the State" [96]. Imitating the doctrinaire approach of those who built Glen Canyon Dam and of those who would strip Black Mesa bare, Abbey intones the Chief's point of view.

A harsh doctrine, you say. Indeed, gentlemen, it is a harsh doctrine—but a necessary one. What is the function of Nature? The function of Nature is to serve the needs of humanity. And what is the purpose of humanity? The purpose of humanity is to serve the aims of society as a whole. As a whole, gentlemen, as a unified, living organism. You say that humanity as presently constituted is anything *but* a unified, organic whole. Quite so. It is our purpose, our duty, as leading and organizing element, to bestow that unity upon mankind. To impose it, if necessary. [96; italics Abbey's]

A modest proposal, the Chief's words mark the cutting edge of irony. But they also, and this fact is crucial, mirror reality. The current United States Secretary of the Interior has affirmed that "man should hold dominion over the earth"; the Chief reproduces James Watt's philosophy almost exactly. Ultra conservative religious leaders today agree that "it is our duty, as leading and organizing element, to bestow" a moral majority's point of view; the Chief voices a similar sentiment. It is possible to find, in every line he speaks, a resonance of contemporary thought. As a vision of our future, he iterates our present. So even though this madman is a visual caricature, and even though he acts both brutally and capriciously throughout the book, he is a mirror of his forerunners. Here, then, is the major source of horror in *Good News:* this megalomaniac represents, not a giant or a dragon, not even a sheriff or a posse, but a diabolical, futuristic vision of what is most depraved about ourselves.

To oppose this curse Abbey sends more people like ourselves, the other side of the human coin, individualists and idealists who battle against the omnipresent corporate power. Representing these ironical anarchists is Noah Rodack, "a heavy, stocky man with gray beard, a bald professorial dome" [66]. The rebel leader oversees a band of incendiaries and revolutionaries, young men and women who would destroy vestiges from the past to make room for an unencumbered future. Such activities, in the Chief's eye, are treasonous and their instigator a traitor. And that is the eye Abbey lets us see through; instead of pronouncing Rodack's politics directly, he refracts the man's philosophy off an antagonistic wall. Except for banal exchanges with his friends, Rodack remains silent, forcing the Chief to interpret the revolutionary point of view. "But you were always so ready with words before," the oligarch taunts his prisoner.

And worse than words, with organized obstructionism. You and your hordes of fearful allies, those vermin from the universities, reservations, ghettos. Who opposed the nuclear industry, the synthetic-fuels industry, the water-diversion projects that might have saved us? Who cried panic every time some reactor malfunctioned? Who kept whining about air pollution and water pollution and food pollution and made it impossible to get our industrial plant modernized? [183]

The Chief angrily catalogues the professor's lawlessness, accusing his enemy of causing confusion and disunity in a once-mighty country: "Leading, step by step, to the loss of power in every form— economic, military, political, spiritual. Decay and disintegration. Exactly what you had wanted and hoped for all along, eh Rodack?" [184].

Both the professor and Abbey refrain from answering. Even though gaping holes of logic crack the Chief's tirade, Abbey makes no attempt to fill them with justifications by Rodack. A world of irony condemns this character as surely as it dooms everyone else. Like other ironical anarchists before him, Rodack breathes a rarefied air high above earth's practicalities. His whole characterization is reminiscent of Paul Bondi's—vague, abstract, more of the spirit than of the flesh despite the violence that surrounds him. Like *The Brave Cowboy's* philosopher too, Rodack disappears into the mists, his fate unresolved and ignored when the story closes. "Art and Rodack fade away under a row of dead and dying eucalyptus trees, through lifeless intersections under bankrupt lights into the gridiron of the tracts" [201], and the reader never hears of them again. This time, though, Abbey controls the disappearance. An ironic pattern, rather than freeing its participants from chaos, often sends them right back into the madness of the ironic world. "The weak, the cynical, the tortured, all seem less in pursuit of a goal than in flight from some terror, and in the struggle to escape they return to the original source of horror."[6] Abbey ensures that Rodack and his compatriots do no less. As flawed as the Chief because they are irrevocably tainted by their own humanity, the ironical anarchists are fated to blow their horns forever at the dark Tower looming before them.

Of course the Tower's defenders are fated too. No one wins in this ironic universe—not Major Roland and the others left behind, not the rabble who oppose him, not even the Chief whose legions will wander from place to place in search of more heavenly pyramids. The Chief's conquistadors, however, are led by the one man in the book with the potential to bridge the enemy worlds. But not surprisingly, Colonel Barnes fails too.

Originally "Captain" Barnes, the soldier looks like a hero—"a tall, thin, young man with sun-bleached hair, sun-bronzed face and hands, . . . he wears the uniform of a desert cavalryman: khakis, sidearm, boots and spurs, a broad-brimmed hat in one hand. His fine, green, intelligent eyes, grave and fearless, contemplate with equanimity the figure of the Chief behind the fortress of his desk" [40]. Alone among his mentor's underlings, Barnes displays some savvy, and so the Chief rewards him.

Barnes pushes back his chair and stands up. The Chief, coming close, looking up, puts a hand on Barnes' shoulder, exerting a powerful pressure downward. For a moment Barnes entertains the silly illusion that the Chief expects him to kneel, like a warrior about to be knighted by his lord. Barnes remains erect, however, and after a moment of hesitation the Chief removes his hand from the young man's shoulder. He takes the eagles from the box and pins the first (removing the double bars) on the right side of Barnes' open shirt collar, opposite the crossed sabers of a cavalry officer. The second he pins—not in regulation, but looking good—onto the front of Barnes' flat-brimmed campaign hat, which he takes up from the table. He embraces Barnes again, with both arms this time, like a European, shakes his hand, steps smartly back, and salutes. [141]

This parody of romance not only turns knighthood into a futuristic joke but also tell the reader exactly what to think of Jack Burns's long-lost son's intelligence. Despite his sensitivity—he calls Brock "a monster, a torturer" [44] and the raid on Rodack's hideaway "ugly" [138]—the colonel cannot comprehend the twisted logic of the path he follows. Whatever his Chief articulates, Colonel Charles Barnes agrees with and obeys. As a sounding board, both for his commander and for his father, he performs his major function, listening intently to their divergent points of view while the reader eavesdrops. He is not, however, a ferryman figure like Sheriff Johnson or Lee Mackie, for he never assumes any directional controls. As an aggressor he fails, following when he should lead, attending when he should act. Barnes is the part of ourselves that goes along with the crowd, the technician whose skills enable a corporate visionary like the Chief to succeed. When *Good News* ends, Barnes has learned nothing. "He turns to the captains behind, . . . and gives them the clenched-fist, rising and lowering arm signal that means, Come on. Move them out. Follow me" [235]. And he follows the Chief.

Presumably the reader does not, for we understand that each recognizably modern element infusing a *Good News* character is ultimately denigrated. The Chief's dream of conquering his environment, Rodack's impotent ironical anarchy, Barnes's man-in-the-crowd acceptance of the status quo, Burns's feudal/futile idealism—each of these fails to sustain Abbey's vision of something beyond their individual, or corporate, limitations. Sympathetic characters carry flaws only slightly less cumbersome than the obvious villains, and no one rides wholly victorious at the story's close (even though everyone still rides, in one way or another). While the Chief, his colonel, and his armies charge forward, Rodack, Art, Sam, and Dixie charge just as determinedly back into the city on the plains.

Confusion and anarchy, not a single individual and not an overriding philosophy, reign supreme.

If irony has an archetypal theme at all, Northrop Frye calls it *Sparagmos:* "the sense that heroism and effective action are absent, disorganized or foredoomed to defeat, and that confusion and anarchy reign over the world."[7] In a word, its theme is chaos. Negativistic pandemonium signifies the crucial difference between *Good News* and its immediate fictive predecessor, *The Monkey Wrench Gang.* While the gang members were antiheroes and their deeds paradoxical, their story made thematic sense. Embroidered with laughter, their idealistic quest not only proved that heroism and effective action can still exist in the world, but their actions traced that romance pattern to a happy conclusion. *Good News,* in contrast, elicits no such approbation for its deeds, advancing instead an unmitigated chaos that exposes its author's irate frustration and angry condemnation of the madness toward which modern man unwittingly heads. Like a vulture picking at the carrion flesh of civilization's corpse, Abbey now scavenges his visionary ruins, alerting his readers to the chaotic carnage he foresees.

> The flies buzz in the heat, murmuring over the spoor of caked blood, the scraps of flesh, the scattered fragments of bone and viscera. The vulture dominates the grave, alert and watchful. Satisfied at last, it begins to scratch at the sand with quick, forceful movements. A man's hand is revealed, rigid fingers clenching the air.
>
> A second vulture appears in the sky. A third. In the immensity of the desert, in the heat of the afternoon, there is no sound but the contented murmur of the flies, the scratching of the vulture, a few sweet and triumphant birdcries. [23]

Stated another way, Abbey gnaws at the skeletal remains of his own romances. Substituting an absurd mission for a heroic quest, a nightmare world for one of dreams, and demoniacal, inadequate characters for more benign, stylized ones, he razes the very structure that has brought his readers into Abbey's world.

The naturalism of the chapter culminating in the two paragraphs quoted above communicates much of his anger and disgust, spelling out gruesome details with graphic particularity, but it also pronounces the book's maliciously paradoxical tone. The shoot-out that precedes the vultures' arrival is no romantic joust, or even a traditional western gunfight; rather, it is a sordid inversion of our expectations. The bad guys ride motorcycles ("The roar becomes violent, tyrannous; five men in black uniforms and helmets painted silver, adorned with painted flames, veer from the decaying pavement and drive into the trailhead" [22]), the good guy gets shot in the back ("A. C. sinks to his knees, eyes dull with shock" [20]), and the carnage is repulsive ("The sun beats down on the two dead men. Interested flies congregate about the wounds, the blackening dribbles of blood, the stains and smell of human excrement" [22]). *Good News* can be nasty, an ironic gospel of the future; its author, "arrogant with indolence, patient, unhurried" [22], a predatory vulture circling a fallen world.

To read irony correctly, the reader must be sensitive to the author's intended point of view. In this passage Abbey's ire leads him to use harsh, vituperative imagery, while elsewhere his tone grows more sarcastic and verbal repartee takes over. The conversation between Jack and Sam that opens the book, although no less piercing and cynical than the darker passages, is flippant and witty. Sam is cooking dinner, part airedale, part coyote: "Eat boss. . . . This dog is good dog. This dog died for our sins. If we do not eat him his death becomes meaningless" [7]. Jack objects to Sam's tone.

"God, there's nothing worse than a smart Indian. And that reminds me of something else. If you're really a goddamn Indian why the hell don't you talk like a goddamn Indian.

"You're a bigot, white man."

"I'm no bigot, I hate *everybody*. Talk like an Indian."

"How? I don't know how. I'm a spoiled Indian. Harvard ruined me."

Burns ruminates, . . . "*My* daddy always said the only good Indian is a dead Indian."

"Mine would've said the only good Indian is a bad Indian. But he was a troublemaker. He was shot dead at Pine Ridge, South Dakota. By good Indians. His last words were, and I quote, 'Let me go my friends, you have hurt me enough!' " [12; italics Abbey's]

But if Sam's tone is caustic, Abbey's is more so. In less than half a page he chastizes white men, red men (both good and bad), their heroic (and not-so-heroic) symbols, and their sacred cows. He inadvertently, too, lets slip an iconoclastic proclamation all his own. Jack Burns says the words—"I'm no bigot, I hate *everybody*"—but Edward Abbey, the ironist, thinks them. Satire has been called militant irony, and in this very militant book the author irreverently attacks every aspect of modernity that affronts him. Hating not everybody, perhaps, but certainly everybody who acts rapaciously, he castigates those who cannot recognize the nightmare he believes must lie ahead. "We have submitted to the domination of an insane, expansionist economy and a brutal technology—*a mad machine* —which will end by destroying not only itself but everything remaining that is clean, whole, beautiful and good in our America. Unless we find a way to stop it" [S, 77; italics Abbey's].

Good News is Abbey's bad news, his particularly ironic way of stopping the mad machine if only his readers will hear. It takes us down a road different from any we have walked before, one with few signposts and one characterized by horseshoe curves and misdirections, but its path has been carefully plotted by the same craftsman who led us from *Jonathan Troy* to *The Monkey Wrench Gang*. Finally, *Good News* arrives at the same destination as Abbey's successes—an imagined new-world hilltop where the view ranges beyond technocracy's control of man toward a vision of man controlling himself. Even though pollution and high-rise machines have limited the horizons of this 1980 satire, and even though his fury sometimes outpaces his control, Abbey still foresees a future of individualistic behavior harmoniously combined. Beyond cognitive boundaries, beyond chaos, *Good News* still predicates some optimistic possibilities.

Two twisted braids of the narrative line give hope. The first skein follows Jack's quest, convoluted as it may be, while the second winds around Sam and Dixie's love. Both insist on a concord between man and the land and between man and his fellow man. Abbey ties that Gordian knot when Jack first confronts his son. The old man speaks quietly. "Come with me, Charlie. Leave these murderers, that dictator Chief. Come with me. I got a little ranch back on the Rio Salado —old Salt Crick. . . . It ain't much but a man can get by there. Two men—with families. Got some good horses, cattle, two good springs, a well. And lots of room. *Lots of room, Charlie!*" [152; italics Abbey's]. Lots of room, a place where a man can raise a family, a reliance on self instead of on the mad machine—even while these seem to lead directly toward genuine happiness and individual contentment, the ironist must disparage the green world idyll. Jack undercuts his supplication by mocking his own methodology: "I got a little ranch . . . Stole it, of course. From the bank" [152]. The colonel responds with more derogation: "We've got the world" [152]. Yet what a world it is, circumscribed by "the barbed-wire gate," "banks of enormous windows," and "the summit of the Tower" [153]. Jack's place, a universe populated by congenial souls, a greater Salt Crick surrounded by family and friends, sounds better; but somewhere, even beyond that—Abbey's world—sounds best of all.

Literally Jack searches for his son, Charlie, but figuratively his quest reaches out to a larger kinship. Carefully interposed among the pages of this irony is a continuing affirmation of a human family —the rebels repeatedly call Jack "Grandfather" [63]—made possible if humans will care for one another. If love and respect can become the norm instead of the aberration then, Abbey infers, a human sacrality can be more than a dream. Just as Ed longed for "a wholesome and reasonable balance between industrialism and agrarianism," a life where one still can "enjoy the advantages of contemporary technological culture without having to endure the overcrowding and the stress [AR, 137], so the characters of *Good News* dream of some place beyond the red world confines of their fallen civilization, some place even beyond the green world idyll. The reader must beware of the crooked path that leads there, though, because everybody stumbles along the land-mined way. "Find somebody," Art Dekker's dying father tells him. "Get some of those kids you went to school with. Bring them back to the place. Then all of you— there's everything there you need. Rebuild it" [21]. Instead, Art finds Jack and Sam and the horrors of guerrilla warfare.

Even so, those horrors cement his need for others—"his aim, now, was to tie in with the 'Robin Hoods,' . . . to join them, fight for them, die with them" [110]. And while the boy's goal sounds like an insane perversion of normalcy to Jack Burns, the cowboy cannot think of a plausible alternative.

> He felt clearly his own growing love for young Art, this lonely and searching boy, who might have been, could have been, his own son. Why not, he thought for one wild moment, why not give up the search for his own, take this lad instead, kidnap him if necessary, take him and the Indian and that girl—Dixie—take them back to his place, where they could hide and work and survive, together, until the madness of civil war passed by them? [110]

Could such a daydream come true? The author answers with an everlasting no—"Futile fantasy; it was already too late" [111]. So Jack rides away from his young friend, keeping his fancy to himself, while overhead "he sees the vultures circling against the blue—black-winged, fierce-eyed, melancholy birds, arrogant in their freedom, humble with hunger" [111]. Equally arrogant, the melancholy, fierce-eyed author brutalizes the green world vision. But this is not to say he brutalizes the dream. If not in the ashes of Phoenix then elsewhere, after Jack's resurrection, some of his hopes may still come true. Like Ed at the close of *Abbey's Road*, like the happy foursome (or fivesome) on *The Monkey Wrench Gang's* final page, Jack and his hypothetical family may still prevail, but only when man commits himself—to preservation of the land and to his own sacrality.

Abbey explains the possibility by means of the Sam and Dixie subplot. The unlikely combination of Harvard-educated shaman and prostitute-turned-sweetheart is part of the author's plan—"two heads touching over the bar" [57]—to protract the Abbeyesque dream.

"We could always leave. Go somewhere else." But at that thought she detects the doubt in his voice.
"Where?"
Sam is silent for a moment. "Yes. Good question. I don't know, Dixie. Come back here, I suppose. Things are bound to get better someday." [81]

Afraid "they could even get worse," Dixie frets while Sam gestures her worries aside. "Then we won't come back here." At that point, their vision reaches only to the "Enchanted Mesa," a green world where red cannot intrude. By the end of their adventures, however, they and their friends perceive someplace far different. " 'No,' Rodack says, 'stop. Let us out. Me and Art. We're going back anyway' " [200]. As soon as Sam and Dixie toy with the fantasy of "going home" [221], they too change their minds. "We made a decision," Dixie reports. "It took us all afternoon to decide but we decided. We decided to go after old Jack and help him find the boy. We're going to find Art and the professor and their gang of outlaws and then—we're going to join them" [238]. And when the barroom pianist challenges this conclusion—"Your part is not to destroy, your part is to bring new life into this corrupt world" [239]—Dixie declares, "I can do both. . . . And I will." So will Abbey, for by writing *Good News* he codifies her affirmation to blend two worlds into one. An ironist, he destroys the corruption he sees around him; a craftsman, he transforms that destruction into vision and art.

Abbey has come a long way from *The Brave Cowboy's* mountain cabin and John Vogelin's pre-air-force ranch, for now he utterly dismisses any life like theirs or Will Gatlin's, any existence insulated from modernity. He knew a quarter-century ago that Voeglin's and Burns's anachronisms could not work, but he had no notion of what would. Now, though, he sees past their limitations to a vision of men and women who will commit themselves to making a contemporary dream, the best of green world and red together, come true. As soon as Ed discovered and rejected the lure of the moon-eyed horse, Abbey allowed himself to speculate. He created Will Gatlin to work through the tragedy of too much isolation, and then he created the Monkey Wrench Gang members to assess the comic outcome of overreaction. Now he has created souls who, like the Rocky Flats protestors he has admired in the past, commit themselves to each other and to the earth's sacrality. Whether they succeed or fail is, ironically, immaterial, because it is now the commitment that counts.

That commitment forces them all to return to the ashes of Phoenix, from which, perhaps, a new civilization will rise. Admittedly, Abbey's mythology grows a bit heavy here. Not only is the parody of Phoenix rising from the ashes obvious, but the resurrection of Jack Burns is excessive. Nevertheless, the author does what a good ironist must do, shifting from realism to myth in a studied effort to pinpoint those social and psychological forces which are causing, in his mind, a twentieth-century catastrophe. Two paragraphs, on two successive pages, exemplify his mode.

Late one afternoon. Once again the sun descends toward the west. One more time the new moon sails high across the sublime, imperial, grandly indifferent blue of the desert sky. Once more, and once again, out of the past and into the unknown, an army departs from a ruined city to seek new adventures, more glorious conquests, greater disasters. Once more and once again, over and over and over again. Seen from the foothills of the mountains, a plume of dust signals the Army's movement, bearing east and northeast toward the high country. The glitter of arms reveals its character. The echo of drums, the bray of horns, announce its purpose. Once more, once again, always and always again. [223]

Men like the Chief will charge forth forever, stamping red reality on an ever-malleable world. No one can stop these armies, no one, the ironist says. But men like Jack and Sam, men like Edward Abbey, are bound to try. "Listen, boss," Sam protests. "I learned one thing at Harvard. There's one thing wrong with always fighting for freedom, and justice, and decency. And so forth." Burns looks up at "the blazing sky," that same existential "indifferent blue of the desert sky," before replying:

"Only one thing? What's that?"
"You almost always lose." The old man laughs, reaches out, and squeezes Sam's near arm. "Well, hellfire, Sam, what does that have to do with it?" [222]

It would be easy to accuse Abbey of more ironical anarchy here. Indeed it would be easy to categorize all his writing as idle gesture that has accomplished nothing, empty words that iterate, "I'm no bigot, I hate everybody." But to do so would mistake his well-wrought words. Always an idealist behind his ironic facade, this contemporary writer is fighting with his pen "for freedom, and justice, and decency." He sees mercenaries marching through his beloved Southwest, carving up mountains and canyons alike, "once more, once again, always and always again," and he cannot stop fighting them, even when destined to lose. "Well, hellfire, . . . what does that have to do with it?" Ironically, nothing. And so he writes an ironic conundrum—armies march, anarchists rebel, and the author throws everyone into chaos. No one actually wins, no one actually loses, although the land itself takes more than its share of the beating. This is the heart of Abbey's warning, though, the sacred fragility of what we should value most. So his combatants are destined to fight forever on that shifting field of red and green, while a romancer-turned-ironist waves his artistic wand across the indifferent sky.

"Is it possible that Phoenix may someday rise from her ashes?" Abbey wrote, almost a decade before *Good News*. "She lives in soot and smoke, dust and confusion and crime, half pickled in sulphuric acid, a city dying from too much gluttonous success" [CC, 43]. For more than a quarter-century now, he has tried with his writings to arrest man's cannibalization of the American West. Varying his artistic technique from book to book, he has tried direct attacks, subtle feints, laughter, and tears. His latest writing is the angriest. Just as Abbey's recent nonfiction hurls invectives at science, that "whore of industry and war" [AR, 125], so *Good News* castigates the effects of scientific "progress"—crowded cities and a landscape devastated by industrialization. Its tone—assaultive, combative, though sad and melancholy too—is a logical choice for an author who knows his words go unheard by the very techno-industrial ears he would most like to reach. Its images—bleak, naturalistic, depressing—are logical too because they emphasize the horrors mankind can perpetuate.

A gust of predawn wind flows down from the mountains. The tail vane of an unlocked windmill turns with the wind; steel grates on rusted steel. The sound is like that of a human groan. The Indian and Burns look toward the corral a hundred yards away and the tall tower—a skeleton of metal—standing within it. There they see, dangling on a rope, black in silhouette against the eastern sky, the first of the hanged men. [15]

It would be inappropriate for Abbey to fill *Good News* with descriptions that revivify the sacred landscape, for that landscape has been consumed and only its skeleton remains. Unlike Ed, Jack and Sam cannot walk "under a wine-dark sky . . . through light reflected and re-reflected from the walls and floor of the canyon, a radiant golden light that glows on rock and stream, sand and leaf in varied hues of amber, honey, whiskey" [DS, 200], because that option no longer exists. In *Desert Solitaire* "the light that never was is here, now, in the storm-sculptured gorge of the Escalante" [DS, 200]; in *Good News* the light has been extinguished. There, in the darkness and with a sound "like that of a human groan," Abbey leaves his fellows, twentieth-century man, slowly twisting in the wind.

It would be a mistake, however, to suppose that Abbey's road terminates at such a juncture. Here is but another waystop on the path to some place better, some place free of selfish appetites and violence to self and land. If *Good News* does not describe such a place specifically, it is only because the author has chosen indirection and chaos as another means of getting there, for, in every important thematic way, this 1980 fiction indicates the proper track.

We can in fact read *Good News* as an all-encompassing march along the many twists and turns of Abbey's road, for this stark and visionary irony includes most of those qualities that characterize its author's prose. Its structure, for example, resembles its predecessors'. The quest design or the search underlies most of Abbey's work, as all his protagonists seek a modern guerdon of one sort or another, but sometimes the earlier fiction stumbled along the way.

Where *Jonathan Troy's* loosely strung episodes hung awkwardly on an ill-conceived narrative chain, the chaos of *Good News* belongs naturally in the book's basic conception. And where the brave cowboy's and John Vogelin's romances ended precipitously and unwittingly, the irony of *Good News* sends its characters forward, beyond its pages and into a viable continuous present that is part of the author's design. Another structural constant for Abbey has been the use of the cowboy tale. Sometimes jocularly, sometimes sarcastically, always intelligently, he has tied four of his six fictions to the conventional Western. In *The Brave Cowboy* he intentionally dropped the form's heroic overtones, in *Fire on the Mountain* he flouted its initiation rituals, and in *The Monkey Wrench Gang* he rode the myth into the twentieth century only to brand the whole process as comically passé. *Good News* takes it a generation further, into an utterly devastating future. Cowboys and Indians fight, not against each other but versus motorcycled horsemen, as modern heroes and villains show definitively that nobility has given way to simple survival tactics and knight-errantry apparently is gone forever. Nevertheless, the mythic design that underlies the plot gives a kind of coherence to its otherwise chaotic format.

Thrusting that plot forward are the characters who move through the ironic universe of *Good News*. Even more intricately stylized than those Abbey created in his earlier fiction—compare, for example, the reconceived one-eyed Jack with his original, or the bombastic Chief with his military forerunners, Desalius and De Salius—the later, more subtly exaggerated figures embellish an artificial madness. No one represents an efficacious mode of behavior and no one functions as Abbey's spokesman, although it is tempting to cast Sam in that role. A shaman, after all, is capable of introducing the earth's sacrality, that commodity extinguished from *Good News*. A shaman's rapport with the earth's spirits brings with it a supernatural inspiration that allows him to cure man's ills, so Sam possesses sacred talents much like an author's—whereas the character changes weapons into creatures and fears into hopes, the writer alters harsh reality into spiritual and artistic vision. Despite this affinity, however, Abbey does not spotlight Sam's achievements. Instead, he treats the shaman as if he were just one more lost soul who, along with the others, fleshes out this incorporeal world. If anything, the men and women of *Good News* are even more abstractly caricatured (and thus more paradoxically drawn) than their fictive ancestors, though they function more concretely within their ironic milieu.

That artistic universe in which they dwell is most important of all. From the rough pictorialism of his early writing through the powerful, sacred descriptions of his later books, this contemporary author has brought the modern West, newly realized, into his readers' living rooms. Abbey's is a West not only of his deepest imaginings but also of an extended vision. Taking what he sees around him, he articulates a tangible landscape of the mind that includes both what he longs for and what he fears. Whereas Jonathan Troy's picture postcard dream, the brave cowboy's mountain, and Billy Starr's New Mexico sketched a part of the horizon, *Black Sun*, *The Monkey Wrench Gang* and *Good News* paint the entire sky. So even though the latter's heavens are clouded by haze and undiluted smog, the artist's hand brushes the pollutants away. "Those distant scenes [may again] be veiled by heatwaves but for the time being remain clear, intricate in detail, glowing with color, infinitely pleasing—because immeasurable—to the mind that can perceive nobility in the undisguised structures of the earth" [134–135]. The Chief misperceives this view, but author and reader do not. Here, in the future, the earth's sacrality may still prevail.

Abbey builds on his sacred vision from book to book, borrowing the strength of rocks, canyons, sagebrush, and mountains to articulate the blessed space. "I've been here before," Jack recalls in a moment of flight, "or a place just like it" [210], but the younger brave cowboy, losing his way, forfeited the very dream that his aging parody so confidently assumes. After Jonathan Troy's rush to the West and until the Monkey Wrench Gang's flight through the Maze, all of Abbey's fictional protagonists sought their dreams unsuccessfully. Now, in *Good News*, that is all changed. On the surface, of course, Sam, Dixie, Art, the professor, and their friends appear thwarted, but ironically enough, they are not beaten where it counts, in their hearts and heads. Like the Ed of Abbey's nonfiction, the rabble of *Good News* march in an emotional and intellectual vanguard, carrying the banner of their creator's soundest ideas.

One might argue that the banner weighs them down. A fiction whose ideas overpower its story line and whose propaganda overwhelms its characters, *Good News* sometimes carries the burden of too much authorial message. Yet, as a fable of the future, this capstone announces Abbey's vision most articulately. "Invisible poisons spread through the atmosphere, borne by the winds from the guilty to the innocent. But all were innocent, all were guilty" [3]. The author himself, innocent yet guilty too, attempts to purge those invisible poisons with the cleansing corrective of his prose. Beneath that shadowed sky, he has given us "good news," a gospel of the future that marks one more tiny sanctuary on the way down Abbey's road. That track, ever indirect, convoluted, twisted, reaches deeply into the American West and pierces to the heart of the American dream. Many years ago, when the fork leading there divided, Ed Abbey made a decision: One sign said, 'Conventional Western Writer;' "the other something like 'Primitive Road, Not Patrolled.' Naturally I took the latter, which looked more interesting and led in the direction I wanted to go" [CC, 26], toward a landscape where at last myth, vision, and reality become the same.

Postscript: A Clean Hard Edge Divides

March, 1989. I learned of Edward Abbey's death from a techno-industrial source. A friend's voice on my answering machine told me he had just heard the news on the radio. Three days later my spring vacation began—a week away from civilization that seemed to me an appropriate kind of farewell, if such a farewell is ever appropriate.

Edward Abbey was never a personal friend of mine. We met, we talked a bit, we corresponded occasionally. My real friend was Ed, the narrator of his nonfiction and the imagined author of his novels. He and I spent a lot of time together—the better part of two years, in fact, while I was writing *The New West of Edward Abbey* and reading and rereading his books. Since my own work has always focused on those books, rather than upon the author, my farewell must celebrate the prose that remains as well as embrace my loss.

Ideally I should have gone to red rock country. But little in this world turns out to be ideal. I went to Death Valley National Monument instead.

Although Ed didn't write much about Death Valley, essays about the place do appear in three of his collections. A straightforward depiction, "Death Valley," was first published in *Sage* in 1967 and ten years later became chapter 7 of *The Journey Home*. A second, more imaginative piece, "Death Valley Junk," forms chapter 17 of *Abbey's Road*. A short portion of "Desert Images" graces a section of *Beyond the Wall*. The first highlights some of the valley's special places, stressing the heat and featuring some powerful description. "Junk" follows a different kind of trip, on LSD, far out on the valley floor. "Images" focuses on the shifting sands. Except for a slap at nearby Las Vegas, none concerns itself with tourism, or environmental problems, or monkeywrenching, or artistic responsibility, or social activism, or any of the issues Abbey liked to stress. Still, I want to imagine these essays as paradigms of Abbey's best work, to reexamine the philosophic thrust, to savor the language, to look into Ed's mind, to predicate the future, and to think of my own Death Valley venture as a characteristic trek along Abbey's road.

We arrived at Scotty's Castle in midafternoon, stepping into eighty-degree heat after a blustery drive from winter. Parking-lot Winnebagos—"big and tin-and-formica cakeboxes on wheels"— dwarfed my pickup truck. Pink-clad, pink-skinned visitors jammed the walkways. Blocking the desert view, a sign proclaimed a two-hour wait before the next available castle tour. Next to the ice cream stand, a small store sold books and peddled information. *Desert Solitaire* was there—two stacks of it, wedged between *Escape from Death Valley* and *Death Valley Lore*. In the midst of personified industrial tourism lay the book that indicts it the most. No one else in the shop recognized the irony.

A baby ranger looked puzzled when we asked about the backcountry—"It's not a people's park, it's a national park." She pointed to the visiting hordes, and firmly directed us to an overflow campground at Furnace Creek. We turned northwest instead, drove half a dozen miles along a disintegrating dirt road, and spent the night. In fact, we spent the entire week of Easter vacation—in defiance of industrial tourism and in celebration of desert solitaire—camped out of sight of any other vehicles.

Further celebration involved a bottle of whisky. Edward Abbey and I had planned several times to sit and talk about Ed and his books. A bottle would advance the quality of the discussion, we believed. Since that conversation never occurred, I had to make it up. Sheltered by a ragged creosote bush, alongside a dry wash with a full moon overhead, I toasted his friends everywhere who had too much to drink in mid-March of 1989. Some lines from "Death Valley Junk" spell out my thought.

"Nothing was happening," wrote Ed twenty years ago. "Except for this cold grip, this icy hand on the back of my neck." He described his perception of "the mountain across the valley, glowing in the sunset light, look[ing] glorious, vividly palpable and tangible." Then he began to lose his sense of time and duration. "There was no duration. I was trapped in limbo between two worlds—a place too queasy and queer to be the waking world, too bright and definite and three-dimensional to be the world of dreams. I didn't know where I was . . . I felt paralyzed." Later Ed reports "pleasure in this miserable, strictured mode of intoxication," a pleasure similar, I suppose, to the headiness I felt last week, and that leads in the essay to a cacophony of writhing trees, palpitating mountains, breathing earth, and stars struggling in a cobweb sky.

The conclusion of "Death Valley Junk," its narrator no longer trapped in a limbo between two worlds, sounds a poignant note today. Ed's experience ultimately collapses into "a shade of disappointment and loss. Some ancient way remembered but not found. The trail was not taken. For me at least, it now seemed clear—there was not going to be any magic shortcut into wisdom, understanding, peace. There would be no easy way." No easy way for Ed to follow Abbey's road, no easy way for his friends to understand a trail that has ended prematurely in disappointment and loss. I spent the next several days trying to find its path.

Following first the popular Golden Canyon route from the valley floor to the Zabriskie Point overlook, we returned to the truck down another, unsigned wash totally devoid of people. Four days later, tracing Salt Creek to its origin, we quickly outdistanced the tentative few who dared to venture more than a hundred yards from their cars. "No more cars in national parks," wrote Ed in *Desert Solitaire*. "Let the people walk." In Death Valley, as in so many other unfamiliar places, not many desert neophytes willingly leave the relative safety of their air-conditioned vehicles. Furthermore, "the motorized tourists, reluctant to give up the old ways, will complain that they can't see enough without their automobiles to bear them swiftly (traffic permitting) through the parks. But this is nonsense." I agreed, watching blindly speeding campers, moving restlessly from Scotty's Castle to Furnace Creek and back again, confirming Ed's prediction. Faster plays better in a U.S. "National Money-mint."

Sometimes trucks are necessary, though, on Abbey's road. Driving along west valley tracks not meant for mortal cars, we at every turn were reminded of the "cactus, sand pits, shock-busting chuckholes, axle-breaking washouts, rocks" of *The Journey Home*'s "Disorder and Early Sorrow." The way was enticing; we kept on going. "And more rocks. Embedded like teeth in the roadway, points upward, they presented a constant nagging threat to my peace of mind." Yet Ed well understood the temptation. In a line reminiscent of so much of his prose, he explains his motivation (and my own). "I had to see what lay behond [beyond] the next ridge."

The next ridge can be even more alluring on foot. "I leave the road and walk out on the dunes." Ed invites his readers to join him as he wanders "past the arrowweed on the salt flats, past the little bosks of mesquite in the foothills of the dunes, up the windward side along the crest where the sand is so firm my feet leave only a faint impression." A light wind comes up, and his tracks begin to soften, to blur, to fade out. He pauses. "I roll over on my back and gaze up at the cloudless, perfect, inhuman, unsheltering sky. The inevitable vulture soars there, a thousand feet above me. Black wings against the blue. I think I know that bird. He looks familiar. I think he's the one that's been following me, everywhere I go in the desert, for about thirty-five years. Looking after me." Looking after Ed too briefly, I'm afraid.

I didn't see his vulture when I walked on the dunes near Stovepipe Wells last week, although the "forms and volumes and masses inconstant as wind but always shapely" sifted everywhere. "Dunes like arcs and sickles, scythe blades and waning moons." Scythe blades and waning moons—the images fit all too painfully with Ed's next words. "Sand and beauty. Sand and death. Sand and renewal."

Death Valley is a place of beauty, death, and renewal. It connotes both the magical dream of sudden wealth and the harsh realities of fool's gold, illusory lodes, heat exhaustion, dehydration, and worse. In *The Journey Home*, Ed describes the latter in terms of five lives claimed by the valley that year, and in a line that recalls the solitary demise of "the Dead Man at Grandview Point," remarks facetiously, "Ah to be a buzzard now that spring is here." Maybe I just didn't look hard enough last week, or close my eyes tightly enough. I wish I could report I had seen that hovering bird.

On the other hand, Ed knew how to follow the Death Valley dream. Seeking a lead and silver diggings, up a nine-mile road built by hand, Ed hikes "far into Hanaupah Canyon to Shorty Borden's abandoned camp." En route, he discovers the kind of surprise that so often punctuates his prose. "That loveliest of desert graces, a spring-fed stream" emerges in the midst of his ascent. "Along the stream grow tangles of wild grapevine and willow; the spring is choked with watercress. The stream runs for less than a mile before disappearing into the sand and gravel of the wash," he reports. "Beyond the spring, up-canyon, all is dry as death again until you reach the place where the canyon forks. Explore either fork and you find water once more—on the right a little waterfall, on the left in a grottolike glen cascades sliding down through chutes in the dark blue andesite. Moss, ferns, and flowers cling to the damp walls—the only life in this arid wilderness."

Shorty Borden's foray into Hanaupah Canyon ended when he "discovered that even with a road it would still cost him more to transport his ore to the nearest smelter than the ore itself was worth." Now his mine is deserted, his track a rock-strewn reminder of man's tenacity. Some day, I expect the boulders and rock slides and scrub brush will reclaim the steep, narrow way, but that day may be many centuries from now. Once disturbed, the desert recovers slowly. So Shorty Borden's road may be fixed as irrevocably as so many other southwest intrusions that Abbey so despised.

No matter. "Almost no one ever goes there. It is necessary to walk for miles." Ed was correct, almost no one ever goes there, except for some of us. I am happy to report that the spring still runs through a choke of wild willows and that, after the canyon forks, the waterfall still drops softly and moss and ferns still cling. Even Shorty's mine remains much as it must have looked when Ed saw it—a slide covering the lower workings, two upper tunnels with intact entrances, some rails, an ore car, and several pieces of equipment too heavy to carry out by hand.

Not all of Death Valley, of course, is filled with such signs of life. Ed called the place "Gravel Gulch," and I can attest to the further accuracy of what he saw when he looked in most directions. Along the Panamints, "there are only the endless barren hills, conventional in form, covered in little but shattered stone. A dull monotonous terrain." Far below, on the valley floor, "swirls of mud, salt, and salt-laden streams lie motionless under a lake of heat, glowing in lovely and poisonous shades of auburn, saffron crimson, sulfurous yellow, dust-tinged tones of white on white." If anything, the grotesque and unforgiving land empowers Abbey's descriptions, honing the syntax and the diction into sharp and salient images. "I descend the narrow gorge between flood-polished walls of bluish andesite—the stem of the wineglass. I walk down the center of an amphitheater of somber cliffs riddled with grottoes, huge eyesockets in a stony skull." Such language reminds me of the best paragraphs in my favorite essay, *Desert Solitaire*'s "Down the River," where he dawdled through a "sculptured landscape mostly bare of vegetation—earth in the nude."

One of Ed's finest gifts, I think, was the incredible freshness of his pictorial eye—the ability to newly imagine for his reader a typical desert scene. Even when a place was less than pictorial, Ed would frame it with words. For example, he never overcame a somewhat negative conception of the lowest spot in the continental United States, but he could paint it for us anyway. "The first impression remains a just one," he said. "Despite variety, most of the surface of Death Valley is dead. Dead, dead, deathly—a land of jagged salt pillars, crackling and tortured crusts of mud, sunburnt gravel bars the color of rust, rocks and boulders of metallic blue naked even of lichen." An appropriate description, an appropriate place, I regret, for this particular trip down Abbey's road.

In the company of Ed, I thought more about the landscape than the novels, more about the man than his characters. But my subconsciousness kept recalling *The Brave Cowboy*'s opening paragraphs, where the prologue begins: "There is a valley in the West where phantoms come to brood and mourn, pale phantoms dying of nostalgia and bitterness." And where the prologue concludes, "it was into this valley of ghosts and smoke and unacknowledged sorrows that The Cowboy rode," just as Ed rode last week with me. Occasionally he and I were accompanied by *Black Sun*'s Will Gatlin, retracing a burning descent. "He was alone in one of the loneliest places on earth. Above him rose tier after tier of cliffs, the edge of the forest barely apparent on the rim of the uppermost wall; around him the gray desert platform where nothing grew but scrub brush and cactus sloped toward the brink of the inner gorge and the unseen river. . . . In all this region was nothing human that he could see, no sign of man or of man's work. No sign, no trace, no path, no clue, no person but himself." Near Badwater, out on the Devil's Golf Course, I found the same emptiness and isolation.

Then I rejected such total nihilism as uncharacteristic. I reminded myself of Hayduke's fortuitous resurrection—"'You believe in ghosts, Doc?' The Doctor thinks. 'I believe in the ghosts that haunt the human mind.'" I fancied Jack Burns after the end of *The Brave Cowboy*, helping out in the pages of *The Money Wrench Gang* and returning to lead the rebellious forces of *Good News*. In the hands of a benevolent author, iconoclasts and cowboys lead charmed lives. At the close of his penultimate novel, one more time, the reader is led to expect that his hero—"there was something shadowy and smokelike about him, something faded, blurred, remembered"—will ride again. "Yes sir, they followed the tracks and they found where the old man was. Found the lance. Dried blood all over the place. But no body." I'm an optimist; I like to think about that ending. I don't like to think about *The Fool's Progress*, or the way I felt last fall when I finished Abbey's latest work of fiction.*

Last week, though, I mostly thought about Ed. I thought about writing this essay, too, and decided that Ed's own words—the final paragraph of *The Journey's Home*'s "Death Valley"—conclude one fool's progress better than I. "The sun goes down. A few stray clouds catch fire, burn gold, vermillion, and driftwood blue in the unfathomed sea of space. These surrounding mountains that look during the day like iron—like burnt, mangled rusted iron—now turn radiant as a dream. Where is their truth? A hard clean edge divides the crescent dunes into black shadow on one side, a phosphorescent light on the other. And above the rim of the darkening west floats the evening star." And now, indeed, a clean hard edge divides.

---

*After I finished this essay, *Hayduke Lives!* was published posthumously, in 1990. There, Jack Burns reappears and plays a significant role.

Afterword

Center for Environmental Arts and Humanities
University of Nevada, Reno

Raconteur and provocateur, Edward Abbey was a master of engaging paradox, an author who used contrasting and often contradictory moods and messages to tease his readers toward independent-mindedness. Few were spared his verbal barbs, his awakening prods—including the community of literary scholars. Although much of Abbey's writing is steadfastly playful and "lowbrow," full of allusions to popular culture and rife with sex and drinking and fighting, he had a serious scholarly background and his work itself has much to offer academic readers. Following military service in Europe, the author attended the University of New Mexico, completing his B.A. in philosophy and English in 1951 and his M.A. in philosophy in 1956, with a yearlong stay in between as a Fulbright scholar at Edinburgh University. He spent 1957 at Stanford University on a Wallace Stegner Creative Writing Fellowship. Complaints against academia aside, this was not an uncultured man.

And yet Abbey seemed to delight in deflecting academic readers' attention away from his work, cautioning them that they were not his intended audience. When *Desert Solitaire,* the book that would ultimately become his chief claim to popular legend and critical longevity, appeared in 1968, he warned in his author's introduction that "serious critics, serious librarians, serious associate professors of English will if they read this work dislike it intensely; at least I hope so" (x). Ann Ronald, like scores of scholars after her, merely smiled at this cautionary statement; she proceeded to write *The New West of Edward Abbey* in the early 1980s, illuminating and contextualizing Abbey's fiction and essays in accordance with scholarly tradition. Although not a monkey-wrencher herself, as she admits in the preface to this study, Ronald is a lifelong hiker and conservationist and a pioneering scholar in the field of literature and environment. "I have ignored his warning as blithely as I ignored the opportunity to pull up survey stakes," she explains. "Instead, this serious associate professor of English has trundled slowly along the path toward Abbey's world, tiptoeing past the places I found incorrigible and rushing pell-mell into those I admired and loved" (xv). Some readers of this book may find it strangely formal in its effort to place Edward Abbey's writing (the fifteen books he had published by that time) in the context of literary history. Abbey's fans and friends might ask, Why does this matter? What does this have to do with good stories and the passionate defense of wild places in the American West?

Writing about *Desert Solitaire,* for instance, Ronald refers to Harry Berger Jr., a scholar of Thomas More, Philip Sidney, Edmund Spenser, and William Shakespeare, who explores the contrasts between created worlds of the imagination and the real, physical world. "By creating a new world of metaphor and myth that is ostensibly a frivolous place," comments Ronald, "the author may either annihilate or affirm those tenets of the real world he images, and may do so through innuendo. Although readers may be unwilling to grant Edward Abbey the company of Shakespeare, Sidney, and Spenser, his adoption of their method is indisputable" (79). As the scholar trundles slowly from text to text in this methodical and comprehensive study, the object of her research—Abbey-qua-literary-artist—assumes his place in a surprisingly rich and significant cultural tradition.

Even as she exhibits her fascination with and respect for Abbey's achievement as a writer, Ronald does not shy away from dispassionate critique. Witness her comments about Abbey's early novel, *Jonathan Troy:*

The causes for *Jonathan Troy*'s failure are many. There is little plot, other than Jonathan's own slow fumbling toward maturity. But since he is no Stephen Dedalus, nor even a Tim Hazzard, although some of his lovesick longings sound like Walter Van Tilburg Clark's trembling hero, the story moves ponderously. In fact, it is difficult to summarize the action because not much happens. Jonathan himself is part of the problem too, for he is not a very likable character. Too self-centered and self-serving, he stumbles from one painful encounter to another, seemingly with little purpose. Meant as a *Bildungsroman*, a novel of a youth's progression to maturity, *Jonathan Troy* succeeds only in expressing an erratic pattern of growth that never persuades the reader of real character development. (6–7)

This sober assessment, and others like it in the study, make it clear that *The New West of Edward Abbey* is not a work of hagiography, a mere celebration of literary accomplishment. Still, in criticizing Abbey's first published novel, which appeared in 1954 when the author was twenty-seven years old, Ronald seeks to be even-handed and to take the work on its own terms, as an effort to write within the tradition of the *Bildungsroman*. If this study is not hagiographic, neither is it narrow-mindedly critical, detracting from Abbey's works because they fail to measure up to external standards or expectations. In fact, one of the aims of *The New West* is to justify Abbey's literary significance by showing how he experiments with and expands the possibilities of several important literary traditions, including the pastoral, the romance, and the Western.

In her comments on mature fictional efforts such as *Black Sun* (1971), Ronald produces a convincing argument that Abbey's successful narrative constitutes a "modern version of the pastoral" (171), refuting Leo Marx's contention that art cannot lead to the alienated individual's reconciliation with society. She praises *Black Sun* as an exemplary work of twentieth-century "pastoral romance" (180). Another of the motifs in Ronald's study is the effort to understand Abbey's work in the context of Western American literature, particularly by comparing his fiction with the conventions of the Western novel. But when Abbey's work appears to deviate from these conventions, the critic does not complain or disparage; in the case of *The Monkey Wrench Gang*, she appreciates how the work "charges past the bounds of conventional western fiction and proposes a new doctrine of frontier behavior" (182). The result, I think, is an impressively fair-minded and respectful work of literary scholarship, one that honors its subject matter without callowly glorifying it. I recall, as a graduate student at Brown University working on the dissertation that would later be published as *Seeking Awareness in American Nature Writing*, reading *The New West of Edward Abbey* and thinking that it was a fine example of what I aspired to achieve as a scholar. My skeptical graduate committee, concerned about the legitimacy of a dissertation on "nature writing," had cautioned me to be cognizant of literary quality in my examination of noncanonical texts. What came to mind was the judiciousness of Ann Ronald's evaluations of Abbey's books. Her study became one of several important models for my own critical writing.

During his life, Abbey enjoyed no shortage of popular notoriety and attention from newspaper critics and fellow authors. Abbey's fascinating, if sometimes troubling, personality has become the stuff of legends, and there are many personal reports about his life and defenses of his iconoclastic views. For example, take a look at the interesting collection of reflections and recollections, *Resist Much, Obey Little: Some Notes on Edward Abbey*, that James Hepworth and Gregory McNamee put together in 1985. However, when Ann Ronald set herself to the task of preparing a serious, book-length, scholarly study of Abbey's work, she was doing something rather revolutionary in moving beyond Abbey's cult of personality to develop a more detached assessment of his literary importance. The value of this approach is that it not only offered an authoritative foundation for future readings of this body of literature—ranging from Abbey's early novels to his major nonfiction of the 1960s and 1970s and his mature fiction—but it signaled the acceptability of this type of serious approach for future generations of literary scholars and teachers, thus helping to make possible the exponential dispersion of Abbey's words and ideas in college and high school classrooms for decades to come.

Ann Ronald was indeed an associate professor of English at the University of Nevada, Reno, when she wrote this book between 1980 and 1982, spending one of these years on sabbatical in San Diego, California. Although she had not previously written on Abbey, Ronald was well prepared for this project, having completed her Ph.D. at Northwestern University in 1970 with a dissertation entitled "Functions of Setting in the Novel," a study of the uses of landscape by Victorian novelists. Many of her seminar papers at Northwestern, preceding the dissertation, had focused on landscape topics as well. It was a logical transition from Victorian fiction to the literature of the American West when Ronald moved to Reno after graduate school to begin her teaching career. A native of Washington State and a graduate of Whitman College and the University of Colorado at Boulder, she was, in a sense, returning to her Western landscape roots by coming to Nevada. Since completing the Abbey project, Ronald has continued her important work in the field of literature and environment, editing the anthology *Words for the Wild* for the Sierra Club in 1987 and authoring a number of articles on Western authors, such as a study of Wallace Stegner, several essays on Nevada literature (including the 1989 piece "Why Don't They Write about Nevada?"), and two omnibus surveys of contemporary nature writing for *Western American Literature.* Recently she has made a compelling foray into nonfiction nature writing with the 1995 volume *Earthtones: A Nevada Album,* which combines her original essays with photographs by the distinguished Salt Lake City writer and photographer Stephen Trimble. At present, she is in the midst of a new project, *GhostWest,* a collection of narrative essays that consider the present-day auras of Western landscapes where significant events (often losses) occurred in the past.

One of the virtues of *The New West of Edward Abbey* is its comprehensive approach to Abbey's writings up to the early 1980s. Readers of this volume can count on a lucid introduction to many of the *central* texts in oeuvre of a *central* figure in the renaissance of American environmental literature during the last quarter of the twentieth century, including such landmarks as *Desert Solitaire* and *The Monkey Wrench Gang.* But Edward Abbey, although ailing, was still alive and writing in 1982 when *The New West* first appeared, and he continued to produce significant work up to his death on March 14, 1989, at the age of sixty-two. Several volumes, including poetry and journals, have appeared posthumously as well.

At the 1995 meeting of the Western Literature Association in Vancouver, British Columbia, Ann Ronald participated in a session devoted to Abbey and offered what she declared to be her final comments on the author. Despite various invitations, she has not wished to return to Abbey and prepare sustained analysis of such works as *The Fool's Progress* and *Hayduke Lives!* for a new, extended edition of this book. She has moved in the direction of her own narrative nonfiction since publishing the initial edition of this study—

has decided that she has other lives to live. I would like, therefore, to say a few words about some of Abbey's significant later and posthumously published volumes, including his final three collections of essays, the two novels mentioned above, the poetry collection *Earth Apples*, and the excerpts from his journals published as *Confessions of a Barbarian*.

In 1982, Abbey published *Down the River*, a miscellany of nineteen essays and book reviews that were collected after appearing in a variety of publications, ranging from *Backpacker* to the *New York Times* and *Rolling Stone*. The book is organized into four sections—"Thoreau and Other Friends," "Politicks and Rivers," "Places and Rivers," and "People, Books, and Rivers"—sandwiched between the preliminary notes, which offer a paean to rivers and river writers Abbey loves, and a whimsical postscript indicating that he is not through running whitewater. The pieces collected here are, for the most part, what the author describes as "environmental journalism" (6) and many seem breezily entertaining or politically motivated; most of the pieces in the book appear not to have been crafted as ambitious literary works. The opening essay in the collection, "Down River with Henry Thoreau," recounts an eleven-day journey down the Green River in southeastern Utah with "five friends plus the ghost of a sixth: . . . a worn and greasy paperback copy of a book called *Walden, or Life in the Woods*." "Thoreau's mind has been haunting mine for most of my life," Abbey tells us. "It seems proper now to reread him" (13). The essay saunters from Thoreauvian topic to Thoreauvian topic, drifting through the text as the boats ride the current, questioning authority, railing against the various forms of slavery, savoring the idea of wilderness. At the same time, he gently teases Thoreau about his Spartan diet, the commercial failure of his writings, and his sex life (or lack thereof). This informal essay has no point except, perhaps, to enjoy anew a tour of Thoreau's words—just as the point of a float trip (especially on a familiar river) may simply be the appreciation of a much-loved landscape and the companionship of fellow travelers. It anticipates, indirectly, such recent works of nature writing as Scott Russell Sanders's chapter "The Flow of the River," from his 1993 volume *Staying Put*, which explores the profound parallels between the movement of narrative and the movement of water. The next essay in *Down the River*, "Watching the Birds: The Windhover," addresses a variety of philosophical topics, from the human tendency to name things in nature to the mysterious inscrutability of the world. Throughout the book, following more mundane narratives of river adventures, essays like this one are sprinkled, reflecting on metaphysical issues. This essay concludes with a familiar tribute to the "humble turkey buzzard" (55), a favorite bird that appears repeatedly in Abbey's books. Should the author happen to be reincarnated, he would prefer to return as a vulture, free to ride the thermals and "contemplate the world we love from a silent and considerable height" (55).

Much as he loves to detach himself from the fray and consider grand ideas and beautiful images, Abbey cannot pull back completely from the political morass of contemporary America. A typical example of the political essays in *Down the River* is "Planting a Tree," which couches the author's anger and frustration with the Reagan administration's M-X Missile plan in a brief story about putting a small tree in his yard on the outskirts of Tucson, hoping that the plant will outlive the foolish human inhabitants of the city, who seem destined to blow themselves and their Soviet counterparts to smithereens. Occasionally, as in the final essay in the book, we find the tender side of Abbey: "Loving one another, we take the sting from death. Loving our mysterious blue planet, we resolve riddles and dissolve all enigmas in contingent bliss" (238). But as many commentators have observed, there is also a recurrent inhumanist streak in Abbey's work, evident earlier in *Desert Solitaire* and noticeable in this collection as well. See, for instance, David Copland Morris's 1997 study, "Inhumanism, Environmental Crisis, and the Canon of American Literature." Abbey's inhumanism appears vividly in the concluding lines of "Planting a Tree," when the essayist remarks that he and his family will never see the cottonwood seedling reach maturity: "But somebody will. Something will. In fifty years Tucson will have shrunk back to what it once was, a town of adobe huts by the trickling Santa Cruz, a happier place than it is now. . . . In that anticipation I find satisfaction enough" (63). Adventure, philosophizing, social commentary—that is the general rhythm of the collection. The three strands come together most eloquently in "Floating," the book's concluding essay, which "floats" idea after idea, only to come crashing into the rocks of physical reality each time; and in the course of savoring this cycle of speculation and realization, an ethic of preservation emerges, the thinker becomes "politicized."

Two years later, Abbey published another nonfiction collection, *Beyond the Wall*. This volume includes ten more magazine pieces and chapters from some of his earlier books, such as *Slickrock, Desert Images, The Hidden Canyon,* and *Cactus Country.* The author jokes in his preface that the photo books, collaborations with distinguished photographers, were too expensive and thus he wanted to make his writings available to a broader audience: "my enemies could buy them but few of my friends" (xi–xii). He also comments tellingly on his desire to publish the essays from the photo books independently of the photographs:

Although it may be true, as Confucius said, that one word is worth a thousand pictures (if it's the right word), it is also true that ordinary prose cannot easily share the pages with the brilliant work of such camera artists as John Blaustein, Ernst Haas, Philip Hyde and David Muench. Yet my words were written to be seen, ingested, mentally processed. . . . I take the liberty of offering these selected essays to the public in a sort of liberated form, free from the domineering, overwhelming presence of true-life, real-color, full-page, scenic landscape photographs. (xii)

The preface to *Beyond the Wall* explains at length the author's attitude toward his previous work, disparaging *Desert Solitaire* and praising such volumes as *Good News, Abbey's Road,* and *Down the River* as "livelier, funnier, more deeply felt, more richly ambiguous, more craftily designed" (xiii)—a set of aesthetic ideals that provides a useful standard for Abbey's writing in general. He also engages aggressively the controversy he first stirred up with *Desert Solitaire* concerning "industrial tourism" and public access to wild places. "Beyond the wall to the unreal city, beyond the security fences topped with barbed wire and razor wire, beyond the asphalt belting of the superhighways, beyond the cemented banksides of our temporarily stopped and mutilated rivers, beyond the rage of lies that poisons the air," he emphasizes, "there is another world waiting for you." This is the world celebrated in the essays collected here: "the old true world of the deserts, the mountains, the forests, the islands, the shores, the open plains" (xiv). Readers interested in literature that considers the relationship between visual and verbal representations of nature will find that several of the essays—such as "Desert Images" and "A Colorado River Journal"—anticipate the work of Barry Lopez, Ann Zwinger, Rebecca Solnit, and William L. Fox. "Down to the Sea of Cortez" and "The Ancient

Dust" echo John Steinbeck and look forward to the fine evocations of Baja California published more recently by Zwinger, Gary Paul Nabhan, Doug Peacock, and Bruce Berger. Apart from the polemical introduction, the focus in *Beyond the Wall* seems to be on telling good stories of wilderness experience, not on driving home abstract arguments in defense of the wild.

Credos and theories of art and nature are what we get in the 1988 book of essays *One Life at a Time, Please*. The collection begins with the text of Abbey's rambunctious 1985 University of Montana presentation, "Free Speech: The Cowboy and His Cow," includes essays on such controversial topics as anarchy, eco-defense, hunting, and immigration, offers several river narratives, and concludes with "A Writer's Credo" and other reflections on art and artists, from Ralph Waldo Emerson to Frederic Remington and Joseph Wood Krutch. As is typical in the introductions to his various essay collections, Abbey delights in providing evidence of how provocative his work has been. In this case, he tells the publication history of the cowboy talk, which appeared, following the Missoula talk, in the pages of *Northern Lights* and later in *Harper's*. The publication resulted in "the usual blizzard of abuse," including a letter from none other than Gretel Ehrlich, who accused him of being "arrogant, incoherent, flippant, nonsensical, nasty, and unconstructive." "'Nasty and unconstructive'—I love that," writes Abbey (3). *One Life at a Time, Please* is a particularly well-organized collection of miscellaneous essays; the structure seems less opaque than that of *Down the River*, less random than the movement from one itinerant narrative to the next in *Beyond the Wall*. Politics, travel, books and art, and nature love: these categories rather nicely sum up the dimensions of Abbey's work.

As he explains in the preface to *One Life at a Time, Please*, Abbey wrote "A Writer's Credo" as a lecture, which he delivered at Harvard University in May 1985. Much of the talk is clearly calculated to stir up what he anticipates to be a mainstream literary audience, just as surely as he expected it to rile up his University of Montana audience a month earlier when, among other things, he stated, "cattle have done, and are doing, intolerable damage to our public lands" (13). Seldom has an American author articulated more forcefully and directly the political nature of literary art than Abbey does in his "Writer's Credo." "It is my belief," he begins the lecture, "that the writer, the free-lance author, should be and must be a critic of the society in which he lives. . . . The more freedom the writer possesses the greater the moral obligation to play the role of critic" (161). Speaking to the literary establishment, he continues, "If literary art, like so much of our poetry, music, and painting, is merely decorative, merely play and no more, then we can get by with wallpaper, polyurethane abstract sculpture, Bloomingdale's catalog, *Vanity Fair,* rock music (music to hammer out fenders by), and Andy Warhol. If literature, on the other hand, is to be more than Muzak, then it must be involved, responsible, committed (O dread clichés!)" (163). Many scholars have noted Abbey's tendency to be indiscriminately provocative, to agitate the left as well as the right, to do anything possible to stir up independent thinking. This is, for him, the essence of political behavior. "By 'political,'" he means

involvement, responsibility, commitment: the writer's duty to speak the truth—especially unpopular truth. Especially truth that offends the powerful, the rich, the well-established, the traditional, the mythic, the sentimental. To attack, when the time makes it necessary, the sacred cows of his society. And I mean all sacred cows: whether those of the public-lands beef industry or the sacred cows of militarism, nationalism, religion, capitalism, socialism, conservatism, liberalism. To name but a few of our prevailing ideologies. (163)

Having stated that his primary goal as a writer is to rouse the rabble and speak the truth (as he sees it), Abbey tempers this assertion by acknowledging that he seeks as well to make things of beauty. He sounds here a bit like Vladimir Nabokov ("For me a work of fiction exists only insofar as it affords me what I shall bluntly call aesthetic bliss" [*Lolita* 286]) and John Hawkes mixed with James Baldwin and Gary Snyder. "I write to make a difference," Abbey concludes: "'It is always a writer's duty' said Samuel Johnson, 'to make the world a better place.' I write to give pleasure and promote aesthetic bliss. To honor life and to praise the divine beauty of the natural world. I write for the joy and exultation of writing itself. To tell my story" (178). Although many of Abbey's essays are written in the first person and do indeed tell parts of his "story," his last three collections of nonfiction offer mostly narratives of specific adventures or glancing philosophical reflections and political diatribes. He turned to the genre of the novel in order to write the encompassing story of his life and to find a way to attach his particular experience to what he took to be the evolving mythos of late-twentieth-century American culture.

In his 1994 biography, *Epitaph for a Desert Anarchist*, James Bishop Jr. quotes Tucson writer Gregory McNamee's informal assessment of Abbey's literary achievement: "Ed's nonfiction is superior to his fiction. It will be what he'll be remembered for. This is not to say that *The Brave Cowboy* and *Fire on the Mountain* weren't good, or that *Black Sun* wasn't a perfectly realized novel. But the apocalyptic novels, *The Monkey Wrench Gang* and *Good News*, his best-known works of fiction, are really little more than comic books, and the writing isn't as sustained as in the essays" (174). This evaluation matches most critics' views of Abbey's work. And yet, much like his contemporary Peter Matthiessen, who disparages his famous nonfiction efforts (such as the Pulitzer Prize–winning *The Snow Leopard*) and prefers to talk about his novels, Abbey himself was passionately devoted to the art of fiction and sought throughout his career to produce a great, memorable novel. As Susan Zakin explains in *Coyotes and Town Dogs: Earth First! and the Environmental Movement*, Abbey was driven, along with the likes of Ernest Hemingway and Norman Mailer, to try writing the Great American Novel, a story that would "capture the myth of a continent and a people" (180). In the end, estimates Zakin, he "may not have reached the level of maturity attained by many great novelists, but by bringing his resonant and moving ideas about the primacy of nature into American discourse, the rebellious and erudite Abbey did more to change society than his contemporaries who produced better-honed work" (180).

The Fool's Progress: An Honest Novel, first published in 1988, was to have been his great novel. He referred to this work as "The Fat Masterpiece" (Zakin 181). During the decade following its publication, the work attracted only modest attention among critics, students, and general readers. Still, when I asked Ann Ronald to provide a brief comment about Abbey's late work, she responded:

> If I were to extend the argument of *The New West of Edward Abbey*, I would most like to write a chapter on *The Fool's Progress*. In that novel, Abbey successfully brought together elements from the romance of *The Brave Cowboy*, the comedy of *The Monkey Wrench Gang*, the tragedy of *Black Sun*, and the satire of *Good News*. Abbey said of Henry Lightcap's escapades, "the best thing I've written yet, and I'm proud of it" (*Confessions of a Barbarian* 330). I agree that *The Fool's Progress* was his most ambitious work

of fiction, and that he indeed should have been proud of his "honest" achievement. (Personal correspondence)

Other longtime readers of Abbey's work, such as Charles Bowden, have offered similar appraisals of their friend's hoped-for magnum opus. James Bishop, who devotes nine pages to an overview of the novel, notes that the initial sketches for the book were prepared years earlier, when Abbey was still a Stegner Fellow at Stanford in 1957. Some passages in the eventual novel emerge directly from drafts written thirty years before.

The roots of *The Fool's Progress* can be discerned in the early years of Abbey's writing career, which coincided with the height of the Beat Movement in the San Francisco Bay Area, a time of postwar, anti-establishment Bohemianism. Like such Beat icons as Allen Ginsberg's "Howl" and Jack Kerouac's *The Dharma Bums,* Abbey's work typically displays a complex tonality that brings together apocalyptic social critique, sweet nostalgia for an edenic era of personal and societal innocence, and almost giddy sensualism. Ann Ronald, in *The New West,* discusses the loose, haphazard "picaresque structure" of such novels as *The Monkey Wrench Gang* and *Good News* (183, 213). Likewise, *The Fool's Progress* contains pronounced aspects of the picaresque in its hero's adventurous journey home from the Southwest, which is the locus of his adult struggles, to the eastern hill country of his West Virginia childhood. The geographical movement from desert Southwest to verdant eastern mountains parallels the narrator/protagonist's quest for innocence and redemption. Bishop's examination of Abbey's private papers brings to light the author's intention, while still a student in Stegner's writing workshop at Stanford, to write of "sub-Bohemian life and the desperate search by young Americans for spiritual enlightenment, emotional fulfillment, and sexual liberation" and to call this work "Down the Road." With 100 pages drafted, the project was shelved as Kerouac's 1955 novel *On the Road* achieved the status of cultural monument. Decades later, no longer a young man, Abbey recast the narrative to express his vision of America as paradise lost.

The Fool's Progress presents Abbey's trademark verbal playfulness and political cynicism, but with a darker, more tired edge than before. When he writes of mortality in *Desert Solitaire,* most notably in the chapter "The Dead Man at Grandview Point," there is a feel of philosophical abstraction to it, a kind of experiential naïveté: "Each man's death diminishes me? Not necessarily. Given this man's age, the inevitability and suitability of his death, and the essential nature of life on earth, there is in each of us the unspeakable conviction that we are well rid of him. His departure makes room for the living. Away with the old, in with the new. He is gone—we remain, others come" (242). In *The Fool's Progress*, as Henry's rickety Dodge pickup makes its way "eastward, eastward," barreling down the east side of the continental divide, "she rocks and rattles over the patches in the asphalt, wheezing, clanking, slowing to sixty, fifty, forty, surrendering (as we all must) to friction and entropy" (168). The truck is on its last legs, the road is disintegrating, and the human occupant, who stops to relieve himself, is preoccupied with mortality: "All forms of excretion are pleasant, said James Joyce. Not always true. I inspect my stool for signs of mortality: it's loose, structurally weak. Unsound. Much too dark" (168). There is, in retrospect, something chilling and sad in the offhand comment, ostensibly from the narrator Henry Lightcap, "My 'irritable colon' is acting up. You might call it that" (168). Chapters later, still en route home, Henry contemplates a highwayside breakfast of greasy bacon and eggs: "No wonder my stomach feels so queer. No wonder that gnawing nagging agenbiting crab deep in my guts won't go away" (437). And finally, in the closing pages, in a chapter called "Judgment Day," there is the hospital scene where Henry is being checked out for "acute pancreatitis" (474). As Henry approaches Stump Crick, West Virginia, and his brother Will's home, "something huge, black, grasping, looming above the trees, blotting out the few dim stars, shambles toward [him] from the forest. . . . Henry, it says, Henry my friend my very best friend, where have you been? I've been looking for you everywhere . . ." (500). A year later Abbey himself was dead, the victim of a disease called "esophageal varices" (Zakin 312).

Ann Ronald notes in *The New West* that Abbey creates a stylized "narrative voice" in such works as *Desert Solitaire*, requiring readers to distinguish carefully between author and narrator/protagonist. In the case of the nonfiction, she refers to the author as "Edward" and the narrator as "Ed" (66). "Insistence upon a separation of author and dramatized narrator may sound trivial," Ronald states.

Although such a distinction is generally made when talking about novels, most readers and critics assume that in nonfiction the two are synonymous. Beneath the solid surface of *Desert Solitaire,* however, viscosity awaits those who innocently believe the author is also the main character. Ed is an original creation . . . , manipulated by Abbey. . . . The author can thus control his audience's attitudes and responses more easily and more effectively. The technique works the way escape fiction does, but with more radical success. (67)

Commentators have noted that *The Fool's Progress* may be Abbey's most autobiographical work, despite its presentation as a novel. The quixotic shifting between first and third person appears to be an undisguised clue that the author and protagonist share a common, or frequently overlapping, identity. Beyond this, Abbey's age corresponds precisely with narrator Henry's, and Stump Crick is a close approximation of Home, Pennsylvania, where the author grew up. Additional projections of the author's life into this archetypal story of a dying man's effort to regain the geography of integrated innocence are too myriad to warrant repetition. What sustains the novel as a work of art is, in part, the controlled structure of alternating chapters, moving between present-day loss and despair in Tucson (and later en route to West Virginia) and systematic, chronological recollections of Henry's childhood and early adulthood. The ability to combine a credible, engaging story with rambunctious wordplay, ever an Abbey trait, is prominent throughout this philosophical novel, a work that is certainly too universal and varied in its themes to be characterized, precisely, as "environmental literature."

I would argue, too, that Jack Kerouac's imprint on this work is inescapable. In other works by Edward Abbey, environmental outspokenness and philosophical sophistication seem uncharacteristic of Beat literature, particularly Kerouac's sentimental, self-consciously ingenuous narrative style. However, *The Fool's Progress* has all the hallmarks of an iconoclastic, individualistic Beat novel, except the narrator here prefers his beat-up Dodge to public transportation (hitchhiking and freight trains). A *beaten* man (and truck and dog) make their way to the East, to the place of origins, in quest of *beatitude.* This is the stuff of myth: the ultimate "nostalgia," the pain of return or the impossibility of true return. Kerouac's *On the Road* depicts the frenzied search for truth on American highways, recounting barely fictionalized jaunts from New York to San

Francisco, back and forth, back and forth, and finally south to Mexico, to the realm of mysterious, beatific, dark-skinned people. The 1950s narrative hopefully identifies a possible new locus of enlightenment, distinct from the decadent materialism of the United States. The progress of Abbey's archetypal "fool" is really a decline into physical and emotional decay; the psychological center of the book is the narrator's memory, the persistent tug of the past and his sense of essential, unrelinquished identity.

Another important Kerouackian motif in *The Fool's Progress*, as in many of Abbey's other books, is the search for and celebration of friendship, of true intellectual companionship. It is ironic, in a sense, that much of this penultimate novel presents a solitary protagonist making his way, with increasing decrepitude, through an isolated landscape; the object of the journey, beyond some vaguely conceived rejuvenation, is a reunion with his older brother William, or "Will," who seems to be the epitome of a good friend. The final lines of the novel, before the "Postlude," suggest tenderly that having "come home," Henry cannot stay for long. Abbey also prophesied his imminent death and underscored his deep attachment to friends in the acknowledgments to *Hayduke Lives!*, the sequel to *The Monkey Wrench Gang* that appeared in 1990: "If friendship is equivalent to wealth and good fortune, then I have been a rich and lucky man throughout my life. Therefore, thinking each new book may be my last (for who knows?—and one does grow weary anyway of this infernal scribbling), I hereby dedicate *Hayduke Lives!* to my loyal friends who have so enriched the Late Middle Ages of my slothful and careless even reckless existence, i.e., viz., and to wit . . ." (n.p.). He then proceeds to name ninety-nine friends, highlighting his fifth wife, Clarke, his five children, and such dear friends as Jack Loeffler, John DePuy, and Doug Peacock.

Hayduke Lives! brings together again the cast of characters modeled rather directly after several of these friends. In her commentary on *The Monkey Wrench Gang*, Susan Zakin invokes Larry McMurtry in support of the idea that "one of the reasons for the Western's durability is that it offers an acceptable orientation to violence" (177). And nowhere in Abbey's work—except perhaps in *Hayduke Lives!*—is violence a more prominent motif than in his action-packed 1975 fantasy of eco-sabotage, *The Monkey Wrench Gang*, a novel that has Hollywood written all over it, as the saying goes, although it has yet to appear on screen. I would argue, though, that

Abbey's Westerns—including *The Monkey Wrench Gang* and *Hayduke Lives!*—are not only excuses to revel in lust and violence but are, more important, occasions to explore the possibilities of friendship. The "gang" of legendary monkey-wrenchers is nothing more than a group of friends, joined by a shared love of place and politicized by what they perceive as the violent abuse of this place. While *The Fool's Progress* certainly embodies Abbey's typical skill at evoking landscapes and portraying the foibles and beauties of the human animal, the late novel was not particularly focused on the region with which Abbey's work is most commonly identified: the desert Southwest. *Hayduke Lives!,* on the other hand, published two years after *The Fool's Progress,* is a thoroughly Southwestern book that picks up, quite literally, where *The Monkey Wrench Gang* left off, after a narrative hiatus of several years (enough time for Doc Sarvis and Bonnie Abbzug to have married and produced a son, Reuben, who is three years old at the book's beginning).

As noted above, Gregory McNamee has described *The Monkey Wrench Gang* as a "comic book." This is an informal, shorthand way of getting at what Ann Ronald explains throughout *The New West* as Abbey's ongoing experimentation with genres. Other friends and commentators have complained that Abbey's fictional characters tend to be walking, talking ideologies, not credible representations of multidimensional human beings. The final novel, *Hayduke Lives!,* certainly deserves this assessment as well, and yet it is also a high-spirited romp, a tall tale of violent eco-defense that at once violates historicity and propriety and incorporates historical reality (rampant urban sprawl and desert mining, gatherings of the Earth First! group that was inspired by *The Monkey Wrench Gang*) into its pages. Perhaps one could argue that the novel seeks to show that old friends, once joined by an important cause, will manage to come together again and fight the good fight, despite the passing of time. *Hayduke Lives!* seems plaintive in its refusal to let the "gang" disperse and move on to new lives. And yet there is also an optimism in the insistence on the possibility of pulling the group back together, this time in support of the veritable army of Earth First! activists that has emerged since the initial, clandestine operations of Sarvis, Bonnie, Seldom Seen Smith, and George Washington Hayduke. In keeping with Abbey's reflections on mortality toward the end of his life, the novel offers several emblems of continuation and longevity: the reappearance of Hayduke (apparently killed at the end of *The Monkey Wrench Gang*) and Jack Burns (a character apparently killed at the end of *Good News*); the spread of the philosophy of monkey-wrenching to Earth First!; and the framing parable of old man tortoise (the symbol of the desert) apparently crushed in the opening pages of the novel by the land-clearing machine-monster called GOLIATH only to emerge "from his grave" (307) at the book's end. For Abbey, though, the narrative suggestions of reincarnation and persistence go beyond the maudlin hope for personal resurrection and imply his more compelling desire that the desert itself, free from human pests, will once again, someday, thrive.

Two other important, posthumous collections of Abbey's private writings and ephemera appeared in 1994, both edited by the author's friend David Petersen. *Earth Apples: The Poetry of Edward Abbey* offers more than seventy brief examples of verse, ranging from ditties and parodies to love songs and tributes (to friends and landscapes). Petersen himself admits at the outset, "This collection, in fact, is something of an anomaly, not proffered as great poetry, but rather, offered as a revealing and entertaining insight into the mind and emotions of a great contemporary novelist and essayist, a great man" (xii). In fact, although the collection focuses on Abbey's poetry, it closely parallels the simultaneous publication of excerpts from his journals. The penultimate poem in the book—a raunchy, eight-line piece called "The Kowboy and His Kow" that concludes with "Yes, give me a home where the grizzer bears roam / Where the bighorn and wapiti play, / Where *never* is seen a hamburger machine / And the cowshit's not stinking all day" (109)—was the last entry to appear in his journal before his death in 1989.

Edward Abbey's journals are now housed in the Abbey Papers at the University of Arizona Special Collections Library and consist of "12.1 feet, 30 manuscript boxes" (*Confessions* ix). Petersen selected approximately one-fourth of the journal material in the Abbey Papers for inclusion in *Confessions of a Barbarian*. The selections reveal a wide range of Abbey's thinking, from the intimate to the professional, the aesthetic to the political. Much of the journal confirms impressions of the man and his work suggested in the earlier, published writings. Of particular interest to some scholars, though, may be the journal passages that reveal the author's own process of deciding not to pursue the scholarly direction that had initially motivated him. On February 10, 1952, for instance, during his year as a

Fulbright scholar studying philosophy at Edinburgh University, he scrawls a brief poem "provoked" by a visit to the library stacks, concluding, "O Lord, preserve me from the fate of these poor hacks / Who waste their lives within library stacks" (22). The following fall, having just begun the Ph.D. program in philosophy at Yale, he explains his decision to leave:

September 20, 1953—New Haven, Connecticut
Today, after two weeks of dilettante study, I withdrew from the graduate school of Yale University. My reasons are several: (1) disenchantment—I had expected, somehow, so much more than is actually here, that the professors would be Platos, the students Aristotles. (2) Realization—I can no longer play at being an academic scholar; from here on, it would require intense and genuine effort, and after all, I want to be a writer, not an academician; I must choose and I have chosen. (3) Financial and temporal expediency—balancing a year at Yale against a year of writing, a year of travel in Europe, a year's delay in returning to the West, I'll give up Yale. (4) An Inner Voice—the sense that my calling and my study lie elsewhere, in the sweet air and under the open sky of the broad world, among my friends and folks, in space and movement and adventure. (111–12)

Abbey was twenty-six years old when he jotted these notes, attempting to plumb the reasons for one of the crucial decisions of his life: his rejection of the academic profession and gravitation toward the grandeur and scary uncertainty of art. The journal selections in *Confessions* go right up to the final month of Abbey's life and offer readers a valuable glimpse into the mind of this unique author. Petersen offers a rich sampling not only of lush nature writing and romantic soul-searching but also of misogynistic quips and anti-liberal rants. While many of Abbey's fictional characters may come across as two-dimensional, comic-book caricatures, the author himself emerges, in the pages of the journals, as a complex and interesting human being. Abbey scholars, of course, would be well advised to go to Tucson and work with the original journals. However, given the limited access to the Abbey archive at the University of Arizona, Petersen has offered a helpful contribution to Abbey studies in the form of this generous collection of journal entries.

As mentioned above, one of the important achievements of Ann Ronald's *The New West of Edward Abbey*, beyond its actual commentary on Abbey's specific works, was how it served to inspire later scholars, myself included, to study (and teach) Abbey's writings and the writings of Abbey's cohorts, from Southwestern authors, such as Charles Bowden and Richard Shelton, to the vibrant community of environmental writers across the country, such as Rick Bass, Wendell Berry, Annie Dillard, Edward Hoagland, Barry Lopez, Peter Matthiessen, Terry Tempest Williams, and Ann Zwinger, to name only a few. The legacy of *The New West* may be glimpsed in the collections of scholarly studies of Abbey's life and work that appeared in the 1990s, moving away from the anecdotal commentaries of *Resist Much, Obey Little* and providing more analytical treatment of the author's publications. Comments on some of the more significant examples of recent Abbey scholarship follow.

In 1993, the journal *Western American Literature* published a de facto Abbey issue that included journal selections edited by David Petersen, a biographical tribute by Jack Loeffler, and two of the best critical articles on Abbey's work, Paul T. Bryant's "The Structure and Unity of *Desert Solitaire*" and David Copland Morris's "Celebration and Irony: The Polyphonic Voice of Edward Abbey's *Desert Solitaire*." In 1998, a new era of Abbey scholarship was swept in when Peter Quigley published a collection of eighteen critical essays by senior and up-and-coming scholars, *Coyote in the Maze: Tracking Edward Abbey in a World of Words.* Quigley discusses Ronald's *The New West of Edward Abbey* at length, calling it a "landmark work" and praising the scholar's "insights regarding the use of irony and the manner in which she carries out a structural analysis" (3). Many of the studies in *Coyote in the Maze* operate with a poststructuralist devotion to the "interwoven and volatile sense of the possibilities of multiple genres" (5), a fascination with what Morris refers to as Abbey's "polyphonic voice." This contrasts with, but does not entirely supplant, the so-called "modernist approach" of Ann Ronald and other critics that seeks to identify the relationship between Abbey's writing and distinct literary traditions, such as the Western and the romance. I would argue that there continues to be a fruitful tension between the New Critical orientation toward "certainty" (*Coyote* 4) and the poststructuralist foregrounding of uncertainty and Bakhtinian heteroglossia. An important aspect of Ronald's study, in fact, is that she discerns in Abbey a recurrent tendency to blur literary genres and test narrative boundaries. *The New West* points the way toward recent readings of Abbey as a quasi-postmodern author.

As we peer into the new millennium, the enthusiastic examination of Edward Abbey's literary works by serious associate professors—and full professors and graduate students—shows no signs of waning. In recent years, fine studies such as Don Scheese's *Nature Writing: The Pastoral Impulse in America* (1996) and Daniel G. Payne's *Voices in the Wilderness: American Nature Writing and Environmental Politics* (1996) have helped to refine our understanding of Abbey's place in the American literary and environmental traditions. Payne, while noting how Abbey's novels helped to inspire the formation of activist groups such as Earth First!, argues that "when evaluated by the usual democratic standards, such as influencing legislation or persuading policymakers to protect land and wildlife, Abbey's political legacy is less clearly discernible. It is far too early to make an informed judgment as to the effect that Abbey's writing will have on environmental policy" ("'Talking Freely'" 45). Frank Stewart's *A Natural History of Nature Writing* (1995) and Peter Wild's *The Opal Desert: Explorations of Fantasy and Reality in the American Southwest* (1999) offer engaging narrative histories of environmental literature, including substantial overviews of Abbey's life and art. Wild, who worked alongside Abbey in the English Department at the University of Arizona, focuses on Southwestern literature and explains how the region's environmental degradation actually appeared to "energize" and motivate the combative author rather than demoralize him (157). Barney Nelson, in her new book *The Wild and the Domestic: Animal Representation, Ecocriticism, and Western American Literature* (2000), highlights Mary Austin, John Muir, and Abbey, complicating the latter's view of ranchers and cattle and suggesting that Abbey, while issuing thoughtful and colorful challenges to rural America, was not a narrow-minded critic of the ranching lifestyle. Nelson suggests, in an essay called "Edward Abbey: Friend or Foe?" that appeared in *Range* while she was drafting her book, that Abbey was as perplexed and conflicted about the vast system of importing exotic treats—coffee, cigars, liquor, and chocolate—as he was about the potential environmental harm that might result from overgrazing (46). James Cahalan's book on Abbey's literary career, forthcoming from the University of Arizona Press, promises to be one of the most definitive and useful new studies.

Although Abbey has been dead for more than a decade, his words and ideas continue to live—and change—in the minds of scholars, students, activists, politicians, ranchers, miners, and lovers of good writing. The present edition of Ann Ronald's foundational study of this important writer and thinker, supplemented with her 1989 essay "A Clean Hard Edge Divides" on the occasion of Abbey's death, will help orient scholars as they make their way into the vibrant topography of his work.

Works Cited

Abbey, Edward. *Beyond the Wall.* New York: Holt, Rinehart, and Winston, 1984.

———. *Confessions of a Barbarian: Selections from the Journals of Edward Abbey, 1951–1989.* Edited by David Petersen. Boston: Little, Brown, 1994.

———. *Desert Solitaire: A Season in the Wilderness.* 1968. Reprint, New York: Ballantine, 1971.

———. *Down the River.* New York: Dutton, 1982.

———. *Earth Apples: The Poetry of Edward Abbey.* Edited by David Petersen. New York: St. Martin's, 1994.

———. *Hayduke Lives!* Boston: Little, Brown, 1990.

———. *The Fool's Progress: An Honest Novel.* 1988. Reprint, New York: Avon, 1990.

———. *The Monkey Wrench Gang.* 1975. Reprint, New York: Avon, 1976.

———. *One Life at a Time, Please.* New York: Henry Holt, 1988.

Bishop, James, Jr. *Epitaph for a Desert Anarchist: The Life and Legacy of Edward Abbey.* New York: Atheneum, 1994.

Hepworth, James, and Gregory McNamee. *Resist Much, Obey Little: Some Notes on Edward Abbey.* Salt Lake City: Dream Garden Press, 1985.

Kerouac, Jack. *On the Road.* New York: Viking, 1955.

Lyon, Thomas J., ed. *Western American Literature* 28, no. 1 (May 1993). Edward Abbey Special Issue.

Morris, David Copland. "Celebration and Irony: The Polyphonic Voice of Edward Abbey's *Desert Solitaire.*" *Western American Literature* 28, no. 1 (May 1993): 21–23.

———. "Inhumanism, Environmental Crisis, and the Canon of American Literature." *ISLE: Interdisciplinary Studies in Literature and Environment* 4, no. 2 (fall 1997): 1–16.

Nabokov, Vladimir. *Lolita.* 1955. Reprint, New York: Berkley, 1983.

Nelson, Barney. "Edward Abbey: Friend or Foe?" *Range* (spring 1996): 46–47.

———. *The Wild and the Domestic: Animal Representation, Ecocriticism, and Western American Literature.* Reno: University of Nevada Press, 2000.

Payne, Daniel G. "'Talking Freely Around the Campfire': The Influence of Nature Writing on American Environmental Policy." *Society and Natural Resources* 11 (1999): 39–48.

———. *Voices in the Wilderness: American Nature Writing and Environmental Politics.* Hanover, N.H.: University Press of New England, 1996.

Quigley, Peter, ed. *Coyote in the Maze: Tracking Edward Abbey in a World of Words.* Salt Lake City: University of Utah Press, 1998.

Ronald, Ann. "A Clean Hard Edge Divides." *Redneck Review of Literature* 16 (spring 1989): 1–6.

———. *The New West of Edward Abbey.* 1982. Reprint, Reno: University of Nevada Press, 1988.

———. Personal correspondence. January 4, 2000.

———. "Why Don't They Write about Nevada?" *Western American Literature* 24, no. 3 (November 1989): 213–24.

Scheese, Don. *Nature Writing: The Pastoral Impulse in America.* New York: Twayne, 1996.

Slovic, Scott. *Seeking Awareness in American Nature Writing.* Salt Lake City: University of Utah Press, 1992.

Stewart, Frank. *A Natural History of Nature Writing.* Washington, D.C.: Island Press, 1995.

Wild, Peter. *The Opal Desert: Explorations of Fantasy and Reality in the American Southwest.* Austin: University of Texas Press, 1999.

Zakin, Susan. *Coyotes and Town Dogs: Earth First! and the Environmental Movement.* New York: Viking, 1993.

Notes

Chapter 1

1. *Jonathan Troy,* p. 310; in this chapter all subsequent quotations from *Jonathan Troy* are cited in text from the first edition unless otherwise noted.

Chapter 2

1. Sources defining the romance are as plentiful as definitions of the term; my own characterization is a compilation of phrases and ideas borrowed from many different critics discussing a wide variety of writers. The list begins with Northrop Frye's influential *Anatomy of Criticism,* closely followed by a lesser-known companion, Robert Foulke and Paul Smith's *An Anatomy of Literature.* Two other useful sources, Gillian Beer's *The Romance* and *Novel and Romance 1700–1800,* edited by Ioan Williams, consider the romance in its British context. Here in the United States, Richard Chase, writing *The American Novel and Its Tradition,* chose the word to isolate certain nineteenth-century American novelists from their contemporaries across the ocean, although Henry James's preface to *The American* had carefully distinguished between the romantic and the real many years before. Chase's well-known book has been praised, supplemented, debated, and debased by a number of scholars, but in the past decade two

books have suggested especially relevant directions for further study. Michael J. Hoffman's *The Subversive Vision* and Richard H. Brodhead's *Hawthorne, Melville, and the Novel*, although dealing with subjects far removed from Edward Abbey's world, are nevertheless expansive and provocative. Finally, any consideration of the Western novel as a particular example of the romance must acknowledge James K. Folsom's conjoining of the terms. In fact, it was the introduction to his excellent book, *The American Western Novel*, that first suggested the general relationship to me.

2. *The Brave Cowboy*, p. 14; in this chapter all subsequent quotations from *The Brave Cowboy* are cited in text from the Zia paperback reprint edition unless otherwise noted.

3. C. L. Sonnichsen, *From Hopalong to Hud*, p. 120.

4. John R. Milton, *The Novel of the American West*, p. 323.

5. William T. Pilkington, "Edward Abbey: Southwestern Anarchist," p. 58.

6. Neal E. Lambert, Introduction to the Zia edition of *The Brave Cowboy*, p. xiii.

7. Levi S. Peterson, "The Primitive and the Civilized in Western Fiction," p. 200.

8. Ibid., p. 199.

Chapter 3

1. C. L. Sonnichsen, *Tularosa: Last of the Frontier West*, p. 290.

2. *Fire on the Mountain*, p. 51; in this chapter all subsequent quotations from *Fire on the Mountain* are cited in text from the Zia paperback reprint edition unless otherwise noted.

3. Garth McCann, *Edward Abbey*, p. 16.

4. Les Standiford, "Desert Places: An Exchange with Edward Abbey," p. 397.

5. Northrop Frye, "The Argument of Comedy," p. 70; see also Frye's *Anatomy of Criticism*, pp. 182–83.

Chapter 4

1. *Desert Solitaire*, p. 6; in this chapter all subsequent quotations from *Desert Solitaire* are cited in text from the Ballantine paperback edition unless otherwise noted.

2. Everett Ruess, *On Desert Trails*, p. 52.

3. Harry Berger, Jr., "The Renaissance Imagination: Second World and Green World," p. 46.

4. I regret any confusion caused by the literal fact that the desert is red

in color. When Abbey paints the Southwest idyllically, it becomes a metaphorical green world; when he taints it realistically, it changes to a metaphorical red one.

5. *Desert Solitaire*, p. 157–71; for further analysis of this chapter see Jerry A. Herndon's " 'Moderate Extremism': Edward Abbey and 'The Moon-Eyed Horse,' " pp. 97–103.

6. *Desert Solitaire*, pp. 233–44.

Chapter 5

1. *The Journey Home*, p. xi; all subsequent quotations from *The Journey Home* are cited in text from the first edition.

2. *Abbey's Road*, p. xv; all subsequent quotations from *Abbey's Road* are cited in text from the first edition.

3. Also a part of *The Journey Home's* Chapter 2, the relevant section was reprinted in *The Sierra Club Bulletin*, July/August 1979, p. 45.

4. Max Westbrook, "The Practical Spirit: Sacrality and the American West," p. 198.

5. Max Westbrook, *Walter Van Tilburg Clark*, p. 12; in this assessment of Clark's writing, Westbrook discusses the term "sacrality" in relation to the works of a single author, while he offers a broader definition and wider range of applicability in his earlier essay, "The Practical Spirit."

6. William T. Pilkington, "Edward Abbey: Western Philosopher, or How to be a 'Happy Hopi Hippie,' " p. 28.

7. "Last Oasis," *Harper's*, March 1977, p. 10.

8. Ibid., p. 10.

9. "Grow and Die," *Penthouse*, September 1979, p. 171.

10. "One Man's Nuclear War: On Civil Disobedience at Rocky Flats," *Harper's*, March 1979, p. 18.

11. S. C., "Review of *Abbey's Road*," p. 38.

Chapter 6

1. In this chapter, quotations from all these books are from the first editions and are cited in text.

2. John F. Baker, "Edward Abbey," p. 6.

Chapter 7

1. Since this chapter was completed, Abbey has published a new collection of essays called *Down the River with Henry David Thoreau and Friends*.

2. Henry David Thoreau, *Walden*, pp. 209–10.

3. Ibid., p. 61.

4. Ibid., p. 91.

5. Ibid., p. 5.

6. Henry David Thoreau, *Civil Disobedience*, p. 243.

7. Ibid., p. 224.

8. Ibid., p. 231.

9. Ibid., p. 236.

10. Ibid., p. 241.

11. *Walden*, p. 129.

12. Joseph Wood Krutch, *The Desert Year*, pp. 5–6.

13. Ibid., p. 39.

14. Ibid., p. 24.

15. Ibid., p. 44.

16. Ibid., p. 209.

17. Ibid., p. 126.

18. See Chapter 11 of *Desert Year*, pp. 169–84.

19. Edward Abbey, "On Nature, the Modern Temper and the Southwest: An Interview with Joseph Wood Krutch," pp. 13–21.

20. Joseph Wood Krutch, *Grand Canyon*, p. 233.

21. Ibid., p. 234.

22. John Muir, *The Yosemite*, pp. 33–34.

23. Ibid., p. 96.

24. Ibid., pp. 99–100.

25. Ibid., p. 16.

26. Ibid., p. 16.

27. Mary Austin, *The Land of Little Rain*, p. 119.

28. Ibid., p. 119.

29. Ibid., p. 152.

30. T. M. Pearce, Introduction to *The Land of Little Rain*, p. vii.

31. *Land of Little Rain*, p. 11.

32. Ruess, *On Desert Trails*, p. 58.

33. *Land of Little Rain*, p. 3.

34. Ibid., p. xvii.

Chapter 8

1. *Black Sun*, p. 43; in this chapter all subsequent quotations from *Black Sun* are cited in text from the first edition unless otherwise noted.

2. Edward Hoagland, "Review of *Black Sun*," p. 6.

3. Thomas J. Lyon, "Review of *Black Sun*," pp. 157–58.

4. Robert Foulke and Paul Smith, *An Anatomy of Literature*, p. 53.

5. Michael Squires, *The Pastoral Novel*, p. 31.

6. Ibid., p. 217.
7. Leo Marx, *The Machine in the Garden*, p. 364.
8. William T. Pilkington, "Edward Abbey: Western Philosopher," p. 31.

Chapter 9

1. *The Monkey Wrench Gang*, p. 26; in this chapter all subsequent quotations from *The Monkey Wrench Gang* are cited in text from the Avon paperback edition unless otherwise noted.
2. John F. Baker, "Edward Abbey," p. 6.
3. Jenni Calder, *There Must Be a Lone Ranger*, p. 7.
4. Ibid., p. 213.
5. Levi S. Peterson, "The Primitive and the Civilized in Western Fiction," pp. 197–207.
6. Calder, *There Must Be a Lone Ranger*, p. 31.
7. Jay Gurian, *Western American Writing—Tradition and Promise*, p. 9.

Chapter 10

1. Northrop Frye, *Anatomy of Criticism*, p. 223.
2. *Good News*, p. 1; in this chapter all subsequent quotations from *Good News* are cited in text from the first edition unless otherwise noted.
3. Robert Foulke and Paul Smith, *An Anatomy of Literature*, p. 865.
4. Ibid., p. 865.
5. Frye, *Anatomy of Criticism*, p. 223.
6. Foulke and Smith, *Anatomy of Literature*, p. 871.
7. Frye, *Anatomy of Criticism*, p. 192.

Bibliography

Whenever possible, I have listed the available paperback edition of each book cited in the bibliography.

Works by Edward Abbey

Abbey's Road. New York: E. P. Dutton, 1979.

Appalachian Wilderness: The Great Smoky Mountains. With Eliot Porter. New York: E. P. Dutton, 1970.

Black Sun. New York: Simon and Schuster, 1971; reprint New York: Avon, 1982.

The Brave Cowboy: An Old Tale in a New Time. New York: Dodd, Mead, 1956; reprint Albuquerque: University of New Mexico Press, Zia Books, 1977.

Cactus Country. New York: Time-Life Books, 1973.

Desert Images. With David Muench. New York: Chanticleer Press, 1979.

Desert Solitaire: A Season in the Wilderness. New York: Simon and Schuster, 1968; New York: Ballantine Books, 1971; rev. ed. Layton, Utah: Peregrine Smith, 1981.

Down the River with Henry David Thoreau and Friends. New York: E. P. Dutton, 1982.

Fire on the Mountain. New York: Dial Press, 1962; reprint Albuquerque: University of New Mexico Press, Zia Books, 1978.

Good News. New York: E. P. Dutton, 1980.

The Hidden Canyon: A River Journey. With John Blaustein. New York: Viking Press, 1977.

Jonathan Troy. New York: Dodd, Mead, 1954.

The Journey Home. New York: E. P. Dutton, 1977.

The Monkey Wrench Gang. Philadelphia: Lippincott, 1975; New York: Avon, 1976.

Slickrock: Endangered Canyons of the Southwest. With Philip Hyde. New York: Sierra Club/Charles Scribner's Sons, 1971.

Studies of Edward Abbey

Abbey, Edward. "On Nature, the Modern Temper, and the Southwest: An Interview with Joseph Wood Krutch." *Sage* 2 (Spring 1968): 13–21.

Baker, John F. "Edward Abbey." *Publishers Weekly*, 8 September 1975, pp. 6–7.

Barbato, Joseph. "Review of *Abbey's Road*." *Smithsonian*, October 1979, pp. 170, 172, 174, 176.

[Clemons, Walter]. "Endangered Air: Review of *The Monkey Wrench Gang*." *Newsweek*, 5 January 1976, pp. 70–72.

Erisman, Fred. "A Variant Text of *The Monkey Wrench Gang*." *Western American Literature* 14 (Fall 1979): 227–28.

Haslam, Gerald. "Introduction" to *Fire on the Mountain*, by Edward Abbey. Albuquerque: University of New Mexico Press, Zia Books, 1978.

Herndon, Jerry. " 'Moderate Extremism': Edward Abbey and 'The Moon-Eyed Horse.' " *Western American Literature* 16 (August 1981): 97–103.

Hoagland, Edward. "Review of *Black Sun*." *New York Times Book Review*, 13 June 1971, pp. 6, 12.

Lambert, Neal E. "Introduction" to *The Brave Cowboy*, by Edward Abbey. Albuquerque: University of New Mexico Press, Zia Books, 1977.

Lyon, Thomas J. "Review of *Black Sun*." *Western American Literature* 6 (Summer 1971): 157–58.

McCann, Garth. *Edward Abbey*. Boise State University Western Writers Series, no. 29. Boise, Idaho: Boise State University, 1977.

Miller, David. "Paeans to the Desert." *Progressive*, January 1978, pp. 48–49.

Miller, Tom. *"Abbey's Road."* *New West*, 23 October 1978, pp. 48–51.

Morgan, Ted. "Subvert and Conserve: Review of *The Journey Home*." *New York Times Book Review*, 31 July 1977, pp. 10–11.

Neiman, Gilbert. "Review of *The Brave Cowboy*." *New Mexico Quarterly* 26 (Autumn 1956): 291–93.

Pilkington, William T. "Edward Abbey: Southwestern Anarchist." *Western Review* 3 (Winter 1966): 58–62.

———. "Edward Abbey: Western Philosopher, or How to be a 'Happy Hopi Hippie.' " *Western American Literature* 9 (May 1974): 17–31.

Powell, Lawrence C. "A Singular Ranger." *Westways*, March 1974, pp. 32–35, 64–65.

Rawlings, Donn. "Abbey's Essays: One Man's Quest For Solid Ground." *Living Wilderness*, June 1980, pp. 44–46.

———. "Anarchic Dreams In Ed Abbey's Wild Southwest." *Living Wilderness*, October–December 1976, pp. 40–42.

S. C. "Review of *Abbey's Road*." *New Republic*, 25 August 1979, pp. 37–38.

Standiford, Les. "Desert Places: An Exchange with Edward Abbey." *Western Humanities Review* 24 (Autumn 1970): pp. 395–98.

Teale, Edwin W. "Making the Wild Scene." *New York Times Book Review*, 28 January 1968, p. 7.

Wylder Delbert E. "Edward Abbey and the 'Power Elite.' " *Western Review* 6 (Winter 1969): 18–22.

Related Works

Austin, Mary. *The Land of Little Rain*. 1903. Reprint Albuquerque: University of New Mexico Press, Zia Books, 1974

Beer, Gilian. *The Romance*. London: Methuen & Co., 1970.

Berger, Harry, Jr. "The Renaissance Imagination: Second World and Green World." *Centennial Review* 9 (1965): 36–78.

Booth, Wayne C. *A Rhetoric of Irony*. Chicago: University of Chicago Press, 1974.

Brodhead, Richard H. *Hawthorne, Melville, and the Novel*. Chicago: University of Chicago Press, 1976.

Calder, Jenni. *There Must Be a Lone Ranger*. New York: Taplinger Pub. Co., 1975.

Chase, Richard. *The American Novel and Its Tradition*. New York: Doubleday Anchor Books, 1957.

Dillard, Annie. *Pilgrim at Tinker Creek*. New York: Bantam, 1975.

Folsom, James K. *The American Western Novel*. New Haven, Conn.: College and University Press, 1966.

———, ed. *The Western*. Englewood Cliffs, N.J.: Prentice-Hall, 1979.

Foulke, Robert, and Smith, Paul. *An Anatomy of Literature*. New York: Harcourt Brace Jovanovich, 1972.

Frye, Northrop. *Anatomy of Criticism*. Princeton, N.J.: Princeton University Press, 1957.

———. "The Argument of Comedy." In *English Institute Essays 1948*, ed. D. A. Robertson, Jr. New York: AMS Press, 1965.

Gurian, Jay. *Western American Writing—Tradition and Promise*. Deland, Fla.: Everett/Edwards, 1975.

Hoagland, Edward. *The Edward Hoagland Reader*, ed. Geoffrey Wolff. New York: Random House, 1979.

Hoffman, Michael J. *The Subversive Vision: American Romanticism in Literature*. Port Washington, N.Y.: Kennikat Press, 1972.

James, Henry. *Theory of Fiction*, ed. James E. Miller, Jr. Lincoln: University of Nebraska Press, 1972.

Krutch, Joseph Wood. *The Desert Year*. New York: Viking Press, 1951.

———. *Grand Canyon*. New York: Doubleday & Company, 1962.

———. *The Voice of the Desert*. New York: William Sloane Associates, 1954.

Marx, Leo. *The Machine in the Garden*. New York: Oxford University Press, 1964.

Milton, John R. *The Novel of the American West*. Lincoln: University of Nebraska Press, 1980.

Muir, John. *The Yosemite*. New York: Doubleday & Company, 1962.

Noble, David W. *The Eternal Adam and the New World Garden*. New York: Grosset & Dunlap, 1968.

Park, Willard Z. *Shamanism in Western North America*. Evanston, Ill.: Northwestern University, 1938.

Pearce, T. M. Introduction to Mary Austin, *The Land of Little Rain*, q.v.

Peterson, Levi S. "The Primitive and the Civilized in Western Fiction." *Western American Literature* 1 (Fall 1966): 197–207.

Ruess, Everett. *On Desert Trails*. El Centro, Ca.: Desert Magazine Press, 1940.

Sonnichsen, C. L. *From Hopalong to Hud*. College Station: Texas A & M University Press, 1978.

———. *Tularosa: Last of the Frontier West*. New York: Devin-Adair, 1960; reprint Albuquerque: University of New Mexico Press, 1980.

Squires, Michael. *The Pastoral Novel*. Charlottesville: University Press of Virginia, 1974.

Stegner, Wallace. *Beyond the Hundredth Meridian*. Boston: Houghton Mifflin Co., 1953.

Thoreau, Henry David. *Walden and Civil Disobedience*, ed. Owen Thomas. New York: W. W. Norton & Company, 1966.

Westbrook, Max. "The Practical Spirit: Sacrality and the American West." *Western American Literature* 3, no. 3 (Fall 1968): 193–205.

———. *Walter Van Tilburg Clark*. New York: Twayne, 1969.

Wild, Peter. *Pioneer Conservationists of Western America*. Missoula: Mountain Press Publishing Co., 1979.

Williams, Ioan, ed. *Novel and Romance 1700–1800*. New York: Barnes & Noble, 1970.

INDEX

197–98, 203, 204, 205, 209,; attitudes in, 182–83, 201–2; caricature in, 197; characterization in, 186–89; continuous present in, 203–5, 206, 208; environmental issues in, 181–82, 183–85, 189–93, 194–96, 199–200, 209; humor in, 183–84, 185–86, 188–89, 200–201, 208; irony in, 184, 189, 193–94, 200; and the law, 182, 196–98; the Lone Ranger in, 184, 187, 188–89, 191, 194, 204–5; paradox in, 185, 188, 192, 194–98; problems with, 190; propaganda in, 198–200; red and green worlds in, 185, 198, 206–7, 208; as romance, 183–84, 188, 191, 198, 200, 202, 205; sacrality in, 182, 185, 199, 206, 207, 208; satire in, 183, 187, 189–90, 192–93, 196–97; structure in, 183, 191–92, 208, tone in, 183; violence in, 181–83, 184, 185–91, 192–98, 201, 202–5, 207–8, 209; vision in, 183, 198–99; as Western novel, 182–99, 203–8; mentioned, xiv, xv, 9–12 passim, 28, 34, 50, 68, 77, 132, 214, 220, 221, 224, 228, 230, 232, 233, 236, 237
Muench, David, 2, 115, 122–24, 127
Muir, John, 64, 140–43, 145, 149

narrative voice: in *Abbey's Road* and *The Journey Home*, 92, 93–94; in *Desert Solitaire*, 66–70, 71–74; in *Fire on the Mountain*, 45–47, 50–51, 54
National Park Service. *See* Park Service
nonfiction, as fiction, 62

On Desert Trails (Ruess), 70
The Ox-Bow Incident (Clark), 197

paradox: in *Desert Solitaire*, 68–69, 85, 89–90, 91; in *Fire on the Mountain*, 52–53; in *The Monkey Wrench Gang*, 185, 188–89, 192, 194–98; mentioned, 56, 59, 70, 84, 85, 88, 128, 144, 213, 214, 228
Park Service, 88–90, 106, 138–39, 200
parody: in *Good News*, 211, 221–27, 233; mentioned, 28, 210, 213, 216
pastoral: novel, 170–71; romance, 169–71, 180; mentioned, 151, 162, 181
pathetic fallacy: and Austin, 142–43; and Muir, 140, 141–42

Pearce, T. M., 143
personal history, xv–xvi, 62, 93–98 passim, 100, 110, 111, 117, 132
photographic essays, 63–64, 113–28; problems with, 124–26; as successful dialogues, 127
picaresque, 183, 190, 213
Pilgrim at Tinker Creek (Dillard), 139
Pilkington, William T., 101, 178
plot: of *Black Sun*, 155–56; of *The Brave Cowboy*, 16–17; of *Fire on the Mountain*, 44; of *Good News*, 211–12; of *Jonathan Troy*, 5–7; of *The Monkey Wrench Gang*, 181–82
Porter, Eliot, 113, 120–21, 127
Portrait of the Artist as a Young Man (Joyce), 86, 87
Powell, John Wesley, 64, 74, 115, 117, 134–35, 140, 144
Prather, John, 44
propaganda, 144, 183, 198–200, 237
prose style: of Abbey and Austin, 142–44; of Abbey and Muir, 141–42; of Abbey and other essayists, 139; in *Black Sun*, 162–64; in *The Brave Cowboy*, 38; describing the land, 144–48; in *Desert Solitaire*, 73–74, 76–78; in *Fire on the Mountain*, 49–52; in *Jonathan Troy*, 5, 7–10, 11–12; in photographic essays, 120–25, 127; mentioned, 2, 4, 38, 64, 127

quest: in *Black Sun*, 162–66; in *Fire on the Mountain*, 47–48; in *Good News*, 211–12, 216–18, 235–36; in *The Monkey Wrench Gang*, 183–84; mentioned, 41, 43, 178, 213, 219, 221, 228, 230. *See also* knight-errantry

red and green worlds: in *Black Sun*, 160–61, 162–67, 168–69, 170–71, 179–80; in *The Brave Cowboy*, 81–82; definition of, 56, 79; in *Desert Solitaire*, 78–90; in *Fire on the Mountain*, 56–58, 59, 78–79; in *Good News*, 230–35; in *The Monkey Wrench Gang*, 184–85, 206–7; mentioned, 24, 62, 95, 107, 146, 149, 153, 170, 171, 198, 206, 208, 221, 231, 232
Richter, Conrad, 192. *See also The Sea of Grass*

216–18, 223–38 passim; in *Jonathan Troy*, 12–13, 14–15; in *The Journey Home*, 94–96, 97–98, 107, 108–9, 111–12; in *The Monkey Wrench Gang*, 183, 198–99, 205–6; for the twentieth century, 148–49; mentioned, 5, 12, 39, 64, 73, 75, 92, 113, 125, 126, 127, 133, 136, 141, 145, 146, 151, 152, 154, 155, 158, 160, 166, 169, 175, 210, 213, 220. *See also* red and green worlds; sacrality

The Voice of the Desert (Krutch), 136

Walden (Thoreau), 66, 129, 130, 140, 170
The Wasteland (Eliot), 220
Watt, James, 224–25
West, the Old and the New, 1–4, 41–42, 52, 53, 76, 108–9, 115, 184
Westbrook, Max, 100
western ethic: anachronism in, 35; in *The Brave Cowboy*, 35–37; new, in *The Monkey Wrench Gang*, 182–83; mentioned, 3, 43

Western novel: definition and pattern of, 16–18, 19–20, 31; *Fire on the Mountain* as, 45–46, 53; inversion of, 17, 228–29; *The Monkey Wrench Gang* as beyond the conventions of, 182–99, 204–8; in the nonfiction, 236; and regionalism, 134; vision in the, 108–9; mentioned, 3, 20, 53, 216–17
Whitman, Walt, 124
wilderness: xii, 45, 61, 76–78, 91, 94, 97–98, 114, 148. *See also* environmental issues
Wister, Owen, 18, 184
The Wizard of Oz (Baum), 159, 166
Woodin, Ann, 117
Wordsworth, William, 116

The Yosemite, 141

Zwinger, Ann, 129